RESOURCE RULERS

Fortune and Folly on
Canada's Road to Resources

Bill Gallagher

Canadian copyright © September 12, 2011 by Bill JW Gallagher # 1089766

First published 2012

All rights reserved. Published in Canada and the United States by
Bill Gallagher. No part of this book may be reproduced, stored in or
introduced into a retrieval system, or transmitted in any form or by any
means (electronic, mechanical, photocopying, recording or otherwise),
without written permission except in the case of brief quotations
embodied in critical articles and reviews.

For information, address Bill Gallagher
14-460 Woolwich Street, Waterloo, Ontario, Canada, N2K 4G8

Cover design by Jesse Senko
Author photograph © Ron Gallagher

Visit Bill Gallagher's website at **www.billgallagher.ca**

ISBN-13: 978-0-9880569-0-9

"For sound wisdom has two sides" (Job 11:6)
Thank you,
Martha, Ron & Claire

CONTENTS

PREFACE

Constitutional change can creep up on us without being formally announced by a constitutional amendment. It can emerge in the changed behavior of key constitutional actors, which reflects changes in political / constitutional culture, by evolving understanding of ancient constitutional documents, and occasionally by the obsolescence of constitutional clauses which speak to yesterday. Indeed, one cannot understand our constitutional history without probing the evolution of the envelope of practices, beliefs and international trends in which the written text is embedded.

A key player in the unending dialectic between the constitution and the underlying society is the Supreme Court which, since 1949, has had the ultimate judicial responsibility of interpreting the constitution, a task which also involves lower courts, and which inevitably nudges the constitution along paths that are not pre-determined. Occasionally, a major constitutional change such as the 1982 Constitution Act, gives the judiciary the invitation and obligation to flesh out the consequences of new constitutional language, which is often no more than a few words, as in the 1982 Charter.

A classic illustration of judicial fostering of a new understanding is documented in Bill Gallagher's masterful survey of the evolution of recent judicial decisions dealing with native rights in resource exploitation. He portrays a remarkable country-wide consistency in positive judicial findings supportive of native claims in resource development. These judicial results reflect what Gallagher appropriately labels native empowerment - the skill and aggressiveness with which First Nations pursued their goals by various measures, most prominently by resort to the courts.

Gallagher's thorough documentation underlines a serious development that is insufficiently appreciated, and is caught in his phrase Resource Rulers, applied to First Nations. In practical terms, this means that vast territories, especially in northern and western Canada, cannot be opened up without the support of the relevant First Nations. The latter have become key players whose support or opposition can determine the future of the proposed opening of a mine, or the construction of a pipeline.

He also points out that the transformation of the criteria through which development possibilities are pursued or rejected is better understood and appreciated by First Nations than by the relevant corporate interests, who seek access to resources. First Nations observe these developments clearly. They understand that they are involved in a social movement which has both national and international roots. In a sense they feel that history is on their side, following a long period in which they were on the sidelines. In contrast, with few exceptions, the economic interests involved in resource development, have not properly appreciated the significance and breadth of the change in indigenous consciousness which is reinforced by judicial decisions, and which translate into the prominent role First Nations are playing in resource development. Governments are also remiss in not appreciating the necessity of coming to terms with this emergent reality.

In the mid 1960s, the Hawthorn Report advocated that Indian peoples - the language of 'Nation' was seldom used at that time - should be thought of as 'Citizens Plus'. In addition to their status as Canadian citizens, they should also have a 'plus' component as compensation for the fact that non-Aboriginal Canadians built a flourishing society on lands on which they had formerly been the sole inhabitants. We - I was a member of the Hawthorn committee - did not specify the contents of 'plus', nor how it should be fleshed out. I repeated the rationale for Citizens Plus in a volume published under that title by UBC Press in 2000. The title *Resource Rulers* of Bill Gallagher's book can be thought of as suggestive of, or a component of, 'plus.'

In other words, Gallagher has reported on a development which helps to flesh out the concept of 'Citizens Plus' that originated in the 1960s, and gained strong Indian support at the time. 'Citizens Plus' was proposed as a term to inform our understanding of how Indian peoples were to fit into the constitutional order. They could be Canadians, but with an important difference rooted in treaties, Aboriginal rights and the evolving content of 'plus.' Originally it was an attempt to define a coexistence in which Canadian citizenship and Aboriginal differences, rather than being seen as rivals - as assimilation assumptions presupposed - could be seen as partners. 'Citizens Plus' was an attempt to respond to a strong indigenous nationalism denied the possibility of independence.

Historically, it is undeniable that Indian peoples have been alienated from the Canadian constitutional order, and have had limited allegiance to the Canadian state. The impact of judicial findings of their status as de facto Resource Rulers will almost certainly weaken their negative views of Canada, given the overwhelming judicial support for their cause.

Nevertheless we remain far removed from a mutual understanding of how we can fruitfully coexist. The route to this hoped-for future is not easily discerned. The lengthy string of judicial triumphs has strengthened First Nations and other Aboriginal peoples in the court of public opinion and in conflict with governments and corporations. Clearly, however, this is not enough.

Muddling through works when the stakes are small, not when they are large, as they clearly now are, particularly in northern and western Canada. We have inchoately fumbled our way into an unhappy situation in which we frustrate each other. We require a clear vision of the direction in which we are heading.

It is clear to me that 'Citizens Plus', coined nearly half a century ago in a government funded independent research project (called the Hawthorn Report), and repeated in my support for the concept in *Citizens Plus* (UBC Press, 2000), helps to locate us. 'Citizens' means no less and no more than that we share membership in a common country. 'Plus' reminds us that Aboriginal peoples carry distinct constitutional identities found in treaties, in Aboriginal rights, in judicial findings, and in the evolving contents of 'plus.' We need to remember that the Charter in s. 25 refers positively to the need to protect "aboriginal, treaty or other rights and freedoms," and that s. 35 of the 1982 Constitution Act recognizes and affirms "the existing aboriginal and treaty rights of the aboriginal peoples of Canada."

The never ending task of nation-building writ large must now address itself to accommodating hundreds of small Aboriginal nations, without whose support large swaths of northern and western Canada have been removed from resource development. Gallagher's book tells us why a policy of drift punctuated by judicial decisions is an insufficient response to the reality that vast areas of Canada are potentially hostile to resource development. The task before Aboriginal peoples, corporate resource interests and governments is to fashion a grand political rapprochement which will reduce the frustration which now bedevils us. The example of Quebec, analyzed in chapter three, shows that it can be achieved. To do so, requires sophisticated statesmanship. It is a political task of the highest order.

Bill Gallagher has removed a blind spot in our understanding of Canada. Although he does not use explicit constitutional language, he has convincingly documented a significant shift in our constitutional life. Both Aboriginal and non-Aboriginal Canadians now have to learn how to make this new reality a positive one.

Alan Cairns

FOREWORD

Who really controls Canada's resources? It's a fair question, especially now, given that natives have amassed the longest running, most impressive legal winning streak over resource access in Canadian history. Their success in the courts has accorded them de facto control over their 'traditional' lands, making them Resource Rulers throughout broad regions of the country. As a direct result, native demands today often challenge the ability of both government and industry to satisfy. Indeed, the rise of native empowerment is dramatically changing the political map of Canada. And new rules of engagement for accessing our natural resources are urgently needed if Canada's resource-dependent economy is to remain competitive in the global marketplace.

This book provides a compass to help the reader navigate the complexities of the vital issues affecting Canada's economic future. In the Canada of yesterday, governments were absentee-landlords who paid little heed to native resource aspirations. However, natives have now rejected this role and its constricting regulatory status quo. By achieving 150 legal wins, they've radically

transformed the corporate/government/native relationship. Today, natives hold the critical balance of power in
deciding the fate of Canada's resource projects.

Unsurprisingly, their legal winning streak coincides
with a long list of lost resource project opportunities and
the toll on Canada's economy has been enormous.
Resource Rulers explores the proposition that natives
have embraced a sophisticated, strategic approach to
achieving their goals. And it offers an in-depth analysis of
the complex dynamics that have set the scene for this
transformation. Hence, the book serves as a users' guide
to develop new rules of engagement for all those involved
in resource development.

In a historical irony, the courtroom has become the
battlefield, the boardroom has become the trading post,
and it's chiefs - not governors - who now recite winning
judgments to the losing side. Moreover, native wins are
often strategically connected. Hence, they cut broad
swaths across government, the resource sector and
professional silos. Still the losing side fails to recognize
the true cause of stock-drops and lost opportunity costs.
It's almost as if these project risk factors are doomed to
remain as perverse and hidden impediments to realizing
the economic benefits of future projects. This book
exposes these risk factors and the consequential folly.

The first chapter provides an overview of significant
events since Trudeau's arrival on the scene in 1968.
Thereafter, the chapters flow from east to west; then go
north, tracking the key events and their strategic inter-
connections. Each chapter emphasizes a different aspect
of this progression: a key cluster of wins regionally
(Maritimes); protest strategies targeting a specific
industry (Ontario), and a premier's costly attempt to
reach out to natives (British Columbia). Each region has
experienced its own share of political folly and lost
fortune. Simply put, it's the Resource Rulers who now

decide who wins and who loses in the road-to-resources sweepstakes.

This book is intended to initiate the necessary dialogue that is so critical to unlocking Canada's resource potential by embracing a common economic strategy that meaningfully engages natives. Until such time as governments and industry come to properly connect the dots, the new Resource Rulers will continue to wield the secret levers of power through the courts.

1

INTRODUCTION: *CANADA'S AWAKENING*

"Trudeau woke us up!" So said Matthew Coon Come upon paying his respects to Pierre Elliott Trudeau who was lying in state on Parliament Hill. It was early October 2000, and a national day of mourning and reflection for the man who had singularly transformed the way Canadians viewed themselves and their country. He also had transformed the way natives viewed themselves and their place within Canada. Here was the former head of the Assembly of First Nations (AFN) referencing Trudeau's role in initiating the remarkable rise of native empowerment.

Trudeau's rise to power is the starting point for understanding the native rights revolution because before him there were just the two solitudes - Quebec and English Canada. For well over a century it had been all quiet on the native front. Indians were administered federally under the Indian Act and were scattered across the country; Eskimos, as they were then called, lived in the arctic, and the Métis were only marginally in the picture in Manitoba. Collectively, natives were powerless, with no access to media, courts or government. And the residential schools had attempted to assimilate them into 'a better life' in mainstream Canada albeit with disastrous results. Until Trudeau, they had been out of sight and out of mind.

Here's how a 1904 Canadian commercial law text profiled their limited capacity to enter into contracts and deal in property, as follows:

> *'Indians' - Contracts cannot be enforced against Indians (living under their tribal conditions) because their property cannot be seized or taken in execution to answer the claim. In theory an Indian's contract is legal and binding upon him, but the government protects his property upon the ground that he has not the sense or discretion enough to take care of it himself. (R. E. Gallagher, Essentials of Commercial Law [Toronto: Warwick Bros. & Rutter, 1904], p. 10) (author's underlining)*

Expo 67, the celebration of Canada's 100th birthday, brought the promise of a new Canada and a new 'with it' generation. The Canadian Pavilion featured many native themes; one video montage poignantly portrayed natives in progressively smaller frames, as if they were being pushed further and further back into the hinterland. Expo was such a national and international success that Canadians everywhere wanted the excitement to continue; the country yearned to be reborn. So it was that Expo 67 heralded Trudeau's arrival and set the stage for his first foray into native policy.

The Just Society

Politically, his election as prime minister the following year kept the party going. He had campaigned on a platform offering social change - The Just Society - and as a political scientist he realized that natives could fit neatly into his platform as a sociological entity. Indeed, they could be especially useful as a template for deflecting the nationalist pressures emanating from Quebec.

Initially, Trudeau had little to say about native policy as he was constantly focused on that other minority – the French Canadians. In his memoires he lumped the two together, as nations only "in the sociological sense" and, more specifically, as not having the identifying attributes of "political sovereignty and independence" (P. E. Trudeau, *Memoirs* [Toronto: McClelland & Stewart, 1993], pp. 73 - 74). Later, in his selected writings, he again insisted that natives had neither specific territory nor governmental powers in the classic "executive, legislative and judicial sense" (P. E. Trudeau, *Against the Current* [Toronto: McClelland & Stewart, 1996], p. 267). His overarching political mantra was: Canada is comprised of two founding nations and that's what had to be reconciled. Of course natives were in the mix - as were multiculturals and women - whose rights were not to be 'overlooked'.

But post Expo, his expressed view became: Why can't we all just be Canadians? To this end he set out to abolish the Indian Act, which was proving to be an embarrassment to Canada's newly burnished image abroad. This was what his 'Just Society' platform promised - equal treatment for all. That stance, as well as his scrapping of the Indian Act, would send an unmistakable message to those wanting special status for Quebec. This approach to reforming native relations could serve as a precedent for reforming Quebec relations as well. Politically, he would be seen to be consistent and fair and philosophically against special status for any group. Viewed in this light, Trudeau's motivation for proposing sweeping native reforms had less to do with reconciling their place within Canada - than with Quebec's.

He made his first moves early on by commissioning a White Paper and appointing a youthful, unilingual French Canadian, MP from Quebec as his Indian Affairs minister. Jean Chrétien was especially useful because above all else he was a Quebec federalist. This parliamentary one/two punch would show Quebec (and the world) that Canada was able to shake off its colonial past by embracing minorities through granting equal treatment to all in an overarching Just Society.

A Turning Point

The White Paper, which proposed sweeping policies designed to totally revamp the status of Indians in Canada, was unveiled in June 1969 but not to an appreciative audience. Indeed, the architects of "The Just Society" were about to get a wake-up call of their own. That's because Harold Cardinal, a young Cree from northern Alberta, had just published his groundbreaking native rights manifesto entitled "The Unjust Society" in direct response to Trudeau's election platform. His book painted a bleak picture of government bureaucracy deadened to the task at hand, and convincingly laid out how Canada was shirking its Indian Act and Treaty obligations. Cardinal's timely book fueled the native rage that was already building against the White Paper; and he was joined by the newly-constituted, National Indian Brotherhood based in Winnipeg (a forerunner to the Assembly of First Nations), which launched a scathing counter-attack with its own, appropriately-titled, Red Paper.

This outpouring of native anger was the historic turning point that Matthew Coon Come had referenced with his "Trudeau woke us up" eulogy, but Trudeau and

Chrétien hadn't seen it coming. The Red Paper united the native leadership as never before. The native leadership maintained that they already had distinct status under treaties, and even under the Indian Act (defects and all). More ominously for the architects of the White Paper, the native empowerment genie was now out of the lamp and ready to be harnessed as an agent of social change by native strategists. In short order, the White Paper was tossed overboard and without a back-up plan, all that was left was the political backstroke. Both Trudeau and Chrétien had struck out on the native file.

But now an even stronger force emerged to preoccupy the government. It was late 1970 and the October Crisis, which necessitated the invoking of the War Measures Act to quell a Front de Libération du Québec (FLQ) uprising, heralded a new and disconcerting era of federal politics. French / English discord over Quebec's place in Canada was boiling over; and, from this point onward, the country would be fixated solely on Quebec, as successive federal governments fought election after election for Quebecers' hearts and minds. Was there any other province in the federation? More to the point, was there anything to be gained in revisiting contentious native reforms?

Remarkably, native strategists in Quebec were quick to realize that the national unity discord held major opportunities for them, if they could only draft in the nationalist slipstream. They saw the obvious similarities between their situation and that of Quebec nationalists for both felt that they had special status. And if Quebec nationalists could assert theirs, so could Quebec natives. Indeed, weren't they here first?

Matthew Coon Come provided another key insight into how Quebec natives came to develop their political activism strategies during the ensuing decades of national disunity when he remarked, "Separatists have given us power!" (excerpt, Miramichi speech, Centre for

Indigenous Environmental Resources conference, 1997). In fact, as reflected below, Canada's Royal Commission on Aboriginal Peoples (RCAP) had drawn a similar conclusion after reviewing the evolution of constitutional developments during this tumultuous period:

> ... *How could first ministers accept the vague notion of Quebec as a distinct society while suggesting that the concept of inherent Aboriginal self-government was too unclear? Aboriginal groups did not oppose recognition of Quebec as a distinct society, so long as Aboriginal peoples were similarly acknowledged through recognition of the inherent right of Aboriginal self-government. ...*
> *(RCAP, 1996, Vol. 1, p. 209)*

The Constitution Act

Now everything focused on Trudeau's constitutional reforms. For it had taken him a decade to deliver - essentially in his last term in office the repatriation and overhaul of the Canadian Constitution in 1981. To this end, native strategists fought for and successfully negotiated the inclusion of aboriginal and treaty rights, as well as blanket protection in the Charter of Rights and Freedoms. These key measures today comprise the fundamental law of Canada and form the underpinnings of the ensuing native legal winning streak. They were also 180 degrees from where Trudeau, the Just Society reformer, had started.

Given that so many precedent-setting native legal wins are grounded in the wording of Trudeau's constitutional initiative, it's worth reviewing the actual text in order to appreciate what native strategists have to work with, as follows:

Constitution Act 1982

Part I: Canadian Charter of Rights and Freedoms

25. The guarantee in this Charter of certain rights and freedoms shall not be construed so as to abrogate or derogate from any aboriginal, treaty or other rights or freedoms that pertain to the aboriginal peoples of Canada including

(a) any rights or freedoms that have been recognized by the Royal Proclamation of October 7, 1763; and
(b) any rights or freedoms that may be acquired by the aboriginal peoples of Canada by way of land claims settlement.

Part II: Rights of the Aboriginal Peoples of Canada

35. (1) The existing aboriginal and treaty rights of the aboriginal peoples of Canada are hereby recognized and affirmed.
(2) In this Act, "aboriginal peoples of Canada" includes the Indian, Inuit and Metis peoples of Canada.
(3) For greater certainty, in subsection (1) "treaty rights" includes rights that now exist by way of land claims agreements or may be so acquired.
(4) Notwithstanding any other provision of this act, the aboriginal and treaty rights referred to in subsection (1) are guaranteed equally to male and female persons.

So Trudeau, who had wanted a Canada without special status for any group, ended up delivering a Constitution that entrenched aboriginal and treaty rights, land claim agreements (present and future) and Charter protection reaching all the way back to 1763 (circa the cessation of

British and French hostilities in North America). And by the time Trudeau took his epoch-ending walk into an Ottawa winter night in 1983, he could rationalize that native rights were now a matter that could be left for the courts to define. As a legal scholar and academic, he would have implicitly trusted the court's judgment. Still it's unlikely that he could have foreseen the flood of native rights litigation, which his constitutional reforms and charter protections would unleash, or that he would have envisioned the breadth and depth of the impact of their winning decisions. Indeed, several of these decisions would turn on the two points that Trudeau had downplayed: geographic territories and governmental powers. He may have understood the rise of French Canadian empowerment, but he was out of his depth with the rise of native empowerment, where issues relating to traditional lands and self-government propelled an emerging third order of government.

In 1984, Prime Minister Brian Mulroney assumed office. He was likewise fixated on Quebec and intent on remedying the constitutional gap left by Trudeau. Mulroney was vexed over the fact that Quebec hadn't signed-on to the Constitution's repatriation. So he set about working-up a new deal for Quebec and, by implication, for all the provinces. Had his Meech Lake Accord succeeded, he would have considered it his greatest success, rivaling Trudeau's constitutional legacy. But Meech Lake had a fatal flaw. While it addressed the unfinished constitutional business of one of the two solitudes, it failed to address those of the third. Again, in the words of the Royal Commission:

The defeat of the Meech Lake Accord was received very poorly in Quebec. Meech was meant to heal the wounds created by the patriation and amendment of the constitution in 1982 over Quebec's objection. For years, Québécois were seeking recognition of their

historic rights - the reality of 'deux nations' - in the
constitution. Aboriginal peoples were unable to have
their nation-to-nation relationship recognized, and
Quebec was unable to have its distinctiveness as a
society recognized. The fate of these two dilemmas
had become inexorably intertwined. ....
                              (RCAP 1996 Vol. 1, p. 213)

The Strength of One

Mulroney had sensed that to seek unanimity on Meech
Lake was a gamble, even admitting that he had rolled the
dice by putting it before the provincial legislatures for
approval. Still, he came very close, as most provinces
quickly approved Meech's constitutional amendments.
But it failed to pass in Manitoba where the provincial
rules required consensus. Specifically, on June 23, 1990
it ran up against Member of the Legislative Assembly
Elijah Harper's "No" vote. Harper sat defiant with an
eagle feather in his hand, indicating that his vote
reflected both his native aspirations and heritage. Here
was a lone native holdout using his vote to admonish
Ottawa over the fact that Meech Lake didn't include
'special status' for natives. Again, according to the Royal
Commission:

The Meech Lake Accord served to galvanize
Aboriginal people, to strengthen their resolve as the
white paper and patriation debates had done earlier.
Aboriginal people were fighting court battles and
engaging in acts of civil disobedience. Canadians
came to know the Gitksan and Wet'suwet'en, who
were fighting in court to affirm ownership and
jurisdiction over their traditional lands; the Haida,
who were standing in the path of logging machines
about to clear-cut their ancient forests; the Lubicon,

who were blocking access to their lands by resource developers, and the Innu, who invaded a NATO air base to protest low-level fighter jet training over their lands and its impact on their hunting economy. By 1990 many non-Aboriginal people also opposed the agreement. Owing to changes in government, the legislatures of New Brunswick and Manitoba had not yet approved the constitutional resolution, and the government of Newfoundland and Labrador had rescinded its original approval.

(RCAP 1996 Vol., 1, pp. 209-210)

Like Trudeau before him, Mulroney had failed to properly appreciate the power that natives had been wielding since the early 80s - namely their ability to thwart the best-laid plans of other players in the political arena. By denying Mulroney his place in the history books, Elijah Harper's "No" represented the high water mark in the rise of native empowerment. In time, this capacity to veto would evolve into a creative force that gave natives the ability to determine outcomes. However, at this point, natives had not yet asserted themselves in a sufficient number of major legal cases in a coordinated fashion. But that step would soon come. It was propelled by the main event in redefining the crown/native relationship - the warrior showdown at Oka!

Oka Warrior Showdown

Shortly after the demise of the Meech Lake Accord, Corporal Marcel Lemay, a Quebec police officer, was shot dead out of a tree in the line of duty while his fellow officers stormed native barricades at Oka, Quebec. The resulting armed stand-off was a searing event that introduced a host of new concepts to Canadians: traditional lands, sacred burial grounds and native warriors. The struggle continued for 78 days (July to September, 1990) and ultimately required 3,700 soldiers and their mechanized equipment to restore law and order. Ostensibly, the dispute was over a golf course expansion by municipal annexation. The back nine holes of which encroached on an area known as "The Sacred Pines," which was a known Mohawk burial ground.

Underneath all the municipal myopia were long-standing unsettled native grievances that went back for centuries. But this time it was non-native Canadians who were given the wake-up call. Most were seeing native warriors in action for the first time. Disconcertingly, the latter seemed to be operating on an ersatz military footing: brandishing high caliber weapons (AK-47s), haphazardly dressed in battle fatigues with face coverings and camouflage paint, using walkie-talkies, draped in warrior flags, with HQ command posts no less. Unlike the Canadian peace-keepers, native warriors excelled at projecting fear: physically in standoffs, in sound bites and in one-on-one stare downs.

Paradoxically, the Prime Minister's calling in the army only served to legitimize their presence in the eyes of native leaders nationally. Many of whom were conducting sympathy blockades along major highways. Canada's image by now was seriously tarnished abroad. The nation of international peacekeepers had been forced to send in its army to confront natives in what was, to most Canadians, an incomprehensible land rights dispute.

Royal Commission on Aboriginal Peoples

In the aftermath of this wanton display of native discontent, Ottawa moved quickly to show that it was taking the threat of more Okas seriously. It launched an inquiry of such scope and energy that its profile resonated internationally. The resulting Royal Commission on Aboriginal Peoples was an ambitious exercise costing $95 million and lasting over five years. In its own words:

> *This Royal Commission on Aboriginal Peoples was born in a time of ferment when the future of the Canadian federation was being debated passionately. It came to fruition in the troubled months following the demise of the Meech Lake Accord and the confrontation, in the summer of 1990, between Mohawks and the power of the Canadian state at Kanesatake (Oka), Quebec. As we complete the drafting of our report in 1995, further confrontations at Ipperwash, Ontario, and Gustafson Lake, British Columbia, signal that the underlying issues that gave rise to our Commission are far from resolved.*
> *(RCAP, 1996, Vol. 1, p. 2)*

Meech Lake's demise was followed a year later by the Charlottetown Accord's overwhelming rejection by Canadians in a national referendum (October 26, 1992). Along with recognizing Quebec as a 'distinct society', it would have offered natives aboriginal self-government constituting one of the three orders of government in Canada. Its rejection ended Mulroney's interest in getting Quebec's signature on the repatriation exercise. But, in hindsight, he should have been just as motivated toward winning native support because it was Elijah Harper's eagle feather veto in the Manitoba legislative assembly that spelled the end of the line for that career-defining gambit.

To these two constitutional failures can be added the Royal Commission's massive and comprehensive report, which ran headlong into the deep constitutional fatigue that followed the Meech Lake and Charlottetown Accord fiascos. Released in 1995, the RCAP report was ignored almost across-the-board due to its overly ambitious recommendations and unrealistic cost projections. So total was the lack of governmental response that a large political vacuum grew, even as native issues became more pressing both regionally and nationally. Its recommendations were left to twist in the wind of native unrest and as a result, two important consequences emerged from this most intentional of political slights.

First, native strategists now had a comprehensive library consisting of five years of value-added legal and historical research, which was readily available for launching legal challenges, and much of it was directly pertinent to their traditional lands and the resources sector. Second, native strategists had begun to share a defining trait with Quebec strategists. This was a deep conviction that they'd been further victimized by the constitutional gyrations that the Meech Lake and Charlottetown Accords had inflicted upon them. Unfinished constitutional business was what they now had in common. And so there were now three solitudes: natives, Quebec, and the rest of Canada.

This sentiment was reflected in the words of former Supreme Court of Canada Justice Brian Dickson who had scoped-out the Royal Commission's terms of reference:

As an ordinary Canadian I feel deeply that this wonderful country is at a crucial, and very fragile, juncture in its history. One of the major reasons for this fragility is the deep sense of alienation and frustration felt by, I believe, the vast majority of Canadian Indians, Inuit, and Métis. Accordingly, any process of change or reform in Canada - whether constitutional, economic, or social - should not proceed, and cannot succeed, without aboriginal issues being an important part of the agenda. (RCAP, 1996, Vol. 1, p. 1)

By now Ottawa had been exposed to a remarkable group of young native strategists who had emerged from the constitutional trenches to take turns at leading the Assembly of First Nations (Ovide Mercredi, Phil Fontaine, and Matthew Coon Come); participating in federal politics (Elijah Harper), and leading the Royal Commission on Aboriginal Peoples (Georges Erasmus). All of whom knew how Ottawa worked and how to manage the media.

Ipperwash Stops the Clock

Then came the Ipperwash debacle. Only this time it was a native, not a Quebec police officer, who was killed in the standoff. The police shooting of Dudley George stopped the crown / native 'relationship clock' on September 6, 1995 and nothing would be the same in Ontario for the next 12 years - not until his death was investigated, redressed and the native burial grounds returned to its rightful owners. In hindsight, the transgression that sparked his shooting appears trivial. After a prolonged occupation of the nearby army base (which had been expropriated during World War II with the promise to be returned) the natives had moved to reclaim another part of the former base that had since been developed as a small provincial park on the Lake Huron shore called Ipperwash Park. Nestled in the rolling dunes at the edge of the beach, it had previously served as a military recreational get-a-way prior to becoming a provincial park. Unquestionably, before the war, it was Indian reserve land containing known and identifiable gravesites.

A narrow public road runs alongside the base down to the park and to the beach and ends in a small parking lot, which is situated on crown land that abuts the park. No more than half a dozen cars can nose up against a very low fence that separates the parking area from the park entrance right in the dunes at the beach. Unbeknownst to the natives, the authorities were treating this low fence as a notional (and literal) line-in-the-sand. If it were to be crossed, then the occupation would be deemed to be spreading from the former base and onto public land. So this low fence became the de facto line-in-the-sand that the authorities would protect by force, if necessary, against any further native encroachment. Having watched the native occupiers expand their control incrementally - first through the army base and then into the small park - the police were not going to allow them to step over this low fence onto crown land. Tragically, in the ensuing melee in the parking lot that erupted on that fateful night, an unarmed Dudley George was shot and killed by a police sniper. The park had already been closed for the season.

As the natives saw it, he died defending their home-lands and his death put aboriginal relations into free-fall across Canada. Ontario natives immediately went to ground in terms of any cooperation with government or industry. In other parts of the country, the national news would soon start reporting lobster wars, fishing wars, wars-in-the-woods, pipeline sit-ins, and mine blockades. These incidents now occurred on a regular basis. There seemed to be no end to the turmoil - especially in the resources sector - where finding work-able solutions proved to be especially elusive.

The Courts Step In

It was at this point in time that the native leadership, having now become highly experienced in addressing constitutional and resource issues, turned to the courts to obtain the clarifications and concessions that they had been unable to achieve at the constitutional negotiation tables. They had their constitutionally protected rights -

albeit undefined - and soon they would realize that taking their chances in court was preferable to lobbying governments for incremental, often piecemeal changes that seemingly led nowhere.

Armed with the Royal Commission's library of research, their application of strategic litigation to define and reinforce their native rights began slowly. Typically, a winning ruling would be followed by Department of Justice head-scratching and then the (by now familiar) political backstroke. But like a popcorn popper reaching full tilt, soon native legal wins began to come faster and faster. In fact, continuous litigation became the defining feature driving native rights forward ultimately putting every government, regulator, and justice department on the defensive. This escalation became all the more evident as the rulings worked their way up through the appeal courts until they finally reached the Supreme Court of Canada.

So this ascendancy was to be Trudeau's unanticipated legacy on the native file. That is, win after win based upon their constitutionally protected rights and charter protection. And this decisive advantage was growing with almost every judgment. This is also the premise upon which Professor Alan Cairns' seminal 2000 text, *Citizens Plus,* was based. His thesis - that natives have been granted rights, entitlements and protections by the crown - resonates still. Indeed, their ensuing legal winning streak supports his far-sighted proposition and analysis.

Now all of a sudden, the Royal Commission's focus on land and resources was required reading for industry executives, because that was now the basis of the native strategy. The Royal Commission's statement with respect to sharing land and resources is given below:

Redistributing Lands and Resources: Most Aboriginal people retain an intensely spiritual connection to the

*land of their ancestors - one that involves both
continuity and stewardship. It is hardly surprising
then, that the most intense conflicts between
Aboriginal and non-Aboriginal people center on the
use and control of land ... Across Canada, <u>Aboriginal
people are pressing for an expanded share - a fair
share - of lands and resources that were once theirs
alone</u>. They were promised as much by the Crown of
England and its successor, the government of
Canada. Some Aboriginal nations signed treaties only
because of that promise.
(RCAP, 1996 Highlights, p. 32) (author's
underlining)*

The Clarity Act

In late 1993, Jean Chrétien followed Brian Mulroney as
prime minister. And it was Chrétien's government that
ignored the Royal Commission's recommendations. But
it couldn't ignore the near miss served up by the 1995
Quebec Referendum that caused the prime minister to
become fixated upon Quebec's proper place within
Canada. In a remarkably strategic move, he and his
intergovernmental affairs minister, Stéphane Dion,
sought direction from the Supreme Court of Canada as
they proposed new federal legislation for governing any
future referendum question and the attendant socio-
political fallout.

By deciding to fight back, Chrétien found a willing ally
in the leader of the Assembly of First Nations, Matthew
Coon Come. The key here was the critical role natives
played in helping his government draft the Clarity Act,
which became such a strategic success that it has most
likely put separatists' dreams on ice. In fact, the
Assembly of First Nations under Matthew Coon Come
worked on key portions of the draft text, which when

passed into law became Chrétien's crowning achievement in bringing closure to the national unity discourse.

Here they were working together in classic 'the enemy of my enemy is my friend' mode in order to establish the official terms governing secession from the federation. In fact, the Clarity Act (as passed) grants natives a legislated say in framing the next referendum question should Canada ever be faced with the possibility of fracture along the Quebec fault line. That's because Quebec contains a native fault line of its own. Indeed, natives can potentially claim 75% of the province's landmass as 'traditional' lands. Here's the relevant wording taken from the Clarity Act, assented to June 29, 2000:

An Act to give effect to the requirement for clarity as set out in the opinion of The Supreme Court of Canada in the Quebec Secession Reference.

Preamble

WHEREAS any proposal relating to the break-up of a democratic state is a matter of the utmost gravity and is of fundamental importance to all of its citizens;

WHEREAS the government of any province of Canada is entitled to consult its population by referendum on any issue and is entitled to formulate the wording of its referendum question;

Other Views to be considered

1.(5) In considering the clarity of a referendum question, the House of Commons shall take into account the views of all political parties represented in the legislative assembly of the province whose government is proposing the referendum on secession, any formal statements or resolutions by the

*government or legislative assembly of any province
or territory of Canada, any formal statements or
resolutions by the Senate, any formal statements or
resolutions by the representatives of the <u>Aboriginal
peoples</u> of Canada, especially those in the province
whose government is proposing the referendum on
secession, and any other views it considers to be
relevant..*

Limitation

*3. (2) No Minister of the Crown shall propose a
constitutional amendment to effect the secession <u>of a
province</u> from Canada unless the Government of
Canada has addressed, in its negotiations, the terms
of secession that are relevant in the circumstances,
including the division of assets and liabilities, any
changes to the borders of the province, <u>the rights,
interests and territorial claims of the Aboriginal
peoples of Canada,</u> and the protection of minority
rights.* (excerpts: Clarity Act (2000, c.26) (author's
underlining)

This is the most significant native legislation since
Trudeau's constitutional rewrite. Natives will now help
frame not only the next referendum question but also the
terms of secession. This was a brilliant strategic coup-de-
grace by the federalists and the AFN. So did the
Assembly of First Nations help save Canada? The
wording of the legislation shows beyond question that
they were instrumental in thwarting secessionist aspirations, an achievement for which Canadians should be
most grateful.

The Governance Act

Only one other legislative initiative merits particular mention here. Robert Nault, Chrétien's Minister of Indian Affairs, championed a comprehensive legislative reform package consisting of four bills designed to revise the Indian Act and related legislation. Representing the Rainy River - Lake of the Woods riding, with the greatest concentration of reserves in Canada, Nault understood Indian Country. And he was committed to getting his department 'out of the way' in terms of letting native communities become more economically self-sufficient. He also wanted to instill a greater degree of accountability in the internal management of native affairs both at the reserve level and nationally. Here's the key provision of his proposed First Nations Governance Act:

> 3. *The purposes of this Act are*
>> *(a) to provide bands with more effective tools of governance on an interim basis pending the negotiation and implementation of the inherent right of self-government;*
>> *(b) to enable bands to respond more effectively to their particular needs and aspirations, including the ability to collaborate for certain purposes; and*
>> *(c) to enable bands to design and implement their own regimes in respect of leadership selection, administration of government and financial management and accountability, while providing rules for those bands that do not choose to do so.*

But the AFN boycotted the bill's discussion, and just when the reform package passed second reading in the Commons, the Liberal Party passed its leader's mantle from Jean Chrétien to Paul Martin. Martin subsequently sided with the AFN, saying he could not support the bill as it stood. The National Post's editorial play-on-words hit the mark:

All For Nault: ... Naturally, the Assembly of First Nations, which represents the same chiefs who Mr. Nault was trying to make more accountable, opposed the First Nations Governance Act. But despite the shrill claims of "colonial" policy making by former AFN Grand Chief Matthew Coon Come, Mr. Nault stood his ground. ... But for ordinary natives, many of whom live in Third-World conditions, the (Martin) government's new approach is a cop-out that will only serve to perpetuate the status quo.
(excerpt: National Post editorial, February 5, 2004)

Robert Nault soon left federal politics - paying the price for his proposed significant reforms. In his exit interview, he reflected on the parliamentary inertia that envelops the Indian Act, as follows: "There's no doubt that it's been frustrating to be the Minister of Indian Affairs knowing that history has not been kind to ministers who try to move an agenda on something they strongly believe in." (Robert Nault as quoted in the National Post, October 11, 2003)

That these reforms failed, paradoxically fueled the native disconnect even more so, since many rank and file native leaders had tacitly supported the initiative. So is the Indian Act simply off-limits? On that point, none other than a former deputy minister of Indian affairs wrote to the *Globe and Mail* offering his insights under the headline: *Indian Act a Victorian Horror:*

... Robert Nault, the Minister of Indian Affairs, is unfortunately correct when he says that the Assembly of First Nations is a lobby group which represents entrenched, Indian Act created-chiefs. This group,

having rejected an invitation to consult, is hardly in a position to claim a violation of rights. ....

The elementary standards for accountability and honesty laid out in the present bill are not perfect, but they represent the first time since 1951 that any minister has had the courage to propose broad changes to the Act. Since the Act is not a treaty, it is not constitutionally entrenched, and therefore it may be further improved as time and experience dictate. (excerpts: Harry Swain, former Deputy Minister Indian Affairs & Northern Development, in a letter to the National Post, June 24, 2002)

So if Robert Nault, a competent and experienced minister couldn't effect legislative changes to his departmental mandate, then, who can? Today, it would appear that only a prime minister can. But how likely is that given Trudeau's and Mulroney's difficulties? Thus, the Indian Act, with all of its inherent defects, may well be with us for a long time to come.

Nault had taken a principled stand in the face of soft polls on the native file. An Ipsos Reid poll taken in 2003 of 3,204 Canadians respecting their assessment of the validity of native land claims was neither flattering nor conducive to effecting change: nearly half of the Canadians polled (49%) took issue with native land rights assertions; 42% felt that treaty and aboriginal rights should be done away with; 63% said fishing and hunting should be the same for all. Of note, this poll represented public opinion at the very moment Paul Martin became prime minister on December 12, 2003. And obviously it came just when Robert Nault's reforms most needed his new leader's full support in getting Canadians onside.

Now seven year later, the demise of the First Nations Governance Act ranks as the most significant missed opportunity for realigning the native relationship. Nothing since comes as close to potentially empowering natives in such a fundamental, and legislated manner. In hindsight, Nault's initiative also stands out as the only principled federal response to addressing the native legal winning streak, which had paradoxically worked-up an even greater head of steam upon the bill's demise. This judicial strengthening is due to the fact that, in the interim, it's been entirely left up to the courts to instill some semblance of order in both the political process and the crown / native relationship. After a rocky start, the courts have proven fairly consistent and, of late, fairly disciplined in instilling that sense of order; because they, too, have been working in the political vacuum created by all the previous failed initiatives (Meech Lake, Charlottetown, the Governance Act, and the Kelowna Accord).

The Kelowna Accord

The Kelowna Accord, announced in late 2005, was Paul Martin's preferred approach to improving the crown / native relationship; given that the AFN had recently 'been there' for the party in the defining event of Chrétien's tenure, which was the Clarity Act. For his part, Martin had spent the best part of two years working up a consensus for its rollout at a special federal / provincial conference dedicated solely to native issues. The Kelowna Accord was developed with close AFN collaboration, and it carried the promise of major spending ($4.5 billion) on a number of key initiatives. However, no sooner was the Kelowna Accord announced that Paul Martin experienced the same political and personal disappointment as had Robert Nault. For Prime Minister Stephen Harper had now arrived on the scene winning the 2006 election and he had campaigned against the Kelowna Accord.

Only now there was a double vacuum undermining the crown / native relationship: a legislative one created by the demise of the Governance Act and a fiscal one due to the 'cratering' of the Kelowna Accord. Tellingly, both had emanated from the highest level of the federal government, the prime minister's office. It's no wonder then that native strategists have overwhelmingly turned to the courts to seek rulings upholding their constitutionally protected rights. Indeed, the courts appear to be the only entity capable of moving the goal posts, a fact that in itself further exacerbates the relationship vacuum by increasing the immense stress on governments to respond to the native legal winning streak.

However, one telling event arose from of the ashes of the Kelowna Accord that went largely unnoticed. The premiers of the principal resource-producing jurisdictions had signed on to the Accord's defining principles: Gordon Campbell (B.C.), Ralph Klein (Alta.), Danny Williams (N.L.) along with a commitment from Jean Charest (Que.) to do likewise. All were vocal in defending the funding allocations behind the Kelowna Accord. These four politicians had come to see the native empowerment 'light' and some had been taught hard legal and civics lessons right in their own backyards. By endorsing Kelowna, they sought to find a way forward with respect to the crown / native relationship and (of course) a measure of economic protection for their resource-based economies.

So Meech Lake, Charlottetown, and Kelowna were all policy failures of the highest order, to which the Governance Act might have been added if it had not been for the Ipperwash death of Dudley George. Who was forever to be known as: "The only native to be killed in defense of a land claim in the 20th century!" The Ipperwash Commission Report into the death of Dudley George called for the immediate legislated overhaul of land claims reform in order to head-off future misguided

policing actions. But thanks to Robert Nault, one of the
Governance Act's suite of bills was already on topic and
on point. And in a rare show of legislative cooperation,
the AFN and the Harper government co-drafted the
Specific Claims Tribunal Act and managed to get it
passed in record time.

Apart from this singular achievement, Canada has
very little to show after almost forty years of political trial
and error directed toward improving the crown / native
relationship. Every prime minister who tried to prioritize
it inevitably found himself mired in a protracted impasse.
Only Stéphane Dion (Clarity Act) and Robert Nault
(Governance Act) stand out as being effective ministers.
By default, almost everything else has been left to the
courts.

Indeed, lost political opportunities may well be the
defining feature of the most important relationship in all
of Canada. This certainly is the case in Canada's
resources sector where the rise of native empowerment
has littered the landscape north of the Trans-Canada
with project 'trainwrecks' and in the process has
transformed natives into Resource Rulers.

The Indian Act

Paradoxically, for native strategists there's a certain logic
in keeping the Indian Act around pretty much 'as is' in
order to coax the courts into providing the requisite
judicial relief by expanding native rights to the
maximum. Time and again, in the media and in the
courts, they invoke the shortcomings of federal government policies (and by implication, the Indian Act) in
order to shape particular outcomes. Perhaps the Indian
Act does for native strategists what Quebec's license plate
(je me souviens) does for nationalist strategists. Since
both have morphed into powerful cultural icons of

political identity. For every social justice movement needs its touchstones, and these two are icons to the two great historic 'minority' wrongs in recent history: Quebec's non-inclusion in the repatriation of the country's constitution, and the Indian Act's blemish on Canada's vaunted human rights record. For Quebec nationalists, their icon harkens back to the founding template of Deux Nations; and for natives, the Indian Act means: shame on Canada for we were here.

But the main reason why the federal government must drive a stake through the Indian Act and dismantle the Department of Aboriginal Affairs is due to the native legal winning streak. Simply, it has created such an extensive body of jurisprudence that the underpinnings of the Indian Act (and of its department) are no longer relevant in the Canada of the 21st century. Thus, the Indian Act serves no go forward purpose. Indeed, it is hindering Canada's economic progress at this critical juncture as native legal wins continue to mount. This blockage is especially relevant with respect to those wins having to do with crown consultation and accommodation now that every court of appeal in the country has held for the native side (except for PEI which has not yet had the opportunity to rule). It's these rulings that urgently need implementation at both the federal and provincial levels if there is ever to be peace and prosperity in the resources sector.

Today, the Indian Act's continued existence appears to serve both sides: governments apparently can live with the international embarrassment as long as ministers are able to keep juggling the issues. In the meantime, natives can invoke the wrong-headedness of Indian Act policy almost at will. In this perverse stalemate, the only time 'a ball is dropped' is when the courts call the government out. Then ministers are able to hold their heads high and announce that they're moving to address the court's edicts. And since ministers barely serve two years in their rotation in and out of this important portfolio, they have little traction to resolve the more fundamental issues and disputes.

Thus, it's the lawyers behind the scenes who are 'driving the bus', and this political dynamic has (in real politick terms) recast the role of the Department of Justice, whose function now is to 'rag the puck' for governments and ministers. This strategy will continue to work just so long as ministers can manage to keep juggling all the issues - or at least until a new portfolio beckons. As it's implicitly understood that all of these headaches can be passed on to successors.

The day after six Peruvian campesinos were killed defending their land rights, the AFN National Chief made business headlines with a passionate call for "*A new approach to resource development*" (Globe and Mail, June 22, 2011). Shawn Atleo specifically drew the link that likewise, here in Canada, conflict directed towards natives draws them together :

> "*We are all treaty people responsible for the land. Land supports the people and conflict is often what drives us together. At times it even costs lives. Canada is an international human rights champion and we have to break this pattern. We have to escape poverty through prosperity.*" (speaking-notes, International Indigenous Summit on Energy & Mining, Niagara Falls June 27, 2011) (author in attendance) (author's underlining)

This, then, is the over-arching backdrop to the record-breaking native legal winning streak, and until it changes fundamentally, natives will continue to take their chances (and will win) in court; or alternatively, take their chances 'on the ground'. For if Canada is ever to realize its full resource potential, we simply have to get natives onside. And in order to do that, we must come to realize that structural changes to the crown / native relationship are long overdue. Indeed, it's a telling commentary on the current state of this vital relationship that almost all of the dialogue that counts - occurs in the courts.

By the time Ottawa convened its (one day) Crown - First Nations Summit in late January 2012, the native legal winning streak was clearly outpacing the event. While ministers and chiefs publicly pledged their support to work on developing a "new relationship", the cumulative impact of this stark legal reality was the elephant-in-the-room. Simultaneously, the rise of native empowerment was cresting over access issues on traditional lands respecting pipelines to both the B.C. west-coast and U.S. gulf-coast for exporting oilsands bitumen to foreign markets. Yet nary a word was mentioned at the Summit about the concerted native opposition that was raging against these projects. Early the next morning, National Chief Atleo made headlines reasserting that natives have the "right to free, prior and informed consent" over these projects. In turn, Prime Minister Harper made headlines days later telling an assembly of global economists that "Canada is, and will remain, open for business". (World Economic Forum, Davos, Jan 28 2012). It appeared that on matters of fundamental import to the country's resource economy, Ottawa and natives seemed predestined to continue their hit-or-miss dialogue in court.

It's one thing for rival leaders to wait for the right moment to issue a strategic sound-bite; but it's another thing entirely for resource proponents who have to bear the media and market fallout from these competing agendas. Thirty four days later, the Enbridge Board of Directors announced the retirement of President (& CEO) Pat Daniel; ironically on the same day that native protagonists were before the United Nations Human Rights Committee in Geneva to condemn Canada's conduct towards them over their opposition to Enbridge's Northern Gateway pipeline. BNN's exit interview with the outgoing President zeroed-in on the "enormously controversial" pipeline project. The elephant-in-the-room had made its presence felt after all.

2

THE MARITIMES: *LOGGERHEADS*

New Brunswick is hardly a hotbed of judicial activism. Rather, it's a province within which powerful corporate agendas have long prevailed, the economy has remained resource dependent, and corporate access to resources has been virtually guaranteed. Within this context, natives were long ago economically marginalized in order to make way for corporate priorities in all resource sectors - especially that of forestry. Indeed, the defining feature of New Brunswick's forests is that just about every tree on crown land is earmarked for one sawmill or another.

'War in the Woods'

So it was a self-described activist judge who challenged the status quo and inadvertently helped launch New Brunswick's 'war in the woods'. The key event was a Court of Queen's Bench ruling delivered October 28, 1997 by Judge Turnbull. The passages that sent native loggers into to the woods with a 'head of steam' are as follows:

*[3] Mr. Paul and with the assistance of several other
Indians had cut three logs of bird's eye maple on land
located approximately ten miles from Bathurst, N. B.
He had no authority from the Minister. The land
where the logs were cut was Crown land that was
licensed to Stone Consolidated (Canada) Inc. to cut
timber. The bird's eye maple is valuable. Mr. Paul
hoped to sell these three logs for anywhere between
one and three thousand dollars. All relevant facts
were admitted by defence counsel and Mr. Paul
confirmed same on the witness stand. (excerpt: R. v.
Paul [1997] N.B.J. No. 439)*

*[20]... I am of the opinion the Indians in New
Brunswick can harvest any and all trees they wish on
Crown lands as an appurtenance to their land rights
under Dummer's Treaty. (Ibid.)*

*[21]... In looking at the larger context I place myself in
the category of "an activist judge," but I make no
apology. History is full of injustices which cannot be
rectified. ... (Ibid.)*

Now the law was on the natives' side! Soon stories of
rampant native logging tore through New Brunswick
coffee shops and, needless to say, Judge Turnbull's
challenge to the century-old status quo in a province
where unfettered access to resources was a corporate
religion stunned the powers that be. Who had even heard
of Dummer's Treaty and how could a judge dredge it up
from the mists of time and expect it to be taken seriously
in reordering something as important as the forest
industry?

Yet it transpired that the New Brunswick government
actually knew quite a lot about the early treaties. That's
because it had intervened to challenge Micmac hunting
rights at the Supreme Court of Canada twelve years

earlier by arguing that the 1752 treaty wasn't valid or, if it were, then natives must revert to hunting the old-fashioned way using bows and arrows. Government litigators had zeroed-in on the words "as usual" in Article 4 of the treaty, as follows: "*It is agreed that the said tribe of Indians shall not be hindered from, but have free liberty of Hunting and Fishing as usual.*"

But the Supreme Court of Canada had to first answer the question as to whether the treaty was binding. It found that it indeed was and provided a history lesson in its ruling, as follows:

[24] The Treaty was entered into for the benefit of both the British Crown and the Micmac people, to maintain peace and order as well as to recognize and confirm the existing hunting and fishing rights of the Micmac. In my opinion, both the Governor and the Micmac entered into the Treaty with the intention of creating mutually binding obligations which would be solemnly respected. It also provided a mechanism for dispute resolution. The Micmac Chief and the three other Micmac signatories, as delegates of the Micmac people, would have possessed full capacity to enter into a binding treaty on behalf of the Micmac. Governor Hopson was the delegate and legal representative of His Majesty The King. It is fair to assume that the Micmac would have believed that Governor Hopson, acting on behalf of His Majesty The King, had the necessary authority to enter into a valid treaty with them. I would hold that the Treaty of 1752 was validly created by competent parties. (excerpt: Simon v. the Queen [1985] 2 S.C.R. 387)

Then, the Supreme Court addressed the contentious wording "as usual" and found instead that the treaty had to be applied "in a flexible way".

[29] First of all, I do not read the phrase "as usual" as referring to the types of weapons to be used by the Micmac and limiting them to those used in 1752. Any such construction would place upon the ability of the Micmac to hunt an unnecessary and artificial constraint out of keeping with the principle that Indian treaties should be liberally construed. Indeed, the inclusion of the phrase "as usual" appears to reflect a concern that the right to hunt be interpreted in a flexible way that is sensitive to the evolution of changes in normal hunting practices. The phrase thereby ensures that the Treaty will be an effective source of protection of hunting rights. (Ibid.)

Thus, twelve years before Judge Turnbull's activist ruling, both the New Brunswick and Nova Scotia governments well knew that:

[36] The Treaty is of as much force and effect today as it was at the time it was concluded. (Ibid.)

Yet nothing was done to educate the citizenry during the intervening decade, a decade that saw: Oka, the Royal Commission on Aboriginal Peoples, the gunfight at Gustafsen Lake and the shooting of Dudley George. All had occurred in the run-up to Turnbull's activist ruling.

To no one's surprise, the New Brunswick Court of Appeal took a dim view of Turnbull's approach (mainly because no expert evidence had been led on treaty interpretation) and in the spring of 1998 he was overruled to considerable rejoicing in corporate board-rooms. But while the status quo was temporarily restored, serious tensions persisted in woodlots where native logging, arrests and equipment seizures continued. Natives were loath to capitulate because an even more important court ruling was pending having to do with the most fundamental concept of all, aboriginal title.

In late 1997, the Supreme Court of Canada issued its momentous judgment that legitimized 'aboriginal title' as a legal precept and provided a test by which it might be established. The Delgamuukw *v.* British Columbia ruling featured a prominent New Brunswick jurist, G.V. La Forest on the bench, whose concluding remarks were undoubtedly made with an eye on the ongoing 'war in the woods' back home:

> *[204] In summary, in developing vast tracts of land, the government is expected to consider the economic well being of all Canadians. But the aboriginal peoples must not be forgotten in this equation. Their legal right to occupy and possess certain lands, as confirmed by s. 35(1) of the Constitution Act, 1982, mandates basic fairness commensurate with the honour and good faith of the Crown. (La Forest J. in Delgamuukw v. British Columbia [1997] 3 S.C.R. 1010) (court's emphasis)*

His summation foretold the legal grounds by which natives would win time and again throughout the next decade in the Canadian resources sector by petitioning the court to tell government to consider their well-being, acknowledging their legal rights to occupy certain lands, upholding their constitutional protections, and at all times demanding basic fairness and honourable dealings especially on the part of the Crown.

Delgamuukw moved the native empowerment yardsticks for the first time in decades, and each province would ultimately have to respond. It was New Brunswick's misfortune to be mired in woodlot tensions just when the Delgamuukw ruling was handed down since native loggers now felt more empowered than ever. If anything, the ruling further polarized the situation. It strengthened the need to recognize native rights on the one hand while respecting the need to recognize corporate property rights on the other. And it left government with the responsibility of trying to recover some semblance of control and legitimacy. But it was only when the province started working to find a formula to guarantee native loggers access to crown timber near their communities (5% of the annual allowable cut) that the 'war in the woods' subsided. Hence, it ensued that sharing the resources pie was seen as doable and the companies, which had managed this transition, emerged no worse for wear. Clearly, the forest industry had been taught a hard lesson. Soon it would be the energy industry's turn.

The Maritimes and Northeast Pipeline Project

Native strategists next turned their attention to the proposed $1.7 billion pipeline mega-project crossing Nova Scotia and New Brunswick. This pipeline project was going to deliver Sable Island gas to New England markets and was a major infrastructure project with all the local spin-offs that such a massive project entailed. There was an offshore component and a New England component. However, it was the middle (and longest) component that traversed treaty lands in crossing New Brunswick and Nova Scotia. And the three components would have to be ready and operating 'in sync' upon the pipeline's commissioning. Hence, time was of the essence. Start-up work focused on resolving all the right-of-way issues so there would no landowner dissenters, especially once the regulatory hearings started. And those hearings would showcase a new cooperative regulatory approach with no less than six federal and provincial government departments and agencies forming one joint public review panel. This streamlined approach would not only minimize the regulatory over-burden, it would defuse the long-standing bureaucratic turf wars. It promised to be cost-effective and thus could become the new review standard.

The panel proceeded expeditiously, addressing the concerns of 107 interveners, of which only two were native. The panel issued its report in late 1997, coincidentally just when the Delgamuukw ruling emanated. Fittingly, the Joint Public Review Panel Report (Sable Gas Project) contained the following comment with respect to how the pipeline proponents had handled the contentious issue of aboriginal relations:

> *... Since the Project did not directly impinge on reserve lands and areas that were the subject of claims negotiations, the Proponents did not initially target aboriginal communities as special interest parties, as they had done for other interest groups. In final Argument the Proponents stated that they were admittedly "slow off the mark" in dealing with First Nations. The Panel believes that this delay was regrettable. ...*

> *Direct, face-to-face contact with aboriginal communities at the Project outset would likely have gone a long way toward alleviating aboriginal peoples' concerns, and avoided mistrust and misunderstanding. The Proponents have belatedly recognized this. ...*

> *The Panel observes that aboriginal people may have special insights on particular cultural, social, economic and environmental impacts of a project and on traditional ways to mitigate these. ... There should be ample opportunity for both parties to develop concrete, effective and feasible ways to achieve this under the umbrella of a protocol or agreement. ...*

Recommendation 45: The Panel recommends that the appropriate regulatory authorities condition their approvals to require the Proponents to submit a written protocol or agreement spelling out Proponent Aboriginal roles and responsibilities for cooperation and studies in monitoring.

Recommendation 46: The Panel recommends that the appropriate regulatory authorities proceed with all necessary approvals ... without further delay.
(excerpts: Joint Public Review Panel Report, June 1, 1997, pp. 90-91)

That last recommendation suggested to markets that the project was a go. But that was not the outcome! The pipeline proponent now had to negotiate a proper native protocol as a condition for operating the pipeline. And just as the stage was set to conclude negotiations, the Delgamuukw ruling reared its 'aboriginal title' head. Imagine the proponent's surprise when three months after receiving environmental approval, all thirteen Nova Scotia chiefs supported by all members of the opposition parties, protested the project on the steps of the Legislative Assembly in Halifax. The minority government of the day had threadbare numbers and would certainly be ousted by the combined opposition numbers if matters ever came to a vote. This was as close as it gets in provincial politics and, unbelievably, the protest was over how the proponents were dealing with natives. Here's the Halifax Daily News coverage:

Angry Micmacs want Sable project stopped: ... Paul [Chief Terrance Paul Membertou band] said several Supreme Court of Canada decisions reinforce Micmac claims to land and resources. He said a March 12 proposal by Maritimes and Northeast Pipeline to waive aboriginal title is unacceptable. "We cannot

*and will not agree to such a waiver."... Membertou
Chief Terrance Paul said ... (excerpt: David Redwood,
The Halifax Daily News, April 1, 1998)*

In late 1998, saying that the protocol negotiations had
broken-down, native strategists launched injunction
proceedings to block the pipeline. But they ran up against
an unexpected procedural issue impeding their ability to
sue. Because they were "intervenors" in the regulatory
proceedings and the rules said that only "parties" had a
right of appeal. Undeterred, they challenged this
procedural prohibition and won a judicial review. With
this legal win in hand, they then went back to court
looking for another. They asserted that the National
Energy Board had breached its duty of procedural
fairness towards them given that it had issued
operational certificates without the proponents having
concluded the required written protocol. Instead, the
proponents had chosen to file the protocol without native
agreement on the basis that it reflected "best efforts";
saying they would undertake all the cited measures
whether natives signed-off or not. As it turned out, the
proponents' optimism was misplaced and native
strategists reminded the court of the wording of
Recommendation 45 (now referred to as Condition 22),
as follows: "The Company shall submit to the Board a
written protocol or agreement spelling out Proponent-
Aboriginal roles and responsibilities for cooperation and
studies in monitoring."

Since an agreement hadn't been reached, the natives
won on this point as well. In fact, the court, in a rare
move, admonished the National Energy Board (NEB)
over its handling of the requirement, as follows:

*[16] In the unique circumstances of this case, before
issuing a decision that the respondents has satisfied
Condition 22, we think the Board was obliged to*

*ensure the applicants had an opportunity to know
specifically what the respondents were submitting
with respect to Condition 22 and to provide the
applicants with an opportunity to respond to it. In
dealing with the respondents and applicants
separately, with neither knowing precisely what the
other was submitting to it, the Board fell into error.
The Board did invite comments from the applicants.
However the procedure it followed did not ensure that
the applicants, in making these comments, knew the
material the Board would be considering as having
satisfied Condition 22. In proceeding in this fashion,
the Board breached the rules of procedural fairness.
(Union of Nova Scotia Indians v. M&NEP [1999] FCA
(Oct. 20)*

These back-to-back native legal wins were a major
embarrassment for the National Energy Board in a
review process that was supposed to be a regulatory
showcase for future mega-projects. Except for the fact
that by now the pipeline was in the ground and ready to
be commissioned - the offshore and U.S. legs were also
ready - as was the Sable Island Production Platform. All
that stood in the way of getting gas to market was the
lack of compliance with Condition 22. It goes without
saying that the native strategists entered the final round
of negotiations from a position of considerable empowerment. Indeed, a special week-long NEB hearing was
scheduled to oversee compliance with Condition 22, and
with everybody watching and waiting, the proponent
needed little incentive to complete the deal. A private
arrangement was struck, regulators were apprised, and
the NEB approvals were re-issued. The project was
finally up and running.

Natives had by now blocked a major pipeline and, by
extension, stalled an offshore gas project, threatened the
tenure of a provincial government, impugned National

Energy Board certificates, and twice prevailed in the Federal Court of Appeal. This was now a major business story and *Canadian Business Magazine* gave the last word to native strategist, Bernd Christmas:

> *The booming energy business in Atlantic Canada has made a serious mistake by treating the Mi'kmaq as just another lobby group.* "What they don't realize is we're not just an interest group," *he says.* "Do other interest groups have constitutionally protected rights?" *(excerpt: Jim Meek, Canadian Business Magazine, November 12, 1999, p. 80)*

Gypsum Mine Precedents

Had the governments, proponents, investors, and analysts conducted due diligence, they would have discovered that the same natives had asserted their rights just two years previous by blocking a gypsum mine expansion on remarkably similar grounds. In 1996, they went to court over the expansion of a Cape Breton gypsum mine which required the deepening of a channel in the northern entrance to the Bras d'Or Lakes in order to accommodate larger vessel trans-shipments. Although the dredging had already been approved by regulators, the natives viewed it as holding the potential to disrupt their traditional fishery. They argued that the environmental review lacked procedural fairness and that their case turned on a key definition in the Canadian Environmental Assessment Act, which they maintained, gave them special standing to be heard. The definition is reproduced here because not only did the natives prevail in this instance, indeed they would do so again and again in future rulings:

"Environmental effect" means, in respect of a project
*(a) any change that the project may cause in the
environment, including any change it may cause to a
listed wildlife species, its critical habitat or the
residences of individuals of that species, as those
terms are defined in subsection 2(1) of the Species at
Risk Act,
(b) any effect of any change referred to in paragraph
(a) on
(i) health and socio-economic conditions,
(ii) physical and cultural heritage,
(iii) the current use of lands and resources for
traditional purposes by aboriginal persons, or
(iv) any structure site or thing that is of historical,
archeological, paleontological, or architectural
significance, or
(c) any change to the project that may be caused to
the environment.
Whether any such change or effect occurs within or
outside Canada; (author's underlining)*

It's clear from this definition that environmental reviews
must specifically address project impacts on "the current
use of lands and resources for traditional purposes by
aboriginal persons." And since that hadn't happened with
the dredging review, the court impugned the Little
Narrows Gypsum expansion project, as follows:

*Procedural Fairness: ... To be informed only after that
meeting that the screening report had been signed off
the previous day and that the authorizations required
under the statutes were expected to be issued, must
have come as a surprise. It is not surprising that the
decision-making process is perceived as unfair by the
applicants. ... (excerpt: Union of Nova Scotia Indians
v. Canada (T.D.) [1997] 1 F.C. 325)*

Fairness and Aboriginal Issues: Surprisingly, the screening report signed off by the Ministers' representatives, makes no specific reference to the use of the Bras d'Or Lakes fisheries by the Mi'kmaq, even in its brief reference to First Nations. ... The potential adverse effects are thus described: "changes to marine waters, fish habitat, and fish migration could adversely impact aboriginal use of marine resources." But the potential for that effect is classed as insignificant, with no cumulative effect. ... (Ibid.)

My conclusion is that despite brief reference in the screening report's table of potential adverse effects, the actual use of fishery resources within the Bras d'Or Lakes by the Mi'kmaq for traditional purposes was not addressed or carefully assessed by those acting for Ministers. ... (Ibid.)

Moreover, the court specifically addressed all the dire corporate warnings as to what would happen if the expansion project stalled, as follows:

For Little Narrows Gypsum it is urged that if the decisions approving the project are set aside, that would inevitably increase the costs of the project, it would create liabilities for Little Narrows gypsum project without any benefit from the project, and it would create uncertainties that could jeopardize long-term prospects of the company and of its employees. Serious as those concerns are, in my view, they are not considerations which should lead this Court to decline to exercise discretion to set aside the decisions to approve the project, particularly where, as I have found, <u>the responsible authorities failed to meet requirements under the CEAA to assess potential adverse economic effects upon the use of fishery resources of the Bras d'Or Lakes for traditional</u>

purposes by the Mi'kmaq people. (Ibid.) (author's underlining)

Here the judge specifically rejected the miner's pleas of undue commercial hardship, doing so because the potential impacts of the dredging on native subsistence had been taken for granted in the regulatory review process. This native empowerment legal preview should have tipped-off Maritimes and Northeast Pipeline that 'unfairness in the process' meant that natives could likewise derail their project; especially since they had already won the following pronouncement:

> *Conclusion: ... It is an aboriginal interest which those acting on behalf of Her Majesty have a fiduciary duty to protect from unwarranted adverse effects of the project, and I have found that those acting [for] the Ministers concerned failed to consider the fiduciary duty here owed. Those failures constituted unfairness in the process and errors in law. (Ibid.)*

Remarkably, this was the very same regulatory misstep (procedural unfairness) that two years later would invalidate the NEB's certificates on the pipeline project. And this legal precedent had been set right in that project's backyard!

On a brighter note, after witnessing this dredging loss, a competing gypsum company in Cape Breton took a proactive approach and negotiated an impact benefits agreement (IBA) with local natives that offered jobs, training, and even a royalty on the tonnage produced. Georgia Pacific's logic for negotiating an IBA was straightforward: since resource projects negatively impact traditional land, natives should receive offsetting commercial benefits. This logic can work wonders, as in this instance eco-activists had pressed to preserve a nearby old growth forest and it was the natives who brokered a solution for the company.

Thus, the fate of these two gypsum mine projects turned on the strength of the native relationship. Success was the outcome where the natives were viewed as allies; failure, where they were taken for granted. Along the way a number a corporate strategies were trashed. There was no point in filing 'best efforts' protocols without native agreement; or in issuing dire economic warnings in the event of a native win; and, last but not least, no point (ever) in expecting natives to waive their aboriginal title. Corporate Canada was now on a steep learning curve.

This early trend in regulatory challenges has since swept westward across the country, where these legal concepts have been embraced in native win after native win. Such concepts include: a) the crown's fiduciary duty, b) the lack of procedural fairness in regulatory proceedings, c) the resulting errors in law, and d) the impugning of board and ministerial approvals. But it was Maritime natives who first taught the mining, forestry and energy sectors their basic lessons in aboriginal law. Soon their target would be government, where once again the lessons of working together and sharing resources would become lost in the fog of war. This time it was a lobster war fought near a small New Brunswick reserve by the name of Burnt Church.

Burnt Church

The history of Burnt Church goes back to the start of European contact. The Company of New France was primarily interested in trade; its charter touted "Paix, Alliance, Confederation" and there likely was a French trading post on Miramichi Bay. Then came the British, whose 'peace and friendship' treaties were intended to militarily neutralize natives in the hope that they wouldn't realign with the French. As a result, British treaties of this early era were not designed to settle native land rights or the question of native land ownership. That they didn't was later clarified by the Supreme Court of Canada in 1985 with the Chief Justice declaring, "None of the Maritime treaties of the 18th century cedes land" (Article 50: Simon v. The Queen [1985] 2 S.C.R. 387). This is why the Delgamuukw ruling landed like a bombshell in the Maritimes in 1997, since it provided an overdue legal test by which natives might assert aboriginal title.

Burnt Church had been under French control up to the fall of Fort Beausejour in 1755, and it probably was named after a British raid that took place around that time. Later, when the Loyalists arrived, most crown land was made available for their re-settlement; thereafter, the demographics and political landscape changed dramatically. Moreover, the newcomers had little appreciation for the earlier treaties and accommodations. By 1844, with Loyalist descendants in charge of the government, the New Brunswick Assembly passed: *An Act to Regulate the Management and Disposal of the Indian Reserves in This Province*. Reserve lands were sold in order to promote further settlement and the proceeds were used to bolster the increasingly destitute (and shrinking) native communities.

New Brunswick natives would remain almost completely removed from the economic mainstream of the province throughout the 20th century; in fact, their exclusion continued right up to the moment that a local native, Donald Marshall Jr., went fishing for eels. The consequences of his prosecution and, more specifically, the native reaction to his subsequent acquittal by the Supreme Court of Canada, put Burnt Church and Canada on a collision course throughout 2000 and 2001. The ruling's opening paragraph, which is provided below, suggests that the primary issues were social justice and livelihood opportunities - not just the purported native law-breaking:

> *[1] On an August morning six years ago the appellant and a companion, both Mi'kmaq Indians, slipped their small outboard motorboat into the coastal waters of Pomquet Harbour, Antigonish County, Nova Scotia, to fish for eels. They landed 463 pounds, which they sold for $787.10, and for which the appellant was arrested and prosecuted.*
> *(excerpt: R. v. Marshall [1999] 3 S.C.R. 456)*

Donald Marshall Jr. was earning pocket change by fishing and selling eels. But the treaty was silent on this point. So did he have a treaty right? The Supreme Court found that the treaty, as written-up, did not reflect the entire (oral) agreement made at the time. This fact is reflected in the following judicial quotations:

> *[12] ... where a treaty was concluded verbally and afterwards written up by representatives of the Crown, it would be unconscionable for the Crown to ignore the oral terms while relying on the written terms (citing Guerin)... (Ibid.)*

> *[14] ... when considering a treaty, a court must take into account the context in which the treaties were negotiated, concluded and committed to writing. The treaties, as written documents, recorded an agreement that had already been reached orally and they did not always record the full extent of the oral agreement (citing Badger) ... (Ibid.)*

The missing clause had to do with establishing a truckhouse (trading post) whereby natives could barter their country food and furs for European goods and supplies. This provision was deemed advisable because the British feared that if the natives weren't properly provisioned, they might resume trade relations with the French, which could greatly destabilize the crown / native relationship throughout the region. In fact, truckhouses were proposed as a way to promote trade and cement the fledging relationship. However, an example of the missing truckhouse clause was addressed in the court's earlier (1985) Simon ruling, which wording is worth noting (see below) since several cases would soon be in dispute with respect to whether natives could hunt, fish, log and trade therein:

> *[6] The Treaty of 1752, the relevant part of which states at article 4 that the Micmacs have "free liberty of Hunting & Fishing as usual", provides: It is agreed that the said Tribe of Indians shall not be hindered from, but <u>have free liberty of Hunting and Fishing as usual and that if they shall think a Truckhouse needful</u> at the River Chibenaccadie or any other place of their resort, then they shall have same built and proper Merchandize lodged therein, to be Exchanged for what the Indians shall have to dispose of, and that in the mean time the said Indians shall have free liberty to bring for Sale to Halifax or any other Settlement within this Province, Skins, feathers, fowl, fish or any other thing they shall have to sell, where they shall have liberty to dispose of to the best Advantage. (excerpt: Simon v. The Queen [1985] 2 S.C.R. 387) (author's underlining)*

So now in Marshall, the Supreme Court of Canada 'read in' the missing truckhouse clause as if it had always been included in the written text, and defined it to mean that the natives had a treaty right to trade for necessaries:

> *[58] The recorded note of February 11, 1760 was that "there might be a Truckhouse established, for the*

*furnishing them with <u>necessaries</u>" (emphasis added).
What is contemplated therefore is not a right to trade
generally for economic gain, but rather a right to
trade for necessaries. The treaty right is a regulated
right and can be contained by regulation within its
proper limits. (excerpt: R. v. Marshall [1999] 3
S.C.R. 456)*

Controversially, the Supreme Court of Canada then went
on to imbue this early era treaty right with a modern day
interpretation, making it tantamount to earning a
"moderate livelihood" and justifying this interpretation
as being the "logical evolution" of the treaty right, as
follows:

*[59] The concept of "necessaries" is today equivalent
to the concept of ... a "moderate livelihood". Bare
subsistence has thankfully receded over the last
couple of centuries as the appropriate standard of life
for aboriginals and non-aboriginals alike. A
moderate livelihood includes such basics as "food,
clothing and housing, supplemented by a few
amenities", but not the accumulation of wealth. ... It
addresses day-to-day needs. This was the common
intention in 1760. It is fair that it be given this
interpretation today. (Ibid.)*

Chaos on the water ensued! Backed with this key legal
justification from the top court, native lobster traps
proliferated in Miramichi Bay. In late 1999, Fisheries and
Oceans' website listed 12,000 native traps (regionally).
The Department attempted to defuse tensions by
underscoring the fact that even with the native trap
increase there was "no threat to conservation or
livelihood" (DFO website).

But the local lobstermen weren't convinced and an
ugly backlash ensued splitting coastal communities,

where seasonal fishing was a primary economic engine in an otherwise depressed region. The resulting incidents of serious violence - vigilantism, beatings, arrests, arson, trap destruction, vandalism, bower desecration, road-blocks, burning barricades, and heavy-handed fisheries law enforcement - took everyone by surprise and were reported nightly on the national news over extended periods. Warriors from all over Canada descended, government ministers and emissaries came and went, and native leaders were prominent in their support. But the local reality was - the poor were fighting the poor!

In 2000, Burnt Church had an 80% unemployment rate, 40% of the population was on welfare and its financial affairs were under third party management (run by outsiders). A review of the headlines printed in mid-August showed how difficult it was to harness native 'on the ground' power:

Boats sunk in Burnt Church fracas (National Post, Aug. 1, 2000)

Attempt fails to ban native men from Miramichi Bay (National Post, Aug. 15, 2000)

'Call off your troops' AFN chief demands of Fisheries Minister (National. Post, Aug. 18, 2000)

Minister refuses to meet natives (London Free Press, Sept. 1, 2000)

The members of the commercial fishing industry were aghast, and in short order managed to get back before the Supreme Court of Canada citing a host of issues that begged clarification. The court itself seemed shaken by the chaotic events playing out in the wake of its ruling. Thus, a second ruling (Marshall 2) was issued just two months later and the court certainly seemed to be in damage control mode. Here's the key passage that tried to corral native expectations:

> *[20] The September 17, 1999 majority judgment did not rule that the appellant (Marshall) had established a treaty right "to gather" anything and everything physically capable of being gathered. The issues were much narrower and the ruling was much narrower. No evidence was drawn to our attention, nor was any argument made in the course of this appeal, that trade in logging or minerals, or the exploitation of offshore natural gas deposits, was in the contemplation of either or both parties to the 1760 treaty; nor was the argument made that exploitation of such resources could be considered a logical evolution of treaty rights to fish and wildlife or to the type of things traditionally "gathered" by the Mi'kmaq in a 1760 lifestyle. It is of course open to native communities to assert broader treaty rights in that regard, but if so, the basis for such a claim will have to be established in proceedings where the issue is squarely raised on proper historical evidence, as was done in this case in relation to fish and wildlife. ...*
> *(excerpt: R. v. Marshall 2 [1999] 3 S.C.R. 533)*

And specifically, with respect to how best to resolve these types of disputes in the future, the court repeated what New Brunswick's noted jurist (La Forest) had advised in Delgamuukw, as follows:

> *[22] On a final note, I wish to emphasize that the best approach in these types of cases is a process of negotiation and reconciliation that properly considers the complex and competing interests at stake. (Ibid.)*

Yet the public couldn't comprehend how a 1760 treaty could be relevant some 240 years later in a prosecution related to fishing for eels. Shortly thereafter, the Minister of Fisheries and Oceans, Herb Dhaliwal, penned an open letter to Canadians headlined: "It's not just about eels." He wanted to signal where the future direction of federal resource management practices were heading and implied that the Crown had learned some hard lessons in prosecuting Donald Marshall Jr. (all the way to the Supreme Court):

> *It's not just about eels: The specific circumstances of the prosecution of Mr. Marshall that led to the Supreme Court's decision did involve the harvesting of eels. But it is clear from the decision that the treaty right affirmed and upheld in <u>Marshall applies to hunting, fishing, and gathering more broadly</u>....* (author's underlining)

> *To go back to court again and again, when we have been admonished to negotiate not litigate, would be both short sighted and inconsistent with the honour of the Crown. ... As a Minister of the Crown, I intend to live up to the same commitment, uphold the Constitution, and discharge the responsibilities of my office. (excerpts: Open letter from Minister Herb Dhaliwal, Fisheries and Oceans, the National Post, February 20, 2001)*

In 2001, the DFO had spent $13 million on fishery enforcement measures alone. Finally in 2002, a negotiated deal terminated the free-for-all with a $20 million cash settlement plus a 13,500 kg band limit for personal food and ceremonial purposes - not for resale. In the end, the real peacemakers at Burnt Church emerged from the native community itself. A local Elder kept the native hotheads in check with his frequent teachings around the sacred fire, and a nearby chief pushed peacemaking to the point that he had to carry a side-arm for self defense. By the time the turmoil at Burnt Church had subsided, over 3,000 natives from across Canada had participated in some way or another and the members of most native communities across Canada could say: "Our flag was there!"

Native Logging

But while hostilities at Burnt Church were over, the repercussions of the Marshall decisions were anything but, as now native strategists headed back to court with two more treaty assertions: a) commercial logging, and b) logging for personal use and consumption. Both issues were again destined for the Supreme Court of Canada, and in 2005 that court took the opportunity to enunciate a stricter approach (cited below) to treaty interpretation; an interesting aspect being its reliance on the common sense observations of the lower court judges:

> *[33] In Bernard, Lordon Prov. Ct. J. made similar findings on similar evidence. He held that on the evidence "there was no traditional trade in logs", while "trade in wood products . . . such as baskets, snowshoes, and canoes was secondary to fur trade and was occasional and incidental" (para. 85). He noted that Chief Augustine had reluctantly conceded that it is "unlikely . . . that the Mi'kmaq contemplated commercial logging during the treaty process" (para. 85). Nor did the evidence suggest that the British ever contemplated trade in anything but traditionally produced products, like fur or fish. (excerpt: R. v. Marshall; R. v. Bernard 2005 SCC 43)*

*[34] These findings were firmly grounded in the
evidence given by expert and aboriginal witnesses at
trial, as well as the documentation and the cultural
and historical background. As Curran Prov. Ct. J.
observed, "[the Mi'kmaq] had no need to cut stands of
trees for themselves. . . . Trees were readily available
and Europeans could cut their own" (para. 92). The
experts agreed that it was probably in the 1780s
before the Mi'kmaq became involved in logging and
then only in a limited fashion as part of British
operations. Logging was not a traditional Mi'kmaq
activity. Rather, it was a European activity, in which
the Mi'kmaq began to participate only decades after
the treaties of 1760-61. If anything, the evidence
suggests that logging was inimical to the Mi'kmaq's
traditional way of life, interfering with fishing which,
as found in Marshall 1, was a traditional activity.
(Ibid.)*

Here were common sense legal interpretations that the
local population could understand and accept. The
second shoe dropped in 2006 when the Supreme Court
of Canada upheld an aboriginal right to harvest wood for
domestic use with the following conditions: a) that it was
only for personal use and consumption for such things as
shelter, transportation, tools and fuel; b) that it came
from traditional territories, and c) that it was not for
profit. Again the lower court's logic of the local judge was
referenced by the top court:

*[15] Arsenault Prov. Ct. J. held that the defendant
benefited from an aboriginal right to gather and
harvest wood for personal use. In finding an
aboriginal right, Arsenault Prov. Ct. J. relied heavily
on the evidence of Mr. Sewell, a Mi'kmaq and status
Indian, recognized as an elder and historian, and
declared as an expert, "regarding oral traditions and*

customs which have been passed down through the
generations and more particularly in the field of
describing practices and customs relating to the use
of and gathering of wood by aboriginals in the
geographical area encompassed by the terms of the
charge" (p. 3). Mr. Sewell's evidence was not
contradicted by the Crown on cross-examination or
by the introduction of any other documentary or
historical evidence. The Crown did not lead evidence
to justify the infringement of the aboriginal right.
(excerpt: R. v. Sappier; R. v. Gray 2006 SCC 54)

Of particular interest here, is the fact that the Supreme
Court repeated the same scolding that it had delivered in
R. v. Simon some twenty years earlier. Then it was
directed at governments attempting to restrict native
hunting rights to "bows and arrows"; and now they
wanted to restrict native logging rights to "baskets and
canoes". Here's the Supreme Court's second admonition:

[49] If aboriginal rights are not permitted to evolve
and take modern forms, then they will become utterly
useless. Surely the Crown cannot be suggesting that
the respondents, all of whom live on a reserve, would
be limited to building wigwams. If such were the case,
the doctrine of aboriginal rights would truly be
limited to recognizing and affirming a narrow subset
of "anthropological curiosities", and our notion of
aboriginality would be reduced to a small number of
outdated stereotypes. The cultures of the aboriginal
peoples who occupied the lands now forming Canada
prior to the arrival of the Europeans, and who did so
while living in organized societies with their own
distinctive ways of life, cannot be reduced to
wigwams, baskets and canoes. (Ibid.) (author's
underlining)

The fact that these judicial admonitions spanned over two decades proves that old attitudes die-hard when it comes to the management of crown resources in the Maritimes. Paradoxically, it's this sort of 'legal constipation' (a term occasionally employed by native strategists to show their disgust as they are about to walk away from the negotiations table) that continues to fuel the native legal winning streak right across the country, giving natives a chance to score on the open net (figuratively speaking) mainly because old attitudes cause governments to ignore the need for the implementation of important rulings that would promote the goal of reconciliation.

Further insight into this dynamic may be gleaned from a 2003 ruling in which the Government of New Brunswick, as part of its legal argument before the highest court in the province, submitted that natives (who were asserting aboriginal title) didn't merit such a finding since historically they were a 'welcoming and sharing people'. In simplistic terms, because natives were friendly, then they weren't landowners. As legal arguments go, this is pure contrivance. Why indeed would there have been the need for 'Peace and Friendship' treaties if the welcome mat had been rolled out? Here's how the Chief Justice of the New Brunswick Court of Appeal responded to the crown's case:

[165] To my mind too, it is a curious proposition indeed. ...

[166] The Crown's argument has the effect of turning the positive benefit actively sought and received by the British into an impediment undermining the Mi'kmaq's claim for aboriginal title. In my view, it is far too late in the day to resort to arguments that undermine rather than advance the objective of reconciliation of aboriginal peoples with Canadian

sovereignty and the "rest of the Canadian society."
That is the purpose that lies at the heart of s. 35(1) [of
the Constitution]. … (excerpts: R. v. Joshua Bernard
2003 262 N.B.R (2d) 1)

Here was the Government of New Brunswick spinning a
Pocahontas version of history in a 2003 court case, right
after 2002 witnessed the climax of hostilities on
Miramichi Bay; and 2001 witnessed the climax of
hostilities in the war-of-the-woods (sporadic gunfire was
featured in both). So not only was this legal bromide
completely out of touch with real-time events, but it also
provided the AFN with a platform to rally its members
nationally as reflected in the following excerpt:

"One of the arguments advanced by the Crown in the
case is that the welcoming and sharing nature of the
Mi'kmaq should be viewed as evidence that they
really didn't have exclusive possession of the
territory; therefore their claim for aboriginal title
must fail" (Phil Fontaine, AFN press release, August
28, 2003).

Another way of critiquing this approach involves
reversing the argument: if "welcoming and sharing"
natives have a weak case for asserting aboriginal title,
then presumably those who were 'on the warpath' have a
strong case. That argument could indeed cover a lot of
geography!

This baffling example of pretzel legal logic, when
coupled with the judicial admonitions, highlights the
obvious shortcomings in litigating native land rights. And
where government missteps have poisoned-the-well in
these types of court proceedings, the overriding effect has
been to increase native resolve to go all the way to the
Supreme Court of Canada making timely reconciliation
all the more elusive. Put another way, if you want to keep

natives going back to court (and walking away from negotiations) this is how to do it.

Native Empowerment Expands

Nevertheless, it was this cluster of important native legal wins in the Maritimes - seven major legal rulings in eight challenges (almost a 90% success rate) that launched the rise of native empowerment nationally. And their momentum soon attracted the attention of local eco-activists. What would happen if they ever became strategic allies? It was Bennett Environmental Inc.'s misfortune to test this equation by running headlong into a joint native / eco-activist campaign with the goal of blocking its proposed state-of-art thermal oxidizer incinerator.

Ground zero in this instance was Belledune, New Brunswick, on the coast of Chaleur Bay. It was once a pastoral landscape; it is now a massive, industrial brownfield site with a lead smelter, fertilizer plant, and a coal-fired power generator all in close proximity. In 2003, Bennett Environmental was welcomed into the nearby industrial park to boost the region's sagging economic fortunes. Bennett's proposed state-of-art incinerator boasted a thermal oxidizer process that treated contaminated soils using very high temperatures. But there were local environmental concerns over what might be going up the stack; natives also expressed doubts with respect to the impact on traditional food sources and human health.

On the other side of the bay, Quebecers had been taken by surprise by the incinerator's rapid approval by the New Brunswick government in late 2003. At the time, Paul Martin was preparing the political ground for his first national campaign, and while visiting the Gaspé region, his motorcade was dogged by anti-Bennett eco-activists. Their actions intensified when they subsequently took their protest right to his Lasalle constituency office in dramatic fashion by chaining themselves by their necks to the office glass doors; forcing police to gain access by busting through a wall in an adjoining office after hours of futile negotiations. Martin now knew that he had a hot campaign issue in a grouping of ridings that could really make a difference in his electoral chances.

It was two months later, on Sunday, May 23, when he (as acting Prime Minister) called the federal election for June 28, 2004. On the Friday before, indeed the last day of official government business, Environment Minister David Anderson announced that there would now be a federal environmental review of the proposed incinerator. Up to this point, the matter had been deemed as being exclusively within provincial jurisdiction. In fact, the incinerator was already in an advanced state of completion. The minister's press release cited "the human health effects in transboundary communities" and the subsequent terms of reference further indicated that the review would also consider native issues. That's because natives had likewise been vocal in raising traditional use issues and had even called upon the United Nations to intervene. The following quotation from the minister's text, which includes reference to natives, is provided below as it's instructive in understanding the evolution of this regulatory process:

The panel, in its review of the project, shall include a consideration of the factors required to be considered under the Act, as they relate to environmental effects in the province of Quebec, on the Pabineau, Listuguj, Eel River Bar, and Gesgapegiag First Nations reserve lands, and in the waters of the Baie des Chaleurs (transboundary environmental effects...). (excerpt: CEAA Draft Terms of Reference June 14, 2004)

It was Bennett Environmental's turn to be taken by surprise as now the project looked like it might have jumped the regulatory gun. Moreover, local opposition had intensified. The company was so frustrated over eco-activist criticism that it launched legal action against a leading environmental naysayer for defamation; which surprisingly prompted an open letter from a local native challenging the company to sue him in order that he could state "the Aboriginal people's case to ownership to the land Bennett Environmental claims to own" (excerpt Dan Ennis, Tobique First Nation, May 30, 2004).

As a result, natives and eco-activists were aligned in a common cause and were waging a fierce public relations campaign against the incinerator; one of the highlights being a huge protest march led by native leaders to the mid-point of the bridge linking New Brunswick and Quebec. The company found itself up against the perfect storm of project opposition: the alignment of native and eco-activist agendas before a federal review process *and* during an election run-up. Presumably to maintain market confidence, the company launched a legal challenge against the federal environmental review process and argued that the review announcement was simply too late given that the facility (costing $27 million) was already 97% complete. And on August 23, 2004 the Federal Court agreed, as follows:

> *[22] I have come to the conclusion that Bennett's facility in Belledune was no longer a "project" when the Minister decided to refer it to a review panel. Since the Act only authorizes him to refer "projects" to a review panel, it follows that he was acting without legal authority, and I so declare. The review panel cannot proceed.*

> *[24] The whole purpose of the Act is to project ahead...*

[26] The facility was past the point of no return, even when the Minister was petitioned to establish a review panel. Although section 28 of the Act requires him to consider such petitions, a petition cannot have the effect of turning back the clock and bringing the facility back into the project stage. (excerpts: Bennett Environmental v. MOE/CEAA 2004 FC 1150)

The ruling was a welcome reprieve for Bennett Environmental; its stock, which had dropped from $28, was now trading in the $6 range. Meanwhile back in Ottawa, Stéphane Dion had become Paul Martin's new Environment Minister and, in what was possibly his very first move, he ordered the appeal of the foregoing ruling:

"The government is appealing the Federal Court's decision to safeguard the integrity of the Canadian Environmental Assessment Act," Minister Dion said... We want to ensure that the application of the transboundary provisions of the Act allows environmental assessments to be undertaken to support sustainable development." (excerpt: CEAA press release, September 28, 2004)

So there was more bad luck ahead for the company and its all-but-completed incinerator. Yet the sequence of political events is telling: pre-election the ordering of the federal environmental review had been the government's last piece of business; and post-election, the ordering of the legal appeal appears to have been the government's first piece of business. Clearly the project's protagonists had both the outgoing and the incoming federal ministers in their corner.

And all the same native interveners would again be involved in the appeal: Eel River Bar First Nation (41 km away); Pabineau First Nation (44 km away); Micmac of Gesgapegiag (32 km away); and the Listujug Micmac

Government. The Belledune Citizens Committee was also
an intervener. All of these parties were steadfastly opposed to the plant and all wanted the federal environmental review process to proceed even though the facility
was now ready to become operational.

However the natives and eco-activists would once
again be disappointed, as the Court of Appeal upheld the
lower court's conclusion for essentially the same reasons
(too late in the day). The appeal judgment's opening
paragraph infers that the press release (in terms of
official paper work) was all there was driving the appeal:

> *[1] A press release issued on June 14, 2004, by the
> Canadian Environmental Assessment Agency says
> that on that day, the Minister of the Environment
> announced "the referral of the Bennett High-
> Temperature Thermal Oxidizer Project, located in
> Belledune, New Brunswick to a review panel".
> Apparently there is no other documentary record of
> the Minister's decision. The stated statutory authority
> for the referral was section 46 and section 48 of the
> Canadian Environmental Assessment Act, S.C. 1992,
> c.37 (the CEAA) (excerpt: MOE/CEAA v. Bennett
> Environmental 2005 FCA 261)*

> *[55] The Belledune HTTO facility was substantially
> complete when the Minister decided to refer it to a
> review panel. As of July 9, 2004, Bennett had invested
> $29 million in the facility. (Ibid.)*

> *[81] In my view, the reason for that particular focus of
> the CEAA is to ensure that the potential environmental
> effects of an activity are assessed in the planning stage.
> This reflects a public policy that favours an
> environmental assessment regime that is both effective
> and efficient, and that respects <u>the need for fairness to
> proponents of projects</u>. (Ibid.) (author's underlining)*

So here's a ruling that highlights the need for procedural fairness for project proponents. Yet it took two legal wins before the company could finally shake off the federal environmental review process. In the interim, the window of opportunity for the project had closed for a variety of reasons. Clearly, one of them was the joint native / eco-activist tag-team that was relentless in pursuing its goal of shuttering the incinerator. The company's year-end results spelled out the final chapters as follows:

> *2005: recorded a loss of $25 million ... the primary reason for these losses - a $15.4 million asset impairment at the facility in Belledune;*

> *2006: recorded a loss of $27.0 million ... the primary reason for the loss - a $12.6 million asset impairment at the facility in Belledune;*

The company had experienced other potentially project-killing problems throughout the ordeal: supply shortfalls and commitment difficulties with respect to securing sufficient amounts of contaminated soil for processing, securities and regulatory problems, as well as serious public relations problems. These issues likewise had much to do with derailing the project. Still the unrelenting native and eco-activist protests, especially the litigation, took a heavy toll. When the dates of the protests and ministerial announcements are overlain on the company's 2004 stock graph, they coincide with (and seemingly precipitate) significant stock drops, indeed the company's stock languished while the two court proceedings dragged on. And even though the company ultimately won both rulings, it nevertheless lost where it counted most - in the court of public opinion.

Thus, the native legal winning streak in the Maritimes holds important lessons for the rest of Canada in understanding the rise of native empowerment. For this is a region where mines, pipelines, forestry, fishing, and state-of-the-art facilities have all stumbled over native rights challenges. Ironically, these same native strategists might well have been potential project allies, appearing with proponents before the same boards, as a form of regulatory insurance. Instead, one project after another ended-up with natives being opposed, first in regulatory reviews, then in court. The losing side consistently made the mistake of taking the treaties, the regulatory process, and the native strategists for granted. They simply assumed that regulators would approve their projects, and they ended up paying a high price for that mistaken assumption. On the other hand, native strategists had figured out how to access the regulatory process and force it to not only prioritize their issues but also to produce satisfactory outcomes.

On the national scene, these Maritime rulings would at times come back to haunt proponents in other regions who seemed heedless of their import and applicability. This phenomenon is known as the 'silo effect' where the next project going forward proceeds as if it were immune to the problems that previous projects encountered. Miners don't share tips with pipeliners, who don't chat with foresters, who never go out in fishing boats. Yet that's exactly how the native legal winning streak became so inter-connected, with one win building upon another in different sectors (silos) right across the country. This interconnectivity also groomed national native leaders for further victories. For example, Roger Augustine, the native peacemaker from the Miramichi and likely the only political leader of any stripe who faced down militant warriors, went on to become Phil Fontaine's chief of staff. It would take another ten years for west-coast natives to win fishing rights off Vancouver Island, which win helped propel Shawn Atleo into the national chief's office.

The elite of the native empowerment movement attended Donald Marshall Jr.'s funeral in Sydney, Nova Scotia, on August 10, 2009. They surrounded his casket as an honour guard with clenched fists raised in a final salute to a native rights trailblazer. Not far away was the municipal park where the deceased (as a 17 year old youth) was charged for a murder that he did not commit and served 11 years in prison as one of the wrongfully convicted. Years later, a Royal Commission exonerated him having this to say in its *Digest of Findings and Recommendations:*

- *that the fact that Marshall was a Native was one of the reasons MacIntyre identified him as the prime suspect.*
- *that MacIntyre accepted evidence that supported his conclusion and rejected evidence that discounted that conclusion.*
- *that the Court of Appeal made a serious and fundamental error when it concluded that Donald Marshall, Jr. was to blame for his wrongful conviction.*
- *that the Court's gratuitous comments in the last pages of its decision created serious difficulties for Donald Marshall, Jr., both in terms of his ability to negotiate compensation for his wrongful conviction and also in terms of public acceptance of his acquittal. (excerpts: Royal Commission on the Donald Marshall, Jr., Prosecution December 1989)*

Donald Marshall Jr. is unique in the annals of Canadian jurisprudence for having had to (successfully) defend his nativeness twice before the Supreme Court of Canada. His acquittals were historic in both the annals of criminal law and natural resources. In the latter, he won a treaty right to fish commercially to earn a moderate livelihood. It was this win in the eel fishing prosecution that drove the rise of native empowerment forward nationally. Reporter Sandra Martin who covered his funeral, captured this telling historical footnote:

> *Mr. Marshall, who had learned the hard way to be wary of authority, phoned his friend Chief Paul and asked his advice. "I told him to keep fishing." Chief Paul said later. "I felt strongly that he had a right to be there and gain a livelihood." (excerpt: Sandra Martin, Globe and Mail, August 7, 2009)*

Two months later, New Brunswick installed a leading Maliseet, Judge Graydon Nicholas from Tobique, as its first native Lieutenant Governor.

3

QUEBEC AND NEWFOUNDLAND:
NO DAM WAY

Quebec and Newfoundland are today locked in a hydro-power race to southern markets; they are bitter rivals in a high stakes competition to maximize their resources and revenues. But the reality from a native empowerment perspective is this: only Quebec is in a realistic position to win because it already has a workable deal with the James Bay Crees who control the critical watersheds located in their traditional lands. In fact, Quebec has a ten-year jump on Newfoundland.

Quebec's enlightened approach on the native file has made all the difference, yet it didn't come easily nor did it happen over night. Yet all that counts in the final analysis is the fact that Quebec identified the paramount role that natives play in the hydropower sweepstakes a decade before Newfoundland did. This is what gives Quebec the competitive advantage today.

It was hydropower that fuelled the rise of native empowerment in both provinces. Natives inhabiting this vast, sprawling territory were amongst the most cohesive societies remaining in North America pursuing traditional lifestyles right up to the 1960s. Massive hydropower developments have landed on their doorstep relatively recently, and were driven by an over-arching sense of entitlement with respect to accessing resources on native 'traditional lands'. This term was an unacknowledged concept at the time since natives were considered to be nomadic - living everywhere and nowhere - rendering them invisible when it came to resource development.

Churchill Falls

This was the era when Newfoundland and Quebec had partnered on the Churchill Falls hydropower project. Hydro-Quebec had agreed to provide funds "over and above" and to "pay the difference" in the event the project defaulted on financing terms. Moreover, Hydro-Quebec had footed the cost of the vast 700KV transmission line crossing Quebec to southern markets. This significant assumption of risk was not lost on the Supreme Court of Canada, as the project would not likely have proceeded otherwise. In a unanimous ruling, the court dismissed Newfoundland's challenge to strike the power purchase contract, as follows:

Until the early 1960's there were two obstacles that stood in the way of developing the water resources of the Churchill River. The first was the problem of transmitting electricity over great distances from the source at Churchill Falls to the nearest market in southern Quebec and the United States without undue loss of power. In the 1960's a feasible means was developed by engineers of Quebec Hydro-Electric Commission (hereinafter referred to as Hydro-Quebec) using high voltage transmission lines (over 700KV) to transmit electricity over long distances without a substantial loss of power. The second

*obstacle in the way of Churchill Falls development
was financial. In order to finance the project CFLCo
had to find a credit-worthy purchaser of its
electricity, one that would undertake to purchase
electric power on a regular basis whether it was
needed or not. (excerpt: reference Re: Upper
Churchill Water Rights Reversion Act [1984] 1 S.C.R
297, p. 303)*

It's this long-term power purchase contract with Hydro-Quebec that remains the frustrating 'legacy issue' today for Newfoundland premiers. That's because the power produced is committed to be sold to Hydro-Quebec at substantially below prevailing market prices until 2041. This was an outcome obviously unforeseen in 1969. The Supreme Court of Canada upheld the contractual arrangement, as follows:

*In 1963 discussions began between Hydro-Quebec
and CFLCo regarding the development of Churchill
Falls and the transmission of power to Quebec. As a
result of these discussions a Letter of Intent was
signed by the parties on October 31, 1966, whereby
they expressed an intent to enter into a contract
which was to be called the Power Contract for the
purchase of hydro electric power by Hydro-Quebec.
The Letter of Intent recognized that the purchase of
power by Hydro-Quebec was essential to the
feasibility of the project and that the Power Contract
would have to meet the requirements of lenders
regarding the security for the repayment of debt. The
Power Contract and the performance of its various
provisions were therefore essential to the completion
of the project and after completion it was of
fundamental importance to its operation.
(Ibid., pp. 303-304)*

It is against this background that the Power Contract between CFLCo and Hydro-Quebec was signed on May 15, 1969. It is a lengthy and detailed document. Under the contract CFLCo agreed to supply and Hydro-Quebec agreed to purchase virtually all of the power produced at Churchill Falls for a term of forty years, which was renewable at the option of Hydro-Quebec for a further term of twenty-five years. The price to be paid for the electricity was to be based on the final capital cost of the project. Provision was made for CFLCo to retain a fixed amount of power for use within Labrador by its subsidiary Twin Falls Power Corporation. In addition CFLCo could recall on three years' minimum notice up to 300 megawatts (MW) to meet the needs of the Province of Newfoundland. (Ibid., p. 305)

But the deal failed to allow for the possibility of Newfoundland gaining independent access to Hydro-Quebec's transmission system in the event of its developing future hydropower sources. This missed opportunity, coupled with the fact that the project's output was (in hindsight) pre-sold at below market prices, makes Churchill Falls the defining resource giveaway of all time. Every Newfoundland premier since has been wary of becoming mired in a similar resource quagmire. The province's current energy plan reflects the ongoing economic and political torment:

The 5,428 MW Churchill Falls power station is a world-class facility. It is the third largest hydro-electric generating station in North America and is the second largest underground power station in the world. However, because of agreements negotiated in the 1960s, the province does not enjoy the full economic or electrical benefit of this enormous asset. ... while the project has generated estimated net

*revenue of $20 billion to the end of 2006,
Newfoundland and Labrador has received about $1
billion. As a result, the Upper Churchill development
has been the subject of much controversy, including
several legal challenges, in the past 30 years. The
widespread dissatisfaction with these arrangements
within the province is one of the primary motivators
behind our resolve to ensure that, in the future, our
resources are developed for the benefit of the people of
Newfoundland and Labrador. (excerpt:
Newfoundland & Labrador Energy Plan 2006-2007,
p. 33)*

It's important to note that nowhere were natives
mentioned as a factor to be considered. The Innu Nation
hadn't been consulted when the Churchill Falls project
created the Smallwood Reservoir, a gigantic man-made
lake in central Labrador that flooded the heart of their
homeland, Nitassinan. Then again, neither had the Crees
when Hydro-Quebec harnessed the fast-flowing rivers
that had likewise resulted in massive flooding in their
homeland. For this was the era of unbridled hydropower
development when natives were sidelined on both sides
of the Quebec / Labrador border. But all that was about
to change.

Cree Empowerment

The catalyst responsible for launching 30 years of
continuous native empowerment in the region started in
1975 with the first land claim settlement in Canada,
which involved the James Bay Crees and the Inuit of
Northern Quebec. That land claim settlement was really
the payoff for the James Bay hydropower project, which
was completed a decade later to great political fanfare.
Now the Quebec government assumed that it had the green

light to move ahead on other hydropower expansions. Thus, in 1989, Premier Robert Bourassa proclaimed his government's mandate to *"conquer the north"* and proposed the Great Whale hydropower project. However, it was never to materialize.

The James Bay Crees by now were fed up with the negative environmental and socio-economic impacts from hydropower expansion and unfulfilled land claim commitments. By combining sophisticated eco-activism, media messaging, public relations campaigns and legal challenges, the Crees mounted the most successful, anti-development campaign ever witnessed in Canada. Their goal was to expose their shoddy treatment by both government and industry to Quebec's most important export market, New England consumers. Paddling their odeyak all the way from James Bay to New York City, they publically embarrassed the Quebec government over their treatment such that the New England governors had second thoughts about locking-up future hydro-power contracts. The Crees addressed state legislators emphasizing the negative human rights reality under-lying any decision to purchase more power from Quebec. Back home, they waged a concerted bureaucratic and legal attack on the project's environmental review criteria, such that Premier Jacques Parizeau, bowing to market pressures, shelved the project indefinitely in 1994!

Referendum Brinkmanship

In any event, Quebec's new premier had bigger fish to fry. Because it was at this juncture that the Parti Québécois was preparing to hold its promised referendum on separation (aka sovereignty-association), once again putting the issue of national unity front and center. However, that initiative precipitated a counter-strike by the Crees and the Quebec Inuit, who conducted their own referendum as a counter-measure to the separatist aim to pull Quebec out of Canada. Their results were strategically released just days before the main referendum, and the Crees polled 96.3% for rejecting Quebec independence. The Crees' straight-forward referendum question was worded as follows:

> *Do you consent as a people that the Government of Quebec separate the James Bay Crees and Cree traditional territory from Canada, in the event of a yes vote in the Quebec referendum?*

Headlines blared the significance of the Crees' referendum result: "The message is clear: 'We won't go': Coon Come has warning after vast majority of Crees reject Quebec independence." (The Montreal Gazette, October 26, 1995). For comparison purposes, here's the official referendum question put to the citizens of Quebec, four days later on October 30, 1995. It's any-thing but straightforward:

> *Do you agree that Québec should become sovereign after having made a formal offer to Canada for a new economic and political partnership within the scope of the bill respecting the future of Québec and of the agreement signed on June 12, 1995?*

Disconcertingly, the Quebec referendum question was defeated only by a very narrow margin: 50.58% had voted "No" and 49.42% had voted "Yes." Now tensions really escalated over the 1975 land claim agreement and its troubled implementation. According to the James Bay Crees, it was honoured more in the breach than not; as a result, they ramped-up one legal challenge after another, alleging *"systemic breaches"* that *"openly and continually violated Cree rights."* Resource projects received the full

court press with a dozen legal challenges in the mix at
any one time. In July 1998, the Crees transformed their
legal assaults into one massive lawsuit demanding full
compliance with the terms of their land claim settlement,
proper dialogue and revenue sharing, promotion of
sustainable resource development, preservation of trap
lines, and a cessation of clear-cutting. Alleging that
industry's practices damaged their way of life, the Crees
specifically targeted the forestry sector and sought
compensation based on stumpage. The Crees were now
the front-runners in the native empowerment movement
nationally and unsurprisingly, their campaign to
destabilize the separatists had won them friends in
Ottawa.

That's because their impressive referendum results,
coming from the Quebec hinterland, constituted key
ammunition for the federalists in their 1998 Secession
Reference before the Supreme Court of Canada. It was
these results that obliged the court to specifically
consider the native land position and the reformulation
of boundaries should Quebec ever split from the rest of
Canada. The Supreme Court specifically addressed these
two points, as follows:

> *[96] No one can predict the course that such
> negotiations might take. The possibility that they
> might not lead to an agreement amongst the parties
> must be recognized. Negotiations following a
> referendum vote in favour of seeking secession would
> inevitably address a wide range of issues, many of
> great import. After 131 years of Confederation, there
> exists, inevitably, a high level of integration in
> economic, political and social institutions across
> Canada. The vision of those who brought about
> Confederation was to create a unified country, not a
> loose alliance of autonomous provinces. Accordingly,
> while there are regional economic interests, which*

*sometimes coincide with provincial boundaries, there
are also national interests and enterprises (both
public and private) that would face potential
dismemberment. There is a national economy and a
national debt. Arguments were raised before us
regarding boundary issues. <u>There are linguistic and
cultural minorities, including aboriginal peoples,
unevenly distributed across the country who look to
the Constitution of Canada for the protection of their
rights.</u> Of course, secession would give rise to many
issues of great complexity and difficulty. These would
have to be resolved within the overall framework of
the rule of law, thereby assuring Canadians resident
in Quebec and elsewhere a measure of stability in
what would likely be a period of considerable
upheaval and uncertainty. <u>Nobody seriously suggests
that our national existence, seamless in so many
aspects, could be effortlessly separated along what
are now the provincial boundaries of Quebec.</u> ...
(Reference re Secession of Quebec [1998] 2 S.C.R. 217)
(author's underlining)*

*[139] We would not wish to leave this aspect of our
answer to Question 2 without acknowledging the
importance of the submissions made to us respecting
the rights and concerns of aboriginal peoples in the
event of a unilateral secession, as well as the
appropriate means of defining the boundaries of a
seceding Quebec with particular regard to the
northern lands occupied largely by aboriginal
peoples. However, the concern of aboriginal peoples
is precipitated by the asserted right of Quebec to
unilateral secession. In light of our finding that there
is no such right applicable to the population of
Quebec, either under the Constitution of Canada or at
international law, but that on the contrary a clear
democratic expression of support for secession would*

> *lead under the Constitution to negotiations in which*
> *aboriginal interests would be taken into account, it*
> *becomes unnecessary to explore further the concerns*
> *of the aboriginal peoples in this Reference. (Ibid.)*

As a direct result of the strategic moves made by the James Bay Crees and the Quebec Inuit, the boundaries of an independent Quebec were no longer a given; quite the opposite, they were going to be negotiable with native interests potentially being first and foremost. This remarkable judicial outcome destabilized the separatist movement, coming as it did just four years after the demise of the Great Whale hydropower project. In fact, these two events now became inextricably intertwined. The Crees' derailment of the Great Whale project signaled the stark reality that Quebec's hydropower options were becoming increasingly limited. In addition, the Secession Reference signaled that natives were largely in the driver's seat when it came to re-drawing the map of Quebec.

Lower Churchill Fiasco

Soon it was Premier Lucien Bouchard's turn to advance Quebec's hydropower agenda, and he proposed a revamped Lower Churchill hydropower agreement with Newfoundland Premier, Brian Tobin. It was touted as a win/win scenario, strengthening Quebec's jurisdiction and borders, while guaranteeing to Newfoundland transmission access across Quebec. The project's launch featured a historic premier-to-premier signing at the scene of the 'original crime' (Churchill Falls) where in front of national media they would attempt to exorcise the ghost that has haunted hydropower relations ever since. But since the premiers had neglected to invite the Innu Nation - the Innu Nation invited themselves.

It was an out and out public relations fiasco! When placard-waving native activists blocked their cavalcade en route to the venue, the two premiers were forced to retreat on foot; Tobin in his sealskin coat with Bouchard holding onto him for support. It was a major humiliation that made national headlines. The premiers never made it to the podium, where later in an impromptu press conference, it was instead the Innu leaders who claimed the high-backed chairs and recited their manifestos. Placards summed it up: "Hydro is a No Go without Innu consent!" Another simply said: "No Dam Way!" Both premiers had received a tough lesson in on-the-ground native empowerment; and, as a result, the Lower Churchill hydropower project aborted that very day. Now both the Crees and the Innu Nation could lay claim to blocking a major hydropower project in their respective homelands.

Home Depot

By early 2000, the James Bay Crees were once again attacking Quebec over its forest management practices and were even using government studies to further their cause, as follows:

> *... In a 1998 internal review document, concerning the entire forestry system in Quebec, the Minister of Natural Resources admitted that current company forest management plans were incomplete and that the existing public consultation process is deficient. ...*

> *This is why we vigorously denounce this deceptive pretense of consultation, which only demonstrates that the Ministry of Natural Resources holds the interests of multi-national corporations above those of the Quebec population and the Crees...*

*(excerpts: Richard DesJardins & Crees' press release,
February 1, 2000)*

Unabated clear-cutting had become the major issue,
inconveniently coming to a head during the height of the
Canada / U.S. softwood lumber dispute. It was at this
critical juncture that the Crees went to Washington to
lobby U.S. legislators and trade representatives, arguing
that Quebec's corporate lumber exports were being
subsidized at the expense of their traditional lifestyle.
The Crees wanted the U.S. government to countervail
Quebec lumber exports with a punitive trade tariff, as
follows:

> *Sam Etapp, Forestry Coordinator with the Grand
> Council, said that "the reason forest products from
> Quebec are so attractive to Americans is because
> there are no social or environmental costs factored
> into the price. Cree hunters and the land bear much of
> the burden of these costs because Quebec favours
> profits over sustainable forest management. The low
> standards of environmental regulation that are
> driving Cree families from their traditional lands
> amount to a <u>trade subsidy</u> for Quebec's forestry
> industry." (excerpt: Crees' press release March 1,
> 2000 Washington) (author's underlining)*

Just days later, the James Bay Crees took the drastic step
of formally repudiating the 1975 James Bay Agreement.
Henceforth, they would assert 'effective control' over
their homelands. This was a serious development given
the key role they had just played in the national unity
debate where they had out-referendumed the separatists
with their own tally of 96%. In June 2000, the Crees
followed through on their warnings of direct action,
putting their consumer boycott strategy into play by
protesting at Home Depot's Annual General Meeting in

Atlanta, where the company president pledged from the podium to "do whatever we can to support you". That event galvanized media support, as follows:

> *For too long, 'sustainable development' has been a pious slogan that politicians use to mask their environmental inertia. Thanks to the Crees' adroit dealing with the corporate world, the slogan 'sustainable development' may at last acquire some substance.*
> *(excerpt: Montreal Gazette editorial, June 5, 2000)*

The Crees had put a tariff cloud over Quebec's lumber exports. Then they won corporate support for their boycott from the world's No. 1 lumber retailer, Home Depot. Back home, influential media sources were now on their side. And soon there would be more to come ...

The Clarity Act

When the Clarity Act became law on June 29, 2000, it formally underscored the pivotal role natives would play should the country ever fracture over Quebec's secession. This important constitutional legislation, in effect a 'poison pill' against future separatist raids on the federation, provides natives with a legislated say in both the formulation of the next referendum question and the proper weighing of the vote result. Prime Minister Jean Chrétien rightly called the Clarity Act his crowning achievement. Here are the key provisions of the Clarity Act that acknowledge the native contribution to national unity, as follows:

> *House of Commons to consider question*
> *Other views to be considered:*

*(5) In considering the clarity of a referendum
question, the House of Commons shall take into
account ... any formal statements or resolutions by
<u>the representatives of the Aboriginal peoples of
Canada</u>, especially those in the province whose
government is proposing the referendum on
secession, ...*

*Factors for House of Commons to take into account
Other views to be considered:
(3) In considering whether there has been a clear
expression of a will by a clear majority of the
population of a province that a province cease to be
part of Canada, the House of Commons shall take into
account ... any formal statements or resolutions by
<u>the representatives of the Aboriginal peoples of
Canada</u>, especially those in the province whose
government is proposing the referendum on
secession, ...*

*Limitation:
(2) No Minister of the Crown shall propose a
constitutional amendment to effect the secession of a
province from Canada unless the Government of
Canada has addressed, in its negotiations, the terms
of secession that are relevant in the circumstances,
including the division of assets and liabilities, <u>any
changes to the borders of the province, the rights,
interests and territorial claims of the Aboriginal
peoples of Canada</u>, and the protection of minority
rights. (excerpts: Clarity Act 2000 c.26) (author's
underlining)*

From this it is abundantly clear that the James Bay Crees
and Quebec Inuit had strategically played off English and
French national unity tensions to emerge as a national
power broker in their own right. Now all of Canada knew

that they were major players on the national scene and without doubt masters in their homeland. As for Quebec, was this not an opportune time for a totally new approach - one that took into account the Crees' strategic and substantial empowerment in the resources sector?

Les Paix des Braves

Then, on October 26, 2001, a remarkable about-face occurred on the floor of the National Assembly. Premier Bernard Landry's environment minister admitted that the government had purposely downplayed Cree studies that established industrial watershed pollution and toxicity, as follows:

> *Environment Minister Andre Boisclair at first tried to dismiss the findings. On Thursday, he admitted the Ouje-Bougoumou Cree are being poisoned, and that the ministry has known about it since at least 1999. "There is a problem," he said. "Their results confirm ours, so there is a problem." (excerpt: CBC News, October 26, 2001)*

Behind the scenes, Premier Bernard Landry proposed to do what was previously unthinkable. He was preparing to forge an entirely new relationship with the Crees. His rough and tumble aboriginal affairs minister, Guy Chevrette, was savvy enough to realize that he also had to be the minister of natural resources, thereby setting native policy in both departments, if anything meaningful was to come of it. He had been through the Baie des Chaleures fishery and lumber blockades and was respected as a no-nonsense operator who could both accept and deliver compromise. It would be an exceptionally small group, and tellingly, Hydro-Quebec was kept completely in the dark. However, what the premier, his minister, and the Crees were about to accomplish would launch Quebec into the big leagues of hydropower development in North America.

On February 8, 2002, Quebecers awoke to spectacular news. Headlines in the February 8, 2002 Globe and Mail declared: "Crees Sign Historic Deal with Quebec - natives to receive $3.5 billion over 50 years and share in the benefits of natural resources." Thus was launched Les Paix des Braves, which was a comprehensive agreement that set out the new relationship between the government of Quebec and the Crees. It was a legacy-defining moment for Premier Landry and a giant step towards securing Quebec's resource future. Ironically, it was a separatist government that finally saw the light; as they well knew that they stood no chance of achieving a credible shot at independence given their shoddy human rights record with respect to natives within their borders.

Native Influence Spreads

On the other side of the country, same-day headlines in the February 8, 2002 National Post announced more troubling economic news for British Columbia: "Broke BC joins the 'Have Nots' - eligible for about $30 million in federal equalization." British Columbia's resource sector had likewise become mired in native turmoil. So, on the very day that Quebec finally managed to reverse the downward slide of its resource sector, that of British Columbia was still in decline. And the main catalyst driving both scenarios was native empowerment.

Nation-to-Nation

In return, the James Bay Crees dropped all litigation and would now participate in environmental reviews for any new hydropower projects. There would be an overhaul of land claims policies as well as a sharing of resource management decision-making and resource revenues; two joint forestry and mineral boards, and the establishment of a mercury pollution fund. In addition, the Crees would assume provincial obligations in social and economic development with $70 million per year being indexed to revenues from Cree lands. Training funds and IBAs with industry were now considered to be essential, as was project contract sourcing to Cree companies. Last but not least, a formal Nation-to-Nation relationship was established. Again, local media supported the new peace agreement: "Mutual self-interest can work wonders. Quebec sees in its northern lands a vast source of exportable energy and other wealth" (Montreal Gazette editorial of October 29, 2001).

There's little doubt that the big winner was the incoming premier, Jean Charest, who had the hydropower expansion stage set for him by the outgoing administration. Hydro-Quebec was approaching its maximum capacity and a major expansion was essential for the province to stay competitive. Les Paix des Braves kick-started the company's multi-billion dollar hydropower projects on the Rupert and Eastmain Rivers.

Quebec's game plan was to become the lowest-cost electricity provider as a prime inducement for attracting industry, with the secondary goal of wheeling surplus power down to New England and over to Ontario. With such an ambitious agenda, Quebec once again had good reason to try and work things out with Newfoundland over the proposed Lower Churchill hydropower project.

The bottom line for Quebec in the hydropower sweepstakes was now clear for all to see. It could either partner with Newfoundland on the Lower Churchill project (assuming that a deal could be worked out), or compete with Newfoundland by prioritizing its other hydro projects. Much would depend upon the same two factors that had derailed the Lower Churchill project previously: the political lay of the land in St. John's and the rise of native empowerment in Labrador. In any event, what gave Hydro-Quebec the upper hand from the outset was having access to the Crees' watersheds - thanks to Les Paix des Braves.

Nitassinan

However, nothing like this power-sharing arrangement existed in Labrador vis-à-vis the Innu Nation. Indeed, the government remained mired in several protracted land use difficulties. Underlying everything else was the long-festering tension over the Churchill Falls hydro-power project that had flooded their homeland years before. Then came the low-level fighter jet training exercises over Labrador for the NATO air forces. Because Labrador resembled the western approaches to the USSR, this was part of Canada's contribution to NATO. Halting these low-level training exercises had become the Innu Nation's priority for asserting their land rights.

Dependent mainly upon traditional food, Innu hunters and their families were being blown out of their camps as fighter jets streaked overhead at tree top level. They were fearful both for their safety and for the ecology. According to their traditional knowledge, the area's wildlife was also experiencing severe stress. So they protested on the base runways at Goose Bay and were arrested time and again. The legitimacy of their cause was reflected in the fact that even their priests went to jail with them. Yet low-level flying continued largely unabated, and more than any other issue, it triggered the Innu Nation's decade-long campaign to reclaim their homeland. As fate would have it, it was against this volatile native empowerment backdrop that a giant nickel / copper mother load was discovered at

Voisey's Bay on the north coast of Labrador in 1995 by two prospectors who were out looking for diamond plays.

To further complicate matters, the Voisey's Bay discovery was also on Labrador Inuit traditional lands. And neither the Innu Nation nor the Labrador Inuit had settled land claims. The Labrador Inuit are coastal hunters and 'people of the ice' who make extensive use of the frozen Labrador Sea. In contrast, the Innu hunted and wintered inland following the central caribou herds. It was a case of Indian Department relocation folly that caused the Innu to end up living on a tiny island off the northern Labrador coast, which they couldn't leave during freeze-up or breakup. Their socio-economic plight became the subject of a Canadian Human Rights Commission ruling that faulted Canada for the many tragedies that befell the inhabitants of Davis Inlet:

I conclude that: the relocation of the Innu to Iluikoyak Island in 1967 and the failure to remedy the living and social condition of the Mushuau Innu on Iluikoyak Island since that time are a breach of the fiduciary obligation of the Crown for which the Government of Canada under its constitutional mandate in respect of aboriginal peoples bears responsibility. (excerpt: 1995 Canadian Human Rights Commission Report on the Complaints of the Innu of Labrador, by Ottawa Law Dean, Donald McRae, p. 48)

As an aside, a footnote in Dean McRae's report reveals attitudes in officialdom that might have impacted the Innu relocation. The text of his report, which is followed by the applicable footnote, is provided below:

<u>*Text*</u>*: This is not to deny those involved in making the decisions for the Innu were acting in accordance with*

what they perceived to be in the Innu's best interests.[146]

Footnote 146. The Innu remain to be convinced of this, particularly in light of statements about the Innu in official documents of the 1950's such as, "in my opinion it would be more merciful to let them die off quickly than to merely prolong the process with inadequate help", (Deputy Minister, Newfoundland Department of Natural Resources to Deputy Minister, Newfoundland Department of Public Welfare, April 16, 1955) and "there is no easy, short term solution, unless it be the solution found for the aborigines of Newfoundland more than a century ago. They, the Beothucks, have been no bother since June 6, 1829. The writer does not advocate this solution for the Labrador Indians..." (Rockwood, Departmental Organization for the Administration of Labrador, June 1959, p. 4). Such comments are viewed as evidence of a callous insensitivity to the Innu that belies a real policy of discrimination if not genocide. (CHRC report, pp. 70-71)

By the time nickel was discovered at Voisey's Bay, Canadians had already come to see the community of Davis Inlet as epitomizing the worst of third world socio-economic conditions. And now it lay in the shadow of a (future) massive industrial footprint. Both Davis Inlet and the Inuit community of Nain were just one day's snowmobile ride from the Voisey's Bay discovery. Clearly, government, industry and natives now had to map out new rules of engagement.

For the miners, the prospect of having two distinct cultural groups in the same neck of the woods was a conundrum, complicated by the fact that the 'people of the ice' had traditional uses that extended well offshore. Their safety while traversing the ice was a major factor since coastal ice crossings were hazardous at the best of times, without having merchant shipping transits thrown into the mix.

Voisey's Bay

By this time, the native legal winning streak was starting to ramp-up in other parts of Canada with several rulings making it all the way to the Supreme Court of Canada. This was a trend not lost on Innu and Inuit strategists. The miners were cautioned not to 'count their chickens' as a result. Indeed, in mid-1997 the Innu Nation and the Labrador Inuit launched a court challenge to the terms of reference of the proposed environmental review process. As the case wound its way through the courts, it triggered a large native protest at the mine site, garnering intense national media coverage. It was while this protest was underway that the highest court in the province weighed-in siding with the natives, as follows:

[85] Likewise, the Inuit and Innu may also be viewed as representing general vital interests. They are understandably pre-occupied with the protection from adverse environmental effects on the immediate area affected, to which their whole cultural, social and economic lives have been linked for generations. Nevertheless, in a very real sense they too are representing the interests of their fellow citizens in this Province inasmuch as the heritage of the environment is a legacy to be preserved for all Newfoundlanders and Labradorians, wherever their abode. Viewed from this perspective the general may be said to transcend the particular environmental concerns more immediately engaged. After all, indiscriminate development without regard to environmental impact translates into agonizing problems for generations yet unborn from every

corner of the Province, whether it be the depleted
fishery; forestry harvesting in the absence of
silvaculture; uncontrolled effluent and emissions
from plants; or the tragedies of flourospar or
asbestos mines. We are sure that all parties involved
would not want to have the mining development at
Voisey's Bay to be placed in the same category.
(Labrador Inuit Association & Innu Nation v. the
Queen & VBNC [1997] September 22, NLCA)

This ruling is now one of the leading benchmarks in the native legal winning streak, because it implicitly endorsed natives as stewards of the land and imbued their role with a serious level of judicial credibility. And the ink wasn't yet dry on this ruling when just three months later the Supreme Court of Canada issued its ground-breaking Delgamuukw decision (December 1997) with its precedent-setting test for determining aboriginal title. Here were back-to-back major legal wins empowering Labrador natives; and soon both would be read from the vacated premiers' chairs during that 1998 Lower Churchill pubic relations fiasco that had sent the two premiers and their hydro project packing.

Hence, the rise of native empowerment had started to make itself felt. The Voisey's Bay project timetable slipped significantly, stock values took major hits, followed by office closures and layoffs. Business head-lines were unrelentingly critical. Over time, it became clear that nothing would happen in the way of project momentum until the natives were brought on board. And the catalyst that accomplished that breakthrough was the successful negotiation of IBAs, which in this instance took a period of years given the deeps roots of mutual mistrust behind the public controversy.

Impact and Benefits Agreement (IBA)

After protracted and difficult IBA negotiations, the St. John's Evening Telegram finally ran the long-awaited headline on November 30, 2001: "Voisey's Bay gets aboriginal support." This was the turning point. Then three announcements came in quick succession - the native deal, the provincial deal, and the project roll out - a pattern that has now become the hallmark for mega-project success. The IBAs had to come first because they represented project insurance that only the natives could provide. In short order, Premier Roger Grimes was at the podium, flanked by native leaders, announcing that the Voisey's Bay project was going ahead. But in native empowerment terms, it was the IBAs that had paved the way and brought closure to what was the most intractable resource dispute in Canada.

A couple of years later, with the project up and running, the miners published a coffee-table retro-spective documenting all the key events - warts and all. It described an earlier native protest in 1995, right after the discovery was made by Diamond Fields, which saw 100 Innu and 60 RCMP officers square off, with sharp-shooters placed on the surrounding hills. While that confrontation ended in negotiations, it nevertheless portended how easy it was for policing situations like this to deteriorate. (Indeed, a year and a half later, Dudley George would be shot and killed by an OPP marksman in a chaotic policing action at Ipperwash Park Ontario). The miners' retrospective, entitled Nickel on the Big Land - the Voisey's Bay Development - offered sage and timely advice for future project proponents: "development could not go ahead without Inuit and Innu consent".

It's a brave assertion! Because today, proponents in other parts of the country are seeing their projects blocked over their refusal to concede on the contentious issue of native consent. Yet it was the singular success of the IBAs that delivered the elusive native consent at Voisey's Bay. Thereafter at resource conferences, federal officials regularly cited these particular IBAs as the preferred industry benchmark. In fact, Voisey's Bay went from volatile native protests to become an international collaborative success story based on the strength of 'Inuit and Innu consent'. What might have once been a corporate leap of faith is now just a prudent business decision. These trailblazing miners led the way!

Premier Danny Williams

Shortly after the Voisey's Bay announcement, Danny Williams took over as premier. Right off the bat, his 2005 Energy Plan promoted the Lower Churchill hydropower project in glowing terms:

> *The Lower Churchill River has two of the most cost-effective undeveloped hydro sites in North America. The 2,000 MW Gull Island site and the approximately 825 MW site at Muskrat Falls. These sites are approximately 200 km and 245 km, respectively, downstream from the 5,428 MW Churchill Falls project. (excerpt: Newfoundland and Labrador Energy Plan Discussion Paper, p. 46)*

After an exhaustive canvassing of potential project partners (who had gone to extraordinary measures and expense to win the government's favour) the premier announced that his province would be going it alone on the Lower Churchill project. By now, Williams' home-grown nationalism had taken hold: Ottawa and Stephen Harper, Quebec and Hydro-Quebec, all were persona non grata. Flag-lowering theatrics aside, the only question left unanswered was whether Newfoundland could really go it alone on such a major hydropower development. That transit corridor across Quebec loomed ever larger as the mega-project's missing link - never mind its (land-locked) questionable economics.

Quebec's "Nationhood"

Yet Premier Williams wasn't the only political leader in the country playing the regional 'nation card'. Six months later on November 25, 2006, Prime Minister Stephen Harper, announced his major national unity concession by granting Quebec: "Nationhood within a united Canada." The declaration signaled that his minority federal government wanted to work with all the provinces - but especially with Quebec. However, a clearly vexed AFN National Chief, Phil Fontaine, fired-off an open letter to all Members of Parliament demanding their reconsideration of the surprise overture to Quebec. For if anyone were to have "nation" status, it was natives:

Dear All Members of Parliament, ...

... Under no circumstances should recognition of the Quebecois be achieved by putting the historical and constitutional status of First Nations at risk. ...

Indeed, the Assembly of First Nations calls upon all Members of Parliament to positively affirm and place on record their recognition of <u>the unique status and rights that First Nations have in Quebec and throughout Canada as the first peoples to inhabit, develop and govern themselves on their lands and as distinct and vital nations unto this day</u>. (excerpts: open letter to MPs. AFN National Chief, November 27, 2006) (Fontaine's underlining)

Even B.C. Premier Gordon Campbell jumped into the fray, responding with an open letter to the National Post supporting the AFN position because he, too, was quickly coming to realize that he needed natives as strategic allies in order to get anything done in his provincial resource sector, as follows:

> *Indeed I would urge the Prime Minister to work with aboriginal leaders to develop a similar motion that offers a positive affirmation of Canada's three founding nations - French, English and aboriginal alike.*
>
> *... It is high time we formally acknowledged Canada's 'third 'solitude' - the aboriginal peoples of Canada. We should do that formally, proudly, and emphatically in a similar resolution that embraces our heritage as a nation of many nations." (excerpts: open letter to the National Post, Office of the Premier, November 27, 2006)*

Of course, the fact that Harper and Charest were now getting along so well would not go unnoticed in Saint John's. Less obvious was the fact that Charest and the Crees were also developing a cordial relationship. For behind the scenes, powerful players in James Bay, Quebec City, Montreal and Ottawa were starting to align their agendas with a view towards promoting new hydro-power projects on Cree lands in Quebec's heartland.

Thus, the stage was set for a race between Quebec and Newfoundland to access new hydropower sources. And this is where Ottawa's according Nationhood status to Quebec comes into play; just as it was Quebec's according 'Nation-to-Nation' status to the Crees. Both moves adroitly prepared the political ground for an emerging federal / provincial / native alliance to promote Quebec's hydropower expansion. Conversely, it was

Premier Williams' go-it-alone stance on the Lower Churchill hydropower project that had sealed the deal. His rebuke to potential partners had forged a common purpose setting into motion the fast-tracking of Quebec's ambition to be the North American leader in hydropower generation. For their part, Hydro-Quebec and the Crees were already working up to this, recognizing that Les Paix des Braves gave them a clear strategic advantage over competing projects. Indeed, by 2005 they appeared together at a World Bank energy conference touting the strategic benefits of their new collaboration:

> *... The Cree of Eeyou Itchee will provide the indigenous perspective on the current development of large hydropower projects and 30 years of lessons learned on the challenges linked to developing these kinds of projects successfully.*
>
> *Hydro Quebec will follow by presenting a new and unique corporate willingness and commitment to building a lasting dialogue and mutual trust, and to addressing the rightful concerns of the Cree of Eeyou Itchee. ... (excerpts: The World Bank Group press, March 14, 2005).*

But while all these progressive steps were being taken in Quebec, the Newfoundland government was vigorously contesting a Metis legal challenge respecting their right to be consulted over fish habitat impacted by the Trans-Labrador Highway construction project. This litigation would be fought all the way to the Supreme Court of Canada, eating up critical time and resources that could have otherwise been better put to fostering a constructive relationship.

Events in Quebec were proceeding at such a pace that an environmental lobby, comprised of no less than 17 constituent organizations from Canada and the U.S., took direct aim at government and industry to expose these rushed hydropower projects as representing more environmental folly. Touting the likelihood of more flooding, more mercury pollution, more river rerouting and more watershed impairment, they were hoping for another U.S. consumer-rejection 'repeat' similar to the one that derailed the Great Whale hydropower project. It had worked last time, only this time Hydro-Quebec shot back taking credit for what it now billed as 'green' energy. That's because the utility was able to invoke the Crees' environmental endorsement, giving its hydro-power projects the 'native good housekeeping seal of approval,' as follows:

Eastmain-1-A /Sarcelle/Rupert is a singular example of Cree cooperation and involvement in a project on Cree territory. The project is at the heart of the Paix des Braves agreement signed in 2002 between the Québec government and the Cree Nation of James Bay. A referendum on the agreement was held beforehand by the Crees in each of their communities. Over two-thirds (70%) of Crees participating in the referendum voted in favour of the agreement, which specifically provided for the Eastmain-1-A/Sarcelle/Rupert project.

Since then, the Crees have been project stakeholders and have participated in all stages of the project, from the design to environmental follow-up.

... [the project] will displace thermal generation in neighboring markets through sales to those markets when appropriate. It is undeniable that the project will help reduce greenhouse gas emissions. (excerpts: Hydro-Quebec, press release of September 12, 2007)

Hydro-Quebec had waited an eternity for the right opportunity to turn the tables on the eco-activists. What a difference having the Crees onside made to their public relations! In one fell swoop, not only were the eco-activists taken out of the equation but, more importantly, hydropower would hereafter be marketed as 'green' energy. So the race was now on in earnest. Quebec had momentum not only because of Cree support but also because of the high-level support it now received from Ottawa. Something in the Ottawa / Quebec City / Cree political alignment was driving hydropower projects forward at record speed. Clearly, the goal was to place Hydro-Quebec in the pole position in the hydropower race to markets.

Labrador Metis Nation

Meanwhile in Newfoundland, the opposite dynamic was settling in. The Court of Appeal had sided with the Labrador Metis Nation in that Trans-Labrador highway challenge, saying that the Metis had been right to demand government consultation. Once again, the highest court in the province used the opportunity to admonish the Newfoundland government:

> *[45] The Crown's analysis should have arrived at the same result, namely, that the respondents have a credible claim which triggers a duty to consult.*
> *(excerpt: Newfoundland and Labrador v. Labrador Metis Nation [2007] NLCA, p. 75)*

Not content with this finding, the province appealed to the Supreme Court of Canada. But that court refused to hear the case, validating the Court of Appeal's ruling.

No doubt feeling the heat from Quebec, Newfoundland's negotiators now conceded to Innu strategists that they indeed held a veto over the Lower Churchill hydro-power project going forward. That key admission finally put things in motion, and by the fall of 2008, Premier Williams was able to announce the Tshash Petapen (New Dawn) Agreement-in-Principle (a 15-page entente) that still required detailed formal text and final Innu agreement. Yet the accord represented a key step in moving the project along. Moreover, the Innu Nation's demands for flood compensation on the initial Churchill Falls project were met.

Quebec v. Newfoundland

By 2009, Quebec was clearly benefiting from a seven-year head start because of 2002's Les Paix des Braves agreement. And now the Lower Churchill project faced even more pressing hydropower competition from Quebec. Premier Charest announced the $6.5 billion Romaine River hydropower project as "the biggest construction project in Canada", while personally cranking-up a massive bulldozer on site. The Quebec government then went public with its marketing strategy:

> *Quebec Energy Minister Claude Bechard is ordering Hydro-Quebec to speed up construction of hydro dams now that the United States is expressing more interest in renewable energy under President Barack Obama. ... "They are more open to green energy, and we want to be one of their best clients," said Bechard. (excerpt: CBC News of February 3, 2009)*

In real politick terms, this was the overarching context when the gloves finally came off between the competing premiers' visions. Precisely because Premier Charest was winning the hydropower sweepstakes, a vexed Premier

Williams launched a blistering counter-attack accusing Quebec of protectionism at his province's expense:

> ... *Danny Williams is accusing Hydro-Quebec of trying to block the Lower Churchill hydroelectric project to protect its own dominance in the marketplace.* ..."*It's a vision about nation-building and not territorial and protectionism by some provinces such as our neighbor Quebec.*" *(excerpt: CBC News, September 3, 2009)*

The last straw was Hydro-Quebec's proposed purchase of N.B. Power, which potentially gave the Quebec utility an infrastructure corridor leading into the New England market. Premier Williams made public his letter to N.B. Premier Shawn Graham warning him about doing deals with the devil:

> ... *Hydro-Quebec is still standing in the way of the legitimate aspirations of a power-exporting province. I have great fears and reservations about the stranglehold that Hydro-Quebec could put in place over the Atlantic region and I hope that you share this concern given your extensive statements on your desire to see your province as an energy hub....*

> ... *I would reiterate that our province feels compelled to look into the potential of anti-competitive behavior on the part of Hydro-Quebec given the potential monopoly that could exist as the result of an agreement between them and N.B. Power.* ... *(excerpts: Premier Williams' open letter of October 28, 2009)*

But the real reason for the premier's fury was Hydro-Quebec's total control of the power transmission corridor that ran from Churchill Falls down to markets in the heavily populated regions of Quebec; and the fact of the matter was that the Lower Churchill hydropower project was not able to gain access to this transmission system. That's because Hydro-Quebec was now flexing its muscle as an outright hydropower competitor. Premier Williams then travelled to New York City where he launched a blistering attack on Hydro-Quebec's (purported) market machinations in front of its targeted customers stating: "We now have a situation where Hydro-Québec believes their current stranglehold is not quite strong enough. ... The state of New York has a direct interest. Market dominance by Hydro-Québec is bad for consumers" (CBC News, November 17, 2009).

Nobody was more elated than Premier Williams when Premier Graham announced in the N.B. legislature on March 24, 2010 that the proposed sale of N.B. Power to Hydro-Quebec was dead! There's little doubt that the Newfoundland premier's very public remarks had helped 'tank the deal' by negatively influencing polling numbers on what was now the biggest political debate of the decade for New Brunswickers, with a provincial election imminent. On September 26, 2010 voters routed the Shawn Graham government. There's also little doubt that Premier Williams' personal and public condemnation of the sale transaction led to his colleague's political demise.

Of course, Premier Williams had earlier tried to rout Steven Harper from office. And this is where his anti-Harper 'Anybody But Conservative' (ABC) federal election campaign came into play. For he was able to deny the prime minister all seven federal Newfoundland and Labrador ridings in the October 2008 national election; paradoxically, leaving himself (Williams) with no representation in the Harper cabinet that could now push for the 'New Dawn's' speedy ratification; so desperately needed in order to close the gap (time lag) on Quebec's rapid hydropower progress.

Because it's an inescapable fact that his anti-Harper ABC campaign helped set the stage for an outcome that would soon backfire on the premier's hydro ambitions. It encouraged Ottawa powerbrokers to join forces with Quebec power-brokers to ramp up their hydropower production. They merged their agendas, under the radar of course, and the Crees were brought on board as equal partners. Indeed, would the Lower Churchill ever see the light of day?

Lower Churchill Announcement

That November, Premier Williams made two back-to-back announcements. His first, touted freedom "from the geographic stranglehold that Quebec has had on us for far too long," as the Lower Churchill hydropower project would now proceed in partnership with Nova Scotia. His second, came a week later when he resigned, declaring that he had "accomplished all that he had set out to do." However, to astute observers, there appeared to be some political sleight of hand at work as to the project's real merits. That's because the Lower Churchill hydro-power announcement was not about the principal Gull Island site being capable of generating 2,000 megawatts. Rather, it was about the much smaller Muskrat Falls site having the potential for only 825 megawatts (all figures taken from the province's 2005 public discussion paper). That's less than one third of the total megawatt capacity that was always touted for both sites - and it verges on a material discrepancy (a serious downsizing) in terms of public messaging.

For their part, the Innu Nation were invitees at the announcement ceremony, using the opportunity to reiterate their insistence that Ottawa first had to come to the table as a 'New Dawn' signatory, before they would sign-off on any hydropower project going ahead on their traditional lands.

Because the newly-downsized project had such daunting economics, the Newfoundland and Nova Scotia premiers had earlier sounded out Ottawa for $375 million to help finance transmission costs. That request prompted Quebec's justice minister to register an official protest with the prime minister saying that it had received no federal help for its transmission line costs. An infuriated Williams retorted that Charest's government was *"bad for Canada."* Here were hydro-power rivals once again at each other's throats.

Over in Quebec, the very week that Premier Williams stepped down, the Grand Council of the Crees opened their official embassy in Quebec City; this was an event that portended such diplomatic significance that every Quebec political leader showed up and pledged support. Nothing like this arrangement exists anywhere else in the country and the formalized nation-to-nation relationship epitomizes the quantum leap that Quebec has over every other resource jurisdiction.

The Lost Decade

Just one hundred days after Premier Williams left office, Ottawa announced that it had found the money to conclude a financial agreement with the Innu Nation on their land claim. This was the last elusive step in reaching an agreement-in-principle and (consequently) winning native support for the Lower Churchill hydropower project. Understanding the cause-and-effect linkage driving this long-awaited announcement is really as simple as 'ABC'; given that Ottawa's fiscal contribution apparently turned on waiting-out Williams' departure.

Danny Williams was barely out of office when Innu Nation strategist, Peter Penashue, ran for the Conservatives in the spring 2011 federal election campaign. Still the results of the vote regionally were almost a replay of the previous ABC campaign, with all six seats on the island of Newfoundland once again snubbing the prime minister. Only Labrador went against the grain with Penashue winning by just 231 votes. He was immediately sworn in as a senior federal cabinet minister and the Innu Nation celebrated his arrival in Ottawa as a transformative day in their turbulent history.

In the span of five months, Williams was out and Penashue was in! Here was the former premier's sparring partner and erstwhile thorn in the side of his government on hydropower development, now poised to fill the very political vacuum that Williams had created (with his ABC campaign). It's poetic justice that the fate of the Lower Churchill hydropower project would now be determined by the Member of Parliament from Labrador.

On Canada Day 2011, the Innu Nation over-whelmingly voted in favour of the New Dawn AIP, the Churchill Falls compensation agreement, and the Muskrat Falls hydropower proposal. The ratification vote was touted as *"the most important decision in the history of our people"* by the Innu Nation's president. Everyone well knew that the project was conditional upon Innu Nation approval; thus, July 1, 2011 marks the moment that Newfoundland's hydropower expansion plans finally broke free to compete with Quebec for market share (a full decade after the Paix des Braves). There's considerable irony in having Minister Penashue at the cabinet table in Ottawa. Not only does it expose the folly of the anti-Harper (ABC) campaign; it could well be the Lower Churchill hydropower project's only shot at getting back into the game. Because the fact remains that, during the critical years of strategizing for these competing projects, the James Bay Cree were hydro-power players and the Innu Nation were not. This is the best single reason for understanding why markets favour

Premier Charest's hydropower fortunes over those of former Premier Williams. More to the point, Quebec's powerful momentum holds real potential to strand the Lower Churchill as a commercially viable project.

In hindsight, Quebec may indeed have bettered its neighbour in what has since turned out to be an unconscionable fiscal windfall on the Churchill Falls revenue split; yet that windfall wasn't apparent at the time the deal was struck. But tellingly, Quebec has another fiscal advantage over its neighbour, as a result of key native settlements that it reached a decade ago. The difference being that the economic upside of those native deals was apparent to anyone attuned to the rise of native empowerment. That's the real Quebec advantage today.

Thus, in native empowerment terms, that "No Dam Way" rebuke back in 1998 was a wake-up call signaling to both governments that they needed to start working collaboratively with natives. Both were given the same unmistakable message, at the same time, and at the same place. Thus that moment represents the proper point of departure for comparing their respective native engagement strategies. The bottom line is that Quebec earned the Crees' support in early 2002; yet for Newfoundland it would still take until mid-2011 to do so. In what has to be the ultimate irony, Quebec woke-up to the fact that natives determined hydropower outcomes a decade before Newfoundland did - at Churchill Falls of all places!

4

ONTARIO: *TIME WARP*

The pivotal event in the rise of native empowerment nationally took place in Ontario. On September 6, 1995, Dudley George, an unarmed native was shot at Ipperwash Park by an OPP TRU (tactical and rescue unit) marksman. At that precise moment, the clock stopped on the native relationship file in Ontario, and nothing constructive would happen until the tragic event was rectified. It would be May 31, 2007 when the Commission Inquiry's report was issued; and May 31, 2009 when its principal recommendation, which was to hand Ipperwash Park back to local natives, was acted upon - a span of 15 years.

Fifteen years is indeed a long time for something as important as the crown / native relationship to lie dormant. In the interim, a vacuum engulfed the province on a host of issues including resource development. And if Queen's Park thought the relationship 'restart' would re-commence as if nothing had happened, it was sorely mistaken, since natives had gone-to-ground in a serious way. New rules of engagement were urgently required, because the worst possible scenario would be a resumption of an unstructured dialogue with everyone picking up where they had left off. Indeed, that was what happened. In the resource sector, industry assumed that it would be business as usual; and if there were to be problems, then government should take the lead in their resolution.

But the landscape had changed. One of the consequences of natives going-to-ground was that the native legal winning streak occurred by in large elsewhere in Canada. In almost every other province, natives were considerably ahead in terms of their legal empowerment. This is the 'time warp' in which Ontario now finds itself. Today the province is largely out of step with the rise of native empowerment nationally. And since Ontario natives lacked comparable legal clout, crisis and chaos would have to reign before the proper balance would be struck to facilitate constructive dialogue. Thus, with the return of Ipperwash Park to the local natives on May 31, 2009, the relationship clock was finally restarted (although in native time it was still September 6, 1995). Now efforts to resume constructive dialogue would have to factor in all the pressures that had been percolating beneath the surface since the shooting. As a result, a proper understanding of the key events at Ipperwash is critical.

Ipperwash

According to the following excerpt from the Call for Applications, published March 18, 2004, the Ipperwash Inquiry was: " ...to inquire and report on events surrounding the death of Dudley George, including the protest by Aboriginal people at the Ipperwash Provincial Park in 1995 where Dudley George was shot. The Commission is also directed to make recommendations aimed at avoiding violence in similar circumstances."

The call for an inquiry also had deep political over-
tones given that the announcement was made on the eve
of a provincial election call and coincided with a last-
minute litigation settlement and compensation payment
made to the George family by Ontario. Now there would
be a full inquiry into the roles and responsibilities of
former Premier Mike Harris, his key ministers and aides
as well as those of the OPP. The Inquiry would be wide-
ranging with no stone left unturned, and its final, five-
volume report would amount to 1,500 pages of detailed
research and analysis.

In effect, the Ipperwash Inquiry was Ontario's Royal
Commission; both were major events in propelling the
rise of native empowerment forward. There's no doubt
that if a native were to be killed in a policing action today
while protesting a resource project, that project would be
derailed along with the careers of all the senior
executives, who's involvement would be exhaustively
investigated. For if nothing else the Ipperwash Inquiry
showed the extent to which such proceedings can become
the focus for human rights lawyers and social justice
activists. All of these agendas merged in the lead-up to
the public inquiry.

Coincidentally, the historical stage was set for the
inquiry just one month prior to its commencement, when
a British auction house announced that a rare medal,
which had been unearthed along the banks of the Detroit
River by a metal detector enthusiast, would be put on the
block. It was an 1814 medal from King George to his
native allies for supporting General Brock in taking Fort
Detroit from the Americans. As the crow flies, that's not
all that far from Ipperwash Park; and it's possible that
some of those natives who fought for King George were
Dudley George's ancestors. Indeed, many natives
appropriated the good king's surname when they
subsequently resettled near Sarnia, which resettlement

was payback by the British for their military services rendered in the defense of Upper Canada.

Still on the subject of archeology, eight days after Dudley George was shot, the Ontario government 'discovered' that indeed it had files documenting the existence of a native burial site in Ipperwash Park. These files had been kept right next to Queen's Park in the Whitney Block. Later on in evidence, the Inquiry heard about how a skull that had been unearthed (back in 1950) from Ipperwash Park ended up adorning the park superintendant's desk. Excerpts from the transcript of that exchange provide yet another time warp dimension, as follows:

Q: And so these -- this skull and partial skeleton that was found in the Park uncovered, I gather, partially as a result of some bulldozing operations, according to the daughter of the Park superintendent, the skull sat on the superintendent's desk for several months.

And we've heard no evidence that anybody in the surrounding First Nations was ever advised that there had been a skeleton found at the time. There's no evidence of that.

Now, would you agree with me that in the situation of finding a -- a skeleton and skull in that fashion, that it was inappropriate, perhaps only in hindsight or perhaps in hindsight, it was inappropriate for the skull to be treated that way and for the First Nations people not to be advised of this? ...

A: Just to be clear, I was never aware of either one of those details.

Q: All right.

*A: On the surface of it, yes, I would agree with you.
(excerpts: Inquiry transcript, cross examination of
former Minister of Natural Resources, Development
and Mines, Chris Hodgson by Murray Klippenstein,
January 17, 2006, pp. 69-70)*

It's speculation of course, but this relic could also have
been one of Dudley George's ancestors. Nevertheless, the
exchange certainly puts the native assertions in
perspective. The facts were that there was a known burial
ground within Ipperwash Park and that the evidence
supporting that fact was easily ascertainable right next
door to Queen's Park.

One problem that hampered the Inquiry was the
evidentiary vacuum created by the intervening deaths of
three of the key OPP players (all had died before the
inquiry convened). Inspector Linton had ordered the
TRU team in; Sergeant Eve had been the on-site
negotiator, and Sergeant Deane was the marksman who
had fired the fatal shots. (Sergeant Eve was killed in the
line-of-duty on highway patrol). Their missing testimony
further complicated the fact that, all told, no less than six
officers had discharged their weapons that night sending
dozens of rounds of ammunition into the darkness. The
scene was chaotic and both sides were traumatized by the
suddenness of the tragic turn of events. In fact, another
officer testified that he had thought (at the time) that he
was the shooter! Here's an excerpt from the inquiry
transcript that gives a sense of what that police officer
experienced when firing point blank into the driver's side
window of a native vehicle:

*Q: ... There's four (4) shots where bullets were lodged
in the side of the car.*

A: Okay.

Q: Okay. There's one (1) that ricochets off of the car. There's at least one (1) to two (2) in the pillar on the driver's side.

A: Right.

Q: And there's a shattered window. Okay, so that's a lot more than you shot with your gun, right?

A: I know I fired four (4), but only two (2) or three (3) at the car.

Q: Okay. So at best, at least two (2), three (3), four (4) or more were fired by others at that car at the driver's side?

A: And I had that sense, that's what I was saying before, about we - I felt that the car was the deceased, because I just had the sense that - when the smoke cleared, I believe there was an officer up with a gun drawn to my left, and at least two (2) to my right standing on the pavement as it was exiting.

So there was three (3) or four (4) of us standing there with our weapons still drawn on that car. (excerpt: Inquiry transcript: cross examination of OPP constable Wade Lacroix by Kevin Scullion May 10, 2006, pp. 260-261)

It's beyond fortunate that this native driver wasn't wounded or killed in the mêlée. (Which is why Constable Lacroix initially thought that his target was the deceased). These events underscore just how chaotic the situation in the dunes was that fateful night.

Political Backdrop

A year before this testimony was elicited, on May 18, 2005, the Inquiry had heard about a taped phone call between two senior OPP officers that had occurred earlier in the evening on the same night as the fatal shooting. Inspector Ron Fox was reporting-in to Inspector John Carson (and Incident Commander) about a meeting at Queen's Park with the premier and senior cabinet ministers that he (Fox) had just left. The following quotations from an article, which appeared in The London Free Press on May 19, 2005, set the stage for the events that occurred later that fateful night:

> *Fox warned Carson that they were dealing with a "red-neck government. They are ... barrel suckers. They are just in love with guns.".... He (Premier Harris) believes that he has the authority to direct the O.P.P. (excerpt: reporter John Miner, quoting OPP inspector, Ron Fox)*

The media obviously sensed that these quotes were a potential indictment of the Harris government's handling of the native occupation; thus the exchange received major national coverage. Paradoxically, this intense media coverage elicited a telling response from out west, where on the very next business day and without any announcement or fanfare, Alberta posted its draft 'First Nation's Consultation Policy' to a ministry website. Which raises the following question: Was Premier Ralph Klein motivated to act by what his colleague (and sometime golf partner) Premier Mike Harris was being put through: enmeshed in native litigation, having to testify as the key inquiry witness, enduring unrelenting and unflattering media coverage, and now being exposed by this latest OPP revelation? Alberta's timing on its own draft native consultation policy was no coincidence.

Of course the Commission Inquiry report focused at length on this late-in-the-day OPP phone call, and the Commissioner ultimately profiled the new Ontario premier as being on the receiving end of unreliable and unfocused information from key officials who obviously should have known better:

> ... *Ministry of Natural Resources officials circulated unverified, inaccurate and extremely provocative reports about automatic gunfire in the park at government meetings. ... MNR officials did not have the expertise to assess the reliability or accuracy of these reports, nor were they aware of the potential implications of passing this unverified information directly to the Inter-ministerial Committee composed of political staff, civil servants and seconded OPP officers, <u>one of whom was in contact with the Incident Commander</u>. Lines of communication and chains of command were blurred. There was also a lack of clarity regarding the relationship between political staff and professional civil servants.*
>
> *Taken together, the interaction between the police and government at Ipperwash created the appearance of inappropriate interference in police operations. (excerpt: Ipperwash Commission Inquiry Report Vol. 1, pp. 676-7) (author's underlining)*

The Commissioner's assessment of the premier's role was direct and to the point:

> *The evidence demonstrated that the Premier and his officials wanted the occupation to end quickly, but there is no evidence to suggest that either the Premier or any official in his government was responsible for Mr. George's death. (Ibid., p. 675)*

To further reinforce these findings, the Commissioner had this to say upon the public release of his report on May 31, 2007:

> ... *It is clear that the provincial government had the authority to establish policing policy and there is no doubt that the Premier, wanted the occupiers out of the park as soon as possible and the occupation ended, but the evidence does not support the claim that he interfered with the O.P.P.'s operation (p. 5).*

> *I have found that both the former Premier and the Minister of Natural Resources made racist comments, in what has become known as "the dining room meeting", although both denied making these offensive comments (p. 5).*

> ... *The O.P.P. decided to march down the road on the night of September 6 because they misperceived the intentions of the occupiers, just as the occupiers misperceived the intentions of the O.P.P. (pp. 8-9).*

> ... *It is impossible to attribute Mr. George's death to a single person, factor, decision or institution. On the contrary, it was the combination of these that made a violent result more likely, particularly when they all came together in the space of a few short days and hours in the context of a highly-charged confrontation. Individuals and institutions need to be held accountable for the consequences of their decisions and actions, whether those consequences were intended or not (p. 11). (excerpts: from the Commissioner's Statement on the public release of his report on May 31, 2007)*

The formal text of the Commission Inquiry Report is significant in that it examines Premier Harris' interaction from several policy and operational angles, as follows:

> *In my view, although Premier Harris was critical of the police, I do not find that he interfered with or gave inappropriate directions to the police at Ipperwash. The Premier conveyed his displeasure that the police had relinquished control of the park to the First Nations people on September 4, 1995. He also said he did not think the OPP had adequately prepared for the occupation. Moreover, the Premier expressed his displeasure that the occupiers were still in the park two days later on September 6. He was undoubtedly critical of the OPP.*
>
> *However, the Premier did not inappropriately direct the OPP on its operations at Ipperwash or enter the law enforcement domain of the police. Although one may disagree with his view, it was legitimate for the Premier to take the position that the First Nations people were illegally occupying the park, and that he wanted them out of Ipperwash Park as soon as possible. He did not give directions on the manner in which the OPP should enforce the law; how, when, and what arrests should be made; tactical decisions; or other actions that should be taken by the police to end the occupation. In my view, the Premier did not give instructions to or interfere with the OPP's operations at Ipperwash in September 1995.*
> *(excerpts: Ipperwash Commission Inquiry Report Vol. 1, Section 12.4.5, p. 371)*

Not to make too fine a point, it is again worth comparing how government officials are portrayed in the formal text of the Commission report:

> *MNR officials circulated unverified, inaccurate and*
> *extremely provocative reports ... did not have the*
> *expertise to assess the reliability or accuracy of these*
> *reports, nor were they aware of the potential*
> *implications of passing this unverified information*
> *directly to the Inter-ministerial Committee ... . (Ibid.)*

While there's more than enough blame to go around, most of it from the Inquiry's perspective appears to lie with the incompetence of government officials and the dubious operational misperceptions of the OPP on site.

Caledonia

The Ipperwash Commission Inquiry report was issued in May 2007, one month before the first National Day of Action. Railroads and highways had been blockaded just the month before over the native occupation at Caledonia, which had already been on the nightly news for over a year. Several other blockades across Ontario were percolating: in the north (Platinex), in the west (Grassy Narrows) and in the east (Frontenac Ventures) as well as in various urban areas (Deseronto, Hagersville and Brantford). Injunctions were flying in the resource sector as the courts were drawn into the unenviable role of referee in one development dispute after another. Over the next eighteen months, Ontario would cycle through no less than three aboriginal affairs ministers, adding to the sense of disarray at Queen's Park. This was the overarching context that greeted the Commission Inquiry's final report. From a media standpoint, it was almost completely upstaged by the shenanigans playing out daily at Caledonia, a rapidly expanding satellite community near Hamilton. And as a direct result, its recommendations about events that transpired in a 1995 context did not gain sufficient traction with the public in a 2007 context. Moreover in an alarming turn of events, Caledonia was now infamous not only for hostile natives - but also for hostile locals.

Henco Industries

On February 28, 2006 while Henco Industries, a local real estate developer, was constructing its first houses in a large open subdivision known as Douglas Creek Estates, the site was occupied by natives out to 'reclaim' their Haldimand Tract lands. Henco quickly obtained injunctions, which the OPP had vetted by the Court for legal clarity purposes. The next day, anticipating local law enforcement, 100 Six Nations women formed a human chain in support of their cause. When a mediator was sent in he was told: "We want the organ grinder, not the monkey!" Days later, the Sheriff was ordered to "step back" while his official documents were dumped on the road and set alight in front of the media. In early April 2006, the local citizenry called upon the OPP to end the occupation, at which point Henco declared that it was "frustrated with authorities at every step." On April 20, 2006, the OPP undertook a pre-dawn massed entry on the contested area, only to be repelled by a larger native contingent. At which point, the native barricades went up.

Newscasts presented a litany of nightmarish images: hydro-electric towers used as barricades to block main roads, burned-out vehicles (one dumped off an overpass onto the highway below), a burning railway trestle (from which firefighters backed away for fear of reprisal), a trenched road, a car crashed into a fenced electrical transformer station followed by a serious fire that resulted in area-wide power blackouts and finally, a half dozen rail lines blocked in sympathy protests (the rail blockade near Belleville impacted some 50 trains and 3,500 travelers).

These events saw native activists arrested and then released by the courts. Local residents were publicly mobilizing, saying "enough is enough" and challenging the OPP to clamp-down. Serious altercations between the two groups ensued that now had the police playing referee to neither side's satisfaction. Police and government both invoked the Ipperwash report. The OPP declared: *"We're the ham in the sandwich."* And the provincial government explained: *"We don't direct police involvement."* It appeared that the Ipperwash report provided both with a Catch-22 'out'. Lost on the media and the public was the post-Ipperwash reality that police and government were now expected to follow a staged, disciplined approach in resolving native land-rights assertions - consisting of facilitation, negotiation, and judicial solutions - before bringing the power of the state to bear.

Moratorium Invoked

In early May 2006, negotiators were finally able to arrange a schedule for discussions. Then just days later, Henco Industries discovered that a Six Nations website had posted a letter from the Minister of Aboriginal Affairs announcing an immediate moratorium on further development on Douglas Creek Estates lands. This was the first Henco had heard of it and they were not even copied on it! (It looked like the moratorium was the trade-off for winning native agreement to the discussion schedule.) In any event, the wording of the letter is highly instructive for project proponents anywhere in Canada who don't have native support, since governments can and will impose a moratorium if it suits their purposes. As such, this letter is a key benchmark in the rise of native empowerment since it exposes the imposition of a moratorium as a potential political project risk factor:

Minister Responsible for Aboriginal Affairs
Office of the Minister
Whitney Block, 99 Wellesley Street West
Toronto, Ontario

May 17, 2006

Haudenosaunee Six Nations Confederacy Council
RR 2
Ohsweken Ontario

Dear Haudenosaunee Six Nations Confederacy Council:

This letter confirms the imposition of an immediate moratorium halting any development on the Douglas Creek lands for a period of time to be agreed upon by the representatives of the Confederacy, Canada and Ontario (the parties). During the period of the moratorium parties will agree to establish a process to deal with the Douglas Creek land rights.

In order for talks on Douglas Creek Estates and the long-term land grievance to proceed, we must see continued progress on removal of the barricades on the transportation corridors.

As the short term discussions proceed, I continue to have full confidence in The Hon. David Peterson and fully support him and the terms and conditions that he negotiates with you.

Hon. David Ramsay
Minister

In early June 2006, on the 100th day anniversary of the barricades going up, 100 chiefs from around Ontario were bused into Caledonia in a display of leadership support. This was yet another wake-up call for the Ontario government. Then on June 27, Minister Ramsay rushed up to northwestern Ontario where a mining dispute was now escalating and where he released the draft of his long-awaited Aboriginal Consultation Guidelines. His trip was most likely in response to these headlines, which appeared in the *Globe and Mail* a few days prior on June 22, 2006: "Ontario faces fresh native-rights storm; mining company and protestors set to square off over property claim."

Finally on July 5, 2006 the Province of Ontario purchased Douglas Creek Estates from Henco for $15.8 million. With Henco out of the picture, the Court of Appeal would now be asked to sort out the legalities of the land reclamation, which was notable for the fact that now Ontario was allowing the native "occupiers" to remain at the Douglas Creek Estates site. In late July 2006, Ontario's Minister of Community Safety became the object of public ridicule by saying: *"The native protest has devolved into a 'symbolic' protest ... there really isn't an occupation."* Caledonia's embattled mayor shot-back with, *"He was not in touch with reality!"* But by this time, the Caledonia conflict had gone international with an article in *The Economist* weighing-in with more unflattering coverage of the situation. Canada was getting another black-eye on the international stage. Ipperwash and Oka were repeatedly referenced in the media. The eyes of the world were watching.

Then, in late August 2006, the Ontario Court of Appeal ruled on the legality of Henco's injunctions to remove the natives. The ruling shows that the court was clearly swayed by the fact that Ontario, now the landowner, was allowing the native occupiers to remain on site:

*[19] The Province owns Douglas Creek Estates. It
does not claim that the protesters are on its property
unlawfully. It does not seek a court order removing
them. It is content to let them remain. We see no
reason why it should not be permitted to do so. If the
protesters cause a nuisance or other disturbance
affecting neighbouring lands or residents of
Caledonia, then action may be required. But no
evidence was presented to us of any current incident
requiring the intervention of the Attorney General,
the Ontario Provincial Police (O.P.P.) or the courts.*

*[22] Here the Province's actions have obviously been
taken to promote the public interest. In discharging
its public duty to address the conflict in Caledonia, the
Province has been required to make some difficult
decisions. These decisions included purchasing the
disputed property, allowing the protesters to remain
on the property, and trying to resolve the ongoing
dispute through peaceful negotiations. These
decisions were taken in the public interest. Some may
disagree with the Province's stance. We do not think,
however, that it is the court's role to question the
wisdom of the government's actions. The motion
judge's order continuing the injunction by making it
binding on the Province, thus leaving the protesters to
face the spectre of ongoing contempt proceedings if
they do not vacate the property, threatens to
undermine the Government's attempts to resolve this
dispute. (Henco Industries Ltd. v. Haudenosaunee Six
Nations Confederacy Council [2006] Ont. CA 82 O.R.
(3d))*

Broad segments of the populace, especially those living
south of the Trans-Canada Highway, interpreted the
Henco rulings as validating a 'two-tier' justice system;
whereby native protesters seemingly received kid gloves

treatment instead of having to face the full force of the law. This sentiment was fueled almost on a weekly basis by the fact that the native protests had intensified during the first six months of 2007.

Indeed, another local real estate development, Sterling Properties, was the scene of a second native occupation. This occupation was newsworthy because of a violent assault perpetrated by natives against a builder that left him badly injured and psychologically traumatized. Soon there was talk of local militia-types organizing to take the law into their own hands. The situation had become so polarized that the roads in and around Douglas Creek Estates warranted round-the-clock police presence. Most of the time the police were on stand-by duty operating on the assumption that there would likely be trouble if the public were left to their own devices. Nobody seemed inclined to fret over the urgent recommendations with respect to policing native protests that had just emanated from the Ipperwash Commission Inquiry; mainly because the Inquiry had been upstaged.

Haldimand Tract

Many of the contentious injunction proceedings over the Douglas Creek Estates reclamation took place in the stately Cayuga courthouse, in front of which stand two 1812- era cannons and a historical plaque that reads:

Haldimand Grant (1784)

Following the American Revolution Sir Frederick Haldimand, Governor-in-Chief of Canada, granted to the Six Nations of the Iroquois a tract of land extending for six miles on both sides of the Grand River from its source to Lake Erie. This grant was made in recognition of their services as allies of the

British Crown during the war, and to recompense them for the loss of their former lands in northern New York State. In later years, large areas of this tract, including portions of the present counties of Haldimand, Brant, Waterloo and Wellington, were sold to white settlers.

Lawyers might have well have introduced this plaque directly into evidence, since much of today's land rights assertions and controversies stem from the arrival of those "white settlers" and their resulting land transactions with Six Nations along the Grand River. The British administrators on the frontier were all military men who understood the win / loss equation of warfare. They viewed Iroquois warriors as being especially valuable allies and developed a workable (quasi-military) relationship with them. After the Thirteen Colonies seceded, it was decided to create a new homeland for their native allies in Upper Canada in recognition of their loyal and faithful service to the Crown. The Iroquois Confederacy comprising Mohawk, Seneca, Cayuga, Tuscarora, Oneida and Onondaga (who were formerly situated in upstate New York) migrated north and took up residence in the Haldimand Tract based on this specific land grant provision:

Whereas His Majesty is pleased to direct ... in consideration of the early attachment to his cause manifested by the Mohawk Indians and the loss of their settlement which they thereby sustained ... to take possession of and to settle upon the banks of the Grand River - six miles deep from each side - to enjoy forever. (excerpt: Haldimand Grant, October 25, 1784)

In fact, two large tracts were purchased from the Mississaugas at either end of Lake Ontario. Today, these two communities are known as the Six Nations of the Grand River (near Brantford) and the Tyendinaga Mohawk of the Bay of Quinte (near Desoronto). Strategically, it was useful for the British to have Mohawks situated at both ends of the lake, as the prospect of encountering warriors would have presented a serious deterrence to the Americans in planning a military invasion of Upper Canada.

The Haldimand Tract extended along the entire length of the Grand River from Lake Erie north to Shelburne; and, at the other end of Lake Ontario, the Simcoe Grant lay in the vicinity of Belleville / Desoronto. Needless to say, numerous parcels in both tracts were wheeled-and-dealed over the ensuing two and a quarter centuries. As is to be expected, the titles to many parcels became factually and legally clouded due to the passage of time; not to mention the many subsequent purchases by bona-fide third parties who rightly assumed that the land registry office afforded them clear title.

The arrival of the Six Nations in Upper Canada coincided with a wave of Loyalist immigration that swept across the region. Having fought for the British, the Six Nations viewed themselves to be in a nation-to-nation relationship with the crown. However, this aspect was lost on the Loyalist settlers who looked to crown land administrators to help them resettle by seeking out the best available land. Throughout Upper and Lower Canada, Loyalist numbers inflated local populations; moreover they had little knowledge of or connection to what had transpired between the British and the Iroquois Confederacy before their arrival. For they too were loyal to the King and eager to start afresh. So it was a generation later, just after the war of 1812, when the era of military alliances with natives drew to a close. Loyalists were now prominent in running state affairs and native administrative matters were relegated to Indian agents who were required to safeguard their rights and document all transactions involving the disposition of tract lands.

Whether the Six Nations today have a valid claim to the Douglas Creek Estates lands has yet to be determined. The issue turns on a historical point of legal conveyance: whether the Plank Road right-of-way was properly divested by the Six Nations in the late 1800s? The road lies within the Haldimand Tract, and as such the Six Nation's consent to convey it was required. Government negotiators appear to believe that the chain of title infers that the right-of-way was properly divested. However, the Six Nations negotiators counter that opinion with the position that it was a leased right-of-way, which should have reverted to their control once the lease had expired. Of note, it was the lack of progress in resolving this particular dispute that prompted the Six Nations land protectors to occupy Douglas Creek Estates, which they viewed as being one of the last available large parcels that could be used to top-up the amount of land owing to them (given that another twenty-eight land disputes remain unsettled). Put another way, the Douglas Creek Estates reclamation sent the native empowerment message that land claim inertia had to be reversed - or else!

City of Brantford

To reinforce this message, from 2007 through to mid-2009, Six Nations 'land protectors' systematically disrupted local real estate developers across the region. The following five headlines tell just a fraction of the complex story:

Six Nations protesters shut down Brantford shopping center construction. (Oct. 24, 2007)

*Grand River plan requires consent, fee: Six Nations
(Feb. 16, 2008)*

*City police have no plans to budge native protesters
(May 5, 2008)*

*Municipality files for injunction to prevent further
'irreparable harm' (May 22, 2008) (all four headlines
from Brantford Expositor)*

*City seeks Armed Forces intervention (May 29, 2008)
National Post*

The following statement from (former) Brantford Mayor
Mike Hancock highlighted the community's stress level:

*"I wouldn't have thought [the comparison to
Caledonia] was possible until today," said Mayor
Mike Hancock, adding that property settlement is a
federal and provincial issue and that officials from
both government ministries have been slow to
respond. "We're collateral damage in all of this and
we feel it." (excerpt: reporters, Craig Offman & Katie
Rook, National Post, July 15, 2008).*

Brantford was now the emerging hot spot in terms of 'on
the ground' native intimidation tactics, and the city
fought back by passing two by-laws: the first, prohibited
interference with development, construction and access
to property; the second, prohibited the collection of
development fees by any organization other than the city
itself. Natives would later argue in court that these by-
laws were not of general application (applicable to all
citizens) but rather that they were specifically designed
to target them as a minority. Yet it was obvious to all that
natives were the ones doing the targeting!

In a surprising turn of events, Brantford found itself on the receiving end of an expensive lawsuit brought by a major developer alleging that the city had failed to provide clear title to its proposed building site. Kingspan Insulated Products now decided not to proceed with its proposed head office and sued for $10 million on account of its having been repeatedly blockaded by native activists. The company blamed the city for its losses, and the mayor blamed the native activists. By year-end 2009, there had been so much native disruption of commercial sites that it prompted the *Brantford Expositor* to publish a lengthy summary of events on a month-to-month basis for its readers. There's no doubt that the city was being handcuffed in terms of development projects; that's because the city itself lay within the Haldimand Tract.

Court proceedings to enforce the by-laws commenced in May 2008, but they wouldn't be finalized until November 2010 - a span of two and a half years. The judge convened 21 days of court time over 22 months; he also appointed an *amicus* to provide independent advice to the court, ordered the parties into facilitation, and eventually succeeded in defusing tensions by handling most of the matters in chambers and out of the public eye. He also ordered the various levels of government to appear in court and explain their delay in addressing land claim issues.

Pembroke Hospital

Just as Ontario was preparing to transfer Ipperwash Park back to local natives and restart the relationship clock, it looked as if a new trouble spot was brewing that bore many frightening comparisons to Ipperwash, Caledonia and Brantford. On April 1, 2009 the front page of the Pembroke Daily Observer ran this headline and story:

Construction Stopped: Authorities are tight-lipped today after construction at the Pembroke Regional Hospital came to a standstill Tuesday following the discovery of an ancient Native burial ground.

According to federal legislation, discoveries of such artifacts are to be treated as national historic sites and must be preserved until archeologists from the Ministry of Natural Resources and Aboriginal Services Canada determine the best course of action. Aside from the loss of productivity and its associated expense, the entire project could be relocated or possibly even cancelled should federal authorities determine the artifacts are too fragile to be handled safely.

Naturally, this has PRH president and CEO Pierre Noel in a state.

"We have a multi-million dollar facility well under way and to contemplate having to postpone or even terminate construction is beyond comprehension." Noel bristled as he hustled into a meeting with government and aboriginal officials.

Kirby Whiteduck, chief of Pikwakanagan band council in Golden Lake, had a different view when arriving for the closed-door session.
"The site holds a great deal of significance for our people and we won't permit it to be damaged any further," he said.

Curiously enough, MPP Cheryl Gallant was not at the meeting but her absence was explained by Chuck Strahl, Minister of Indian Affairs and Northern Development, who represented the federal government at the meeting.

"She's just too pale to be at the table," Strahl explained.

The meeting broke up around midnight with police protecting the controversial site while Native protestors set up tents across the road to keep tabs on the location.

Calls to Mr. Noel, Mr. Whiteduck, Mrs. Gallant, and Mr. Strahl were not returned, as apparently all had better things to do on April Fools Day than talk to us. Hopefully they like you dear readers, will enjoy this little spoof on April 1! (editor: Pembroke Daily Observer, April 1, 2009)

Not everybody got the joke! Certainly native leaders weren't laughing. Moreover it's doubtful that the mayors of Caledonia, Hagersville and Brantford found it amusing. In Caledonia, the tab to taxpayers was now reaching $60 million (excluding the Henco buyout). Although lame, the spoof conveyed an aura of realism due to all the hot buttons thrown into the article for good measure: "burial ground", "native protestors", "tents across the road", and "police protecting the controversial site". Native leaders were outraged and the newspaper belatedly apologized saying on its website that "... it was intended to amuse and entertain, and not meant to offend anyone." Still it was published at the very moment that Ontario's relationship clock was poised for restart. Thus this bit of media folly begs the question: If it's just a joking matter, why would police ever put themselves in harm's way in future standoffs?

Frontenac and Platinex

The editorial was all the more remarkable given that the City of Pembroke had a serious native protest underway on its doorstep. A uranium exploration company, Frontenac Ventures, had been blockaded for months over watershed protection issues and had petitioned the courts to compel native compliance under the 100-year old Mining Act. The same scenario was playing out in northwestern Ontario involving another explorer, Platinex Inc. Here were native leaders protecting traditional watersheds on two fronts, and it appeared that eco-activists were supporting them every step of the way. Indeed, the perfect storm had blown in; and its aftermath would see the map of Ontario fundamentally changed. Moreover, the Ipperwash Inquiry had foreseen the coming chaos and had urged Ontario to take a proactive role in settling the Platinex dispute before things got out of hand:

> *The confrontation at Big Trout Lake and the judicial decision in the Platinex case <u>should serve as a call to Ontario to take the initiative in meeting its obligations</u> to ensure that meaningful, good-faith efforts are made to accommodate the interests of Aboriginal peoples and to respect their rights in the course of managing natural resource development. (excerpt: Ipperwash Commission Inquiry, Volume 2, p. 112) (author's underlining)*

However, the reality was that the Ontario government had been missing-in-action in the native consultation department all along. And that left the now stressed corporate - native relationship up to the courts to sort out. Both cases would ultimately be heard together before the Court of Appeal; but by then, the native leaders in both blockades had already been incarcerated for their admitted contempt of the lower court injunctions (favouring the mining companies). However, in the forum of public opinion, their plight had become a highly visible and emotionally charged human rights cause. Huge public rallies in front of Queen's Park involving thousands of concerned citizens and lasting over a period of days protested their incarceration both as victims of the judicial system and of an antiquated Mining Act. The Court of Appeal reduced their 6-month sentences to time already served and tellingly referred to the "eloquent Report of the Ipperwash Inquiry". The court declared with respect to Frontenac Ventures:

> *[65] ... there was no need to bring down the hammer of long jail sentences and very substantial fines.*

> *[66] For these reasons, I conclude that the custodial and monetary components of the sentences imposed on the appellants were too harsh. ...*
> *(excerpts: Frontenac Ventures v. Ardoch Algonquin First Nation Ont CA July 7, 2008, 91O.R. (3d), p. 1)*

Then the Court of Appeal echoed Platinex's submission on sentencing:

> *[3]... Platinex Inc. informed the court that it would not be opposing the appeal because "the appellants have spent enough time in jail, the matter will ultimately be settled only through negotiation, and no good purpose would be served by keeping the appellants in jail any longer." (excerpt: Platinex Inc. v. Kitchenuhmaykoosib Inninuwug First Nation Ont CA, l July 7, 2008, 91O.R. (3d), p. 18)*

The native leaders were immediately released to a tumultuous public reception on the courthouse steps, coincidentally right on the eve of the 2nd National Day of Action. They were now rising-stars in the native empowerment movement and were regularly referred to as 'political prisoners in Canada' in supportive press releases. Thus it's important to understand their prior actions in order to appreciate how the map of Ontario would soon be changed as a result.

The specific incident that gave rise to the jail sentences in the Platinex case was the eviction of Platinex's CEO, and an archeologist (as well as the author) from conducting a court ordered site survey - for cultural impacts and burial sites - in order to set the stage for exploratory drilling to proceed. This type of survey was a prime recommendation of the Ipperwash Inquiry and it would have been an omission of corporate - native protocol had it not been undertaken. In fact, the site survey was specifically ordered to proceed by the judge as a preliminary step under the court's ongoing case supervision. Instead, Platinex's CEO was blockaded at the community airstrip and served with a formal eviction notice: *"You are hereby ordered by chief and council to leave Kitchenuhmaykoosib Reserve # 84 immediately."* Moreover, the court had also sanctioned a consultation protocol that was supposed to be complied with.

Perhaps the best source for explaining the way events subsequently played out comes from the Ipperwash Inquiry itself. For at the closing of the argument phase, a key submission was made by the northern native police services board warning the Inquiry that resource companies were being specifically 'targeted' by native strategists. The following transcript excerpts are from the same police board that subsequently dealt with the fallout from the Platinex eviction:

> *Nishnawbe-Aski Police Services undertook the task of addressing confrontations, protests, and road blockage over resource development.*

> *... Today, First Nations traditional land occupiers have re-emerged and revitalized their rights to their traditional lands.*

... At times it appears to First Nations that Ontario is taunting them to take more aggressive actions.

[The] Nishnawbe-Aski police services examined three (3) road blockages erected by First Nations in Northern Ontario ... we have included certain parts of Kitchinumaykosib Inninuwug (Platinex) protest.

Ontario and resource developers are the two (2) main proponents consistently targeted in the direct actions. Ontario government has been consistently negligent through its policies and regulations to accommodate First Nations and their interests in the planning of natural resources.

This has led to complete marginalization of the First Nations resulting in abject poverty, anger and frustration, that developer interests have been targeted because of continual negligence to comply or meet undertakings according to negotiated terms and conditions of agreement. Direct action has been a means to force the developer to the table.

Many times First Nations have been considered on an afterthought basis. Ontario has intentionally ignored Supreme Court of Canada rulings on First Nations rights. Ontario needs to be compelled.

As stated previous without drastic changes in laws and policies to accommodate First Nations, direct actions in various forms will continue and escalate. (excerpts: submission by Nishnawbe-Aski Police Services Board, Chief Mike Metat, Ipperwash Commission Inquiry transcripts, pp. 61-74, August 24, 2006)

Thus from no less an authority than the Ipperwash Inquiry itself comes the strategic insight that Platinex was "targeted" in "direct actions" by native leaders who were willing to go to jail in order to "compel Ontario" to safeguard the environmental integrity of their traditional lands. However, throughout this tumultuous period, Ontario was nowhere to be seen in the consultation and accommodation department (until it was far too late in the day). Indeed, the court was prompted to deliver the following series of admonitions that singularly blames Ontario in no uncertain terms for the ensuing mining controversy, as follows:

> *[93] Although the Ontario government was not present during these proceedings, the evidentiary record indicates that it has been almost entirely absent from the consultation process with KI and has abdicated its responsibility and delegated its duty to consult to Platinex while, at the same time was making several decisions about the environmental impact of Platinex's exploration programmes, the granting of mining leases and lease extensions. Both before and after receiving notice of KI's TLE claim.*

> *[94] In the several years that discussions between Platinex and KI have been ongoing, the Crown has been involved in perhaps three meetings. There is no evidence that the Crown has maintained a strong supervisory presence in the negotiations despite Platinex having expressed its concerns to Ontario on a number of occasions.*

> *[96] Despite repeated judicial messages delivered over the course of 16 years, the evidentiary record available in this case sadly reveals that the provincial Crown has not heard or comprehended this message and has failed in fulfilling this obligation.*

*[97] One of the unfortunate aspects of the Crown's
failure to understand and comply with its obligations
is that it promotes industrial uncertainty to those
companies, like Platinex, interested in exploring and
developing the rich resources located on Aboriginal
traditional land. (excerpts: Platinex v.
Kitchenuhmaykoosib Inninuwug. Reasons for
Judgment Superior Court of Justice, July 28, 2006)*

These admonitions were handed down just one month
before the Nishnawbe-Aski police services board made
its representations before the Ipperwash Commission
Inquiry - in effect validating every point that had befallen
Platinex. Ontario's abdication of responsibility had
meant that Platinex was left to fend for itself and, as a
direct result, taxpayers picked up the tab when Ontario
subsequently bought out Platinex's interests in the
disputed properties in a multi-million dollar legal
settlement. By the time of the payout, the province was
onto its fourth aboriginal affairs minister in as many
years, underscoring the revolving door on native
priorities at Queens Park.

The Litigator's Toolbox

In the wake of the release of the native leaders, one
ruling stands out as potentially the most significant of all
in the native legal winning streak. It has to do with
Frontenac Ventures immediately moving to have its
native protagonist, Robert Lovelace, re-incarcerated. The
company clearly wanted to send an unmistakable
message of corporate power and legal clout. Thus it
motioned to have the Supreme Court of Canada consider
having him serve the full six-month sentence. But
Frontenac's strategy failed and here's the Court's one-
sentence ruling, as follows:

Application For Leave to Appeal to the Supreme Court of Canada - Dismissed
Frontenac Ventures Corp. v. Ardoch Algonquin First Nation, 91 O.R. (3d) 1
Application for leave to appeal dismissed with costs to the respondents Ardoch Algonquin First Nation, Robert Lovelace and Paula Sherman December 4, 2008 (excerpt: Binnie, Deschamps and Abella JJ.)

Frontenac's Venture's application to Canada's top court brought into play the biggest tool in the corporate litigator's toolbox - the power to incarcerate. Indeed, Robert Lovelace had defied the court's authority and refused to purge his contempt. Yet the Supreme Court of Canada indicated that it would not reconsider the Ontario Court of Appeal's disposition of his sentence. Thus, not only was Robert Lovelace's six-month sentence reduced to time-served but also the admonition of "no need to bring down the hammer of long jail sentences and very substantial fines" now stood as the law of the land.

Two years later, in the Supreme Court of Canada's very next ruling on the 'duty to consult', it had this to say on how it views native legal defences:

[33] The duty to consult described in Haida Nation derives from the need to protect Aboriginal interests while land and resource claims are ongoing or when the proposed action may impinge on an Aboriginal right. Absent this duty, Aboriginal groups seeking to protect their interests pending a final settlement would need to commence litigation and seek interlocutory injunctions to halt the threatening activity. These remedies have proven time-consuming, expensive, and are often ineffective. Moreover, with a few exceptions, many Aboriginal groups have limited success in obtaining injunctions

> *to halt development or activities on the land in order*
> *to protect contested Aboriginal or treaty rights.*
> *(excerpt: Rio Tinto Alcan Inc. v. Carrier Sekani Tribal*
> *Council, 2010 SCC 43) (author's underlining)*

It's obvious from these observations that the Supreme Court of Canada is not going to countenance heavy-handed legal proceedings against natives by industry. There's little doubt as a result of Frontenac Ventures' prior motion to re-incarcerate, that the corporate litigator's hammer has now been reduced to a fly-swatter. In fact, it was folly to incarcerate them in the first place.

Because it wasn't long before that Frontenac Ventures judicial admonition was legally turned-back against industry by native strategists in yet another dispute. It happened in a major court challenge in British Columbia, where both the logging company and natives sought interim injunctions, each against the other. But now it was the natives who won, and the ruling makes it clear that the judicial admonition in Frontenac Ventures helped them turn the tables on Canfor:

> *[133] However, in respect of the admonition at para.*
> *48 of Frontenac Ventures ...*

> *[136] Canfor's application for an interim injunction*
> *against the Sam defendants ... is dismissed.*

> *[137] The Kelah plaintiffs' application for an interim*
> *injunction ... to restrain Canfor from engaging in*
> *timber harvesting within CP324 is allowed. (excerpts:*
> *Canadian Forest Products Inc. v. Sam 2011 BCSC 676)*
> *(author's underlining)*

Nothing better demonstrates the cause-and-effect relationship of how the native legal winning streak plays out regionally and nationally. The ruling in Frontenac

Ventures now helps native strategists! But this was not how it was meant to unfold when it was launched by corporate litigators in order to punish native land rights activists. Proving as postulated herein, that the corporate litigator's toolbox is vastly overrated as a bulwark against the rise of native empowerment in the resources sector.

Ontario's Belated Response

Now the modernization of the Mining Act became a legislative priority, highlighting the need for native consultation and dispute resolution. Likewise, the Far North Act proposed to put half of northern Ontario under a complete anti-development land freeze. Ontario now proposed a $30 million resource revenue-sharing fund for natives. These measures were really the result of native strategists and eco-activists merging their agendas; and they both succeeded in effecting major policy and legislative changes. The inter-connectivity of events was such that these new policies were announced immediately after the release of the jailed natives. Here's the premier's declaration that northern Ontario was about to go 'green':

Ontario will protect at least 225,000 square kilometers of the Far North Boreal region under its Far North Planning initiative. ... Permanently protecting these lands will also help a world wrestling with the effects of climate change, as they are a globally significant carbon sink. Protecting this region is a key part of the Ontario government's plan to fight climate change. (The region absorbs approximately 12.5 million tonnes of CO_2 from our atmosphere each year). (excerpt: Premier's press release July 14, 2008)

Paradoxically, the proposed freeze area is about the same size as the Cree homelands that the Quebec Government had succeeded in opening-up to hydropower and resource development in 2002, because of Les Paix des Braves.

Yet one year later, northern natives were taking a decidedly less enthusiastic view of the anti-development freeze. They now saw future resource opportunities drying up along with their ability to shape their own economic fortunes:

Grand Chief [Beardy] clarifies NAN's position on Far North Land Use Planning bill:

"I want to make it very clear that at no point have I said that NAN has endorsed, has supported or has been behind this legislation ...

The Far North is our homeland and has been kept pristine by the Cree and Ojibway people for generations. We recognize the Far North's ability to absorb the effects of climate change, but this legislation protecting 225,000 square kilometers of our territory has potential to block us from developing our communities so the carbon sink can remain intact to right the environmental wrongs of the industrialized south.

We are not opposed to the goals of conservation, but Ontario's efforts to save the planet must not come at First Nations' expense." (excerpts: Nishnawbe Aski Nation press release, June 3, 2009)

Northern natives now understood that they had been boxed-in in terms of realizing their future economic development potential. Three months later during the Standing Committee hearings on the Far North bill, eco-activists, native strategists, and industry executives had little choice but to abandon all alliances and promote their own interests. First up were the environmental strategists promoting the premier's green vision:

We want to see this bill substantively improved, not withdrawn, as others have recommended. ... Make it clear that First Nations will be enabled to establish and manage a permanent network of interconnected protected areas - areas free, essentially, of industrial development. That would be consistent with the Premier's vision. (excerpt: CPAWS Wildlands League presentation to standing committee, August 13, 2009)

The president of De Beers Canada pointed out the importance of protecting the company's $1 billion Victor Diamond Mine investment:

Bill 191 sets out to protect at least 50% of the area of the undertaking; however, there are no specific details on how this is going to be achieved other than that it will not permit mines or other industrial development. ... In terms of the balance, we do not believe it provides balance to provide certainty and stimulate interest in investing in the far north. (excerpt: De Beers Canada presentation to standing committee on August 13, 2009)

Then northern natives, asserting their role as resource gatekeepers across the entire region, sternly rebuked the standing committee, as follows:

Nishnawbe Aski chiefs-in-assembly have condemned Bill 191 and instructed me and my staff to take all steps necessary to stop the bill from becoming law. Nishnawbe Aski chiefs demand a fresh, meaningful government-to-government dialogue based on our treaty-making relationship. Bill 191 tries to govern

land use planning in what you call the far north.
Virtually every single community there is a
Nishnawbe Aski First Nation. (excerpt: NAN
presentation to standing committee on August 6,
2009)

Clearly, northern natives now felt duped. The anti-development moratorium was the last thing they wanted. In this, they could commiserate with De Beers, who two years before had likewise felt duped over the government's tax reversal having to do with its Victor Diamond Mine - namely the first northern Ontario mine.

De Beers

De Beers had been caught by surprise when, without prior notice and just as its Victor mine was about to go into production, the Ontario government negated the tax incentive it had established to promote new mining investment in northern Ontario. This reversal was done with such sleight of hand that De Beers went public with a play-by-play write-up in its Diamond Focus media release issued on the mine's opening. In their own words:

As of May 22, 2007, diamonds were taxed at 10%,
and the Victor Mine was recognized as a remote
project and eligible for a 5% rebate. This was the case
when Victor was discovered and when the decision
was made to build a $1 billion diamond mine.

On May 23, 2007, that all changed. Buried in the
government of Ontario's 2007 budget was an
announcement that caught De Beers Canada and the
people of northern Canada off guard. Diamonds
would be removed from the Mining Tax Act and be
taxed separately according to a new formula.

The net effect of the new diamond royalty would be:

- *The Victor Mine would lose its remote status.*
- *The nominal tax rate would rise from 5% to 13% on a sliding scale.*
- <u>*Less profit would leave less money to be shared under Impact Benefits Agreements (IBAs) with local Aboriginal communities.*</u>
- *Discouraging further development on new mines in Ontario. (author's underlining) (excerpts: De Beer's Diamond Focus, 2007/08)*

The budget itself was headlined: "Ontario's tax system supports expanded prosperity." But that's not the way the Attawapiskat chief saw it who sided with De Beers in no uncertain terms:

Native community decries 'tax grab' at diamond mine:

"You and your officials are well aware that the only diamond mine in Ontario, and thus the only one to be immediately impacted by your decision, is located in the traditional territory of the Attawapiskat First Nation. Given the obvious importance of this project to our community and to future exploration in our lands, we should have been consulted". Chief Carpenter wrote in an April 4 letter to the Premier. (excerpt: reporter, Andy Hoffman, Globe and Mail, April 10, 2007)

From the chief's perspective, here was critically needed economic development money being siphoned-off in a last minute tax reversal; a tax reversal specifically directed at one mine and consequently at one native community. He correctly saw it as a tax grab by Ontario that negatively impacted his community's IBA revenues from the mine. Coincidentally, these events took place just when the Assembly of First Nations launched its Corporate Challenge Program designed to get natives and project proponents working together. Here's what National Chief Phil Fontaine had to say about the Victor mine just a few months later in an open letter to the National Post:

> *Economic development at the cost of our human rights is a non-starter. This is not to say that we are "anti-development" or "anti-industry". First Nations want to enjoy the economic benefits of resources just as Canada has. For example in my recent visit to the Victor Diamond Mine in Attawapiskat First Nation in northern Ontario, I saw an excellent example of how the private sector and First Nations can work together in partnership. The mine will create hundreds of jobs, more than a decade of employment, and make a significant contribution to the economies of Canada, Ontario and the First Nation. (excerpt: AFN National Chief's letter to the National Post, January 25, 2008)*

But the unsettling reality was that yet again, the Ontario government appeared to be undermining the potential for an important corporate - native economic partnership to take root. Four years later, this tax-grab was completely missed by media commentators who freely and extensively critiqued the goings-on in Attawapiskat while its 'state of emergency' made nightly headlines during the winter of 2012. Surely if this community suffered such hardship in close proximity to a major mine (notably where De Beers has gone the extra mile) then there's little reason to expect other northern native communities to 'roll out the red carpet' for the next proposed mine. It's resource management folly of the highest order.

'Ring of Fire'

Getting mining up-and-running in the 'Ring of Fire' (central Ontario northlands) will now be the litmus test especially in light of the region's socio-economic short-comings and lack of physical infrastructure. Grand Chief Stan Beardy's remarks at a 2010 'Ring of Fire' mining conference set the bar high as he again profiled natives as de facto resource rulers, as follows:

There are two defining characteristics for understanding us - our special relationship to the Creator and our special relationship to the land. Government has a legal duty to consult with us - and it's a major issue with industry as well. We are insisting on having 'free, prior and informed consent' which is now an international standard - noting that Canada still refuses to sign the U.N. Declaration of Indigenous Rights.

Mining takes a toll on our people and the environment. Yes we're interested in benefits and partnerships - not handouts - but our consent is still required. We see chromite-fever everywhere these days and we're concerned that there's the appearance of a 'green light'. There is much to be done on pre-planning efforts (not off to a good start).

We have a lot to learn from the Voisey's Bay experience - there the company did many things to optimize First Nations participation and we need the same tools and capacity. Moreover, without supporting First Nations - Canada's economy will never prosper! (excerpts: speaking notes, NAN Grand Chief Stan Beardy, Thunder Bay, February 10, 2010)

Seven months later the gloves came off when the Far North Act passed over the objections of northern natives, who issued a flurry of press releases that foretold a pessimistic future for the new map of Ontario, as follows:

> ... *uncertainty and unrest are imminent* .... *The legislation will be opposed by any and all means necessary.* ... *The law can be passed by the Province of Ontario but this does not promise industry free access to our lands* ... *(We) do not and will not recognize this legislation on our homelands.* ... *The real fight is just beginning. (excerpt: NAN press releases. September 22/23, 2010)*

The government moved quickly by designating a 'Ring of Fire' coordinator, whose specific role was to lead industry and natives into a new era of cooperation and mutual respect. But that's not how native strategists saw it:

> *"The Premier of Ontario continuously talks about this so-called 'new relationship' with First Nations and yet again he unilaterally makes a decision without consultation with NAN First Nations," said NAN Grand Chief Stan Beardy. "We are disturbed that the Premier can express his willingness to create a true partnership and yet leaves us out of this critical process. We need to ensure that our objectives and our plans for anything in our territory are adequately represented. We should have been a part of the selection of the person to fill this critical position." (excerpt: NAN press release September 30, 2010)*

The natives had a valid point given that this key appointment drew upon the same senior office that the Superior Court in the Platinex ruling had previously admonished for being "almost entirely absent from the consultation process." This ongoing state of affairs presented an unflattering picture of Ontario in that it appeared to still not be getting the court's key message.

Native press releases in the spring of 2011 were replete with the same wording used five years previously at the Ipperwash Inquiry: threatening "direct actions" to "compel" Ontario to engage in constructive dialogue. (Chiefs of Ontario press release, April 14, 2011).

Moreover, native opposition to provincial legislation expanded to other sectors, notably the Forest Tenure Modernization Act, as follows:

"We will not be subject to yet another piece of one-sided legislation that challenges our constitutionally protected Aboriginal and Treaty rights to be properly and adequately consulted and accommodated on matters such as forestry," said NAN Grand Chief Stan Beardy. "We will exercise our own jurisdiction in determining what is best for the resources in our traditional territory - not what the province thinks is best. Bill 151 must be scrapped and replaced with a Bill that reflects the recommendations by First Nations." (excerpt: NAN press release May 6, 2011)

Back to Brantford

The City of Brantford's controversial by-laws were up-held in the fall of 2010 in a ruling that clarified a number of legal points in contention, which are listed below:

[6] The respondents ... systematically blockaded these development sites commencing in 2007. ... (excerpt: City of Brantford v. Montour et al., 2010 ONSC 6253)

[25] [the city alleged civil conspiracy] ... this tort has merit. (Ibid.)

*[26] [the city alleged public nuisance] ... this tort
would also appear to have merit. (Ibid.)*

*[35] In my view the City will suffer irreparable harm,
if that has not already occurred, if this situation is
allowed to continue. I find as a fact, on the evidence
before me, that the economy of this small city is at
risk; the employment of members of the community
are likewise at risk; the reputation of the City as a
place to live, work and invest is at risk; the tax base is
at risk; all as a result of the City being unable to
regulate development, provide a conflict free
environment for investment, employment and the
raising of families, and the inability of the City to
ensure to local residents and the investment
community that the rule of law prevails. (Ibid.)*

*[50] The City of Brantford was established within the
lands described by Ms. Holmes (a court expert). That
is, within the lands that she opines the Six Nations
agreed to surrender for sale and were indeed sold.
(Ibid.)*

*[54] I conclude, by way of my preliminary
assessment, that the claim for title, or the return of
these lands to the respondents, (natives) is
exceedingly weak. ... (Ibid.)*

*[55] ... For more than 150 years the Six Nations did
nothing to indicate to innocent third-party
purchasers that there was any problem with title to
their lands. ... (Ibid.)*

*[60] ... The lands in question have long since been
altered and acquired by private landowners. The only
issue, in reality, is one of possible compensation if the
respondents (natives) can prove their claim. (Ibid.)*

It remains to be seen whether the City of Brantford and Six Nations can work out their differences. Brantford is one on the most historic settlements in the country in terms of the crown / native relationship. General Brock visited there and entreated with Six Nations while en route to take Detroit from the Americans in 1812 with their help. Two hundred years later, less than 5% of the Haldimand Tract remains with Six Nations. Today this is the country's largest native community; in need of more land for its growing population. There's a shared history that goes back to the founding of Canada. Tellingly, during the climax of tensions at Caledonia, a local roadside sign read: "If you love Canada - thank a native"!

Niagara's Transmission Corridor

In late 2011, Provincial Energy Ministry Brad Duguid stated that Ontario was not prepared to "risk lives" to finish the hydro transmission corridor proposing to cross Six Nations reserve lands. The two hydro towers required to complete the line are likely the same ones barring the entrance to Douglas Creek Estates all these years later. Here was the Energy Minister linking the shooting death of Dudley George in 1995 - to the fracas in Caledonia in 2006 - explaining his government's inability to complete an important $116 million hydropower hook-up in 2011.

Another Moratorium!

In March 2012, Ontario moved to head-off yet another native vs. mining dust-up by unilaterally declaring an area four times the size of P.E.I to be under moratorium. This was in the same region where Platinex had previously been bought out; and now God's Lake Resources were given a similar fiscal incentive to relinquish its rights in the interests of a peaceful outcome. Notably, that company had just issued a press release stating that it was "canvassing Security Companies to ensure the smooth completion of its drill program" (March 01 2012) which statement potentially portended serious resource folly (!) In any event, it was up to the sixth Aboriginal Affairs minister in six years to stick-handle that messy public relations situation; thus the latest moratorium and multi-million dollar payout.

Henco, Platinex, God's Lake: in a span of six years each dispute served up an anti-development moratorium and each corporate interest was bought-out by Ontario at considerable taxpayer expense (approximately $24.5 million in total). Along the way, the map of northern Ontario was fundamentally redrawn in apparent denial of legitimate native concerns and priorities. In due course, that might well prove to be the biggest economic hit of all; as vast tracts are off-limits to development. Moreover, if missteps continue, the region might well become a low-conflict zone adding another order of resource complexity entirely.

It's abundantly clear that Ontario has paid a very high price for its mishandling of its most important relationship. Unlike other parts of the country, the rise of native empowerment in Ontario didn't occur as a result of one legal win after another. It happened as a result of the wrongful shooting of Dudley George at Ipperwash Park by the OPP, which tragic event greatly fueled native anger. That anger has not been allowed to dissipate; instead, perversely, it is regularly stoked by the systemic political and bureaucratic incompetence that pervades Queen's Park. Thus native anger continues to be the defining feature of the crown / native relationship. And until such time as this situation is massively rectified, Ontario will remain in the grip of its self-made and self-sustained 'time warp'.

5

THE PRAIRIES: *RAILROADED*

The main driver behind the need for the prairie treaties was the railroad. It facilitated the opening-up of land for westward immigration, since transporting homesteaders to create western markets for eastern goods was essential for the railway to pay for itself. Thus the numbered treaties started in southern Manitoba and stopped at the Rockies - as did homesteading. The northern treaties came later but their driver was resource discoveries and the need for ready access to Klondike gold fields and Mackenzie Valley oil (Norman Wells).

In settling the prairies, Canada competed head-to-head with the United States for homesteaders. As a result, the amount of land offered to settlers (and similarly to natives as an inducement for settling down on reserves) tended to reflect whatever the United States was offering its homesteaders at the time. Consequently, the land grants vary in some of the prairie treaties. Another factor explaining the land quantum variations had to do with the rise of Métis nationalism and the need to secure a military access corridor running west from Ontario into the prairie heartland.

The combined effect of these two pressures explains why the treaties on either side of Treaty 1 in southern Manitoba provided natives with more 'settler' land than Treaty 1 did. Treaty 3 to the east was negotiated when Métis leader Louis Riel posed a threat to westward expansion; and Treaty 2 to the west reflected what the U.S. was offering settlers during a homesteader rush. Sandwiched between the two, Treaty 1 natives have long harboured the view that they were shortchanged. Compared to the U.S., natives didn't receive sufficient land under any of the treaties. According to the Royal Commission, as follows:

> ... *Aboriginal lands south of the 60th parallel (mainly Indian reserves) make up less than one-half of one percent of the Canadian land mass. By contrast, in the United States (excluding Alaska), where aboriginal people make up a far smaller portion of the population, they hold three percent of the land. (excerpt: highlights from the RCAP report, pp. 32-33)*

Traditional Lands

The treaty-making process on the prairies essentially worked like this: treaty commissioners urged natives to become farmers, promising that they could continue to free-range across their traditional lands for subsistence purposes, even though they were relinquishing their land in exchange for treaty rights and land grants (which were to comprise reserves). They were given assurances to this end, and the formal wording was written-up with the caveat that their surrendered lands could nevertheless be used for settlement and development:

> *[4]... the said Indians, shall have the right to pursue their avocations of hunting and fishing throughout*

the tract surrendered ... saving and excepting such
tracts as may, from time to time, be required or taken
up for settlement, mining, lumbering, or other
purposes ...
(excerpts: R. v. Sundown [1999] 1 S.C.R., p. 393).

Twelve years ago the validity of this wording was upheld
by the Supreme Court of Canada, making this promise as
relevant today as it was in the 1870s. As a result, natives
today expect to be consulted and accommodated on
matters impacting their traditional lands. However,
many Canadians mistakenly view treaty rights as being
applicable only within reserve boundaries, and do not
appreciate that hunting, gathering, and fishing rights
extend to traditional lands. In the words of the Royal
Commission:

> *Treaty agreements did not end the conflict. Indeed, it*
> *became sharper as settlers took up residence next to*
> *Aboriginal people, who had not foreseen how deeply*
> *settlers' ways would clash with their own. They*
> *thought that the Crown's treaty promises would be*
> *enough to ensure their survival and independence.*
> *They were wrong. ...The conflict became more deeply*
> *entrenched when the Constitution Act, 1867 - drafted*
> *without discussion with Aboriginal people - assigned*
> *legal ownership of all Crown lands to the provinces.*
> *(excerpt: highlights from the RCAP report, p. 34)*

Treaty Rights v. Property Rights

The same Supreme Court of Canada ruling made one of
the most important judicial pronouncements ever for
propelling the rise of native empowerment forward:

[35] ... Treaty rights, like aboriginal rights, must not
be interpreted as if they were common law property
rights. ...

Aboriginal and treaty rights cannot be defined in a
manner which would accord with common law
concepts of title to land or the right to use another's
land. Rather, they are the right of aboriginal people
in common with other aboriginal people to
participate in certain practises traditionally engaged
in by particular aboriginal nations in particular
territories. (excerpts: R. v. Sundown [1999] 1 S.C.R.)

The combination of these two legal concepts - rights over
traditional lands and rights to traditional practices -
added significant clout to the native legal winning streak.
For many a corporate litigator would miss the court's key
distinction that treaty rights are not akin to common law
property rights. That's because resource rights are
singularly premised upon property law; whereas native
rights are founded upon constitutionally protected
treaties and aboriginal rights, the honour of the Crown,
and the implied duties to consult and accommodate. The
Royal Commission paid particular attention to southern
Manitoba and the Métis as well:

Similarly, Métis people who believed that they had
won the right to their own lands and resources in the
bargain with Ottawa that led to the Manitoba Act,
were driven further and further west - and ultimately
dispersed as a people - by the largely fraudulent
manner in which that bargain was administered.
(Ibid., pp. 33-34)

Treaty 1

To those in the know, Treaty 1 has long been the cauldron of native empowerment nationally. And it was native strategists in southern Manitoba who built the political base for the ensuing successes in the courts. The National Indian Brotherhood, based in Winnipeg, kicked things off in 1968 with its Red Paper, which challenged Trudeau's White Paper. Out of that came the formation of the Assembly of First Nations in 1982 that was later to be led by two national chiefs from Manitoba: Ovide Mercredi (two terms) and Phil Fontaine (three terms). From the Manitoba Legislature, Elijah Harper emerged as the face of native empowerment during the failed Meech Lake and Charlottetown constitutional initiatives. Throughout this extended period, the Assembly of Manitoba Chiefs served as an incubator for national and regional leaders who subsequently became instrumental in propelling the rise of native empowerment forward.

Rail Blockades

April 2006 saw the first rail blockade in eastern Ontario, some 50 trains and 3,500 passengers were disrupted in a Caledonia 'sympathy' protest. These events signaled a marked uplift in native on-the-ground empowerment. One month later, the Assembly of Manitoba Chiefs launched a direct challenge to Prime Minister Harper's Accountability Act. Feeling that natives were being singled-out, the Assembly of Manitoba Chiefs responded with a full-page open letter in newspapers challenging the government, as follows:

> *Open letter to the Members of Parliament of Canada:*
> *... It is of grave concern to us that the Government of*
> *Canada would consider weakening the position of*

*Aboriginal business in Canada, especially after
making great strides toward Aboriginal capacity
building, particularly with the success of the current
contract. The planned procurement disregards the
established Government policy, ignores the resolution
of the Assembly of First Nations and contravenes
accountability legislation.*

*Since the first priority of the Government of Canada
is to enact and enforce the Federal Accountability Act,
we therefore pose the question: Where is the
accountability on this matter? (excerpts: Grand Chief
Ron Evans Assembly of Manitoba Chiefs, Globe and
Mail, May 18, 2006)*

One month later, it looked like native activists would
again be targeting railroads. More specifically, they
focused on the trunk lines crossing the Treaty 1 corridor.
However, CN managed to reach a last minute settlement
on the courthouse steps:

*"The Assembly of Manitoba Chiefs has agreed that
there will not be a blockade of CN lines in the
foreseeable future," CN spokesman Jim Feeny told
reporters outside Winnipeg's main courthouse.*

*"In addition, CN has agreed to write a letter to the
minister of Indian and northern affairs, asking the
minister to do everything in his power to speedily
resolve the issues that are presently before the First
Nations and the Government of Canada." (excerpts:
CP Canada News June 28, 2006)*

Over the next few months, Canadians witnessed an
escalating war-of-words in newspapers, starting with this
'shot across the bow' from the federal Indian Affairs
minister:

I was surprised to read that Assembly of First Nations National Chief Phil Fontaine has targeted June 29 as a "national day of action ... to disrupt road, rail and port service from one end of the country to the other.".... Working together to find solutions is a much more constructive way of dealing with issues than planning blockades.

I hope none of the $27- million in grants and contributions received annually by the AFN will be used in planning illegal blockades. The government is committed to finding solutions to difficult issues, not by announcing grand, unachievable goals, but by tackling them one step at a time. Good progress has been made. Chief Fontaine and I are working on housing, water, land-claims reform and many other issues that require collaborative solutions. Threatening a summer of discontent does nothing to create an atmosphere to move things forward. (Indian Affairs Minister, Jim Prentice, open letter to the Globe and Mail, March 28, 2007)

Two days later, the National Chief responded with his own open letter, as follows:

Indian Affairs Minister Jim Prentice ... quotes from a John Ibbitson column saying that June 29th is "a national day of action ... to disrupt road, rail, and port service from one end of the country to the other." This is not in any way my statement, nor the AFN-led position.

The Chiefs-in-Assembly passed a resolution to have June 29 as a Day of Action to raise public awareness of First Nations issues. There are no Assembly of First Nations-led plans to conduct illegal activities. As national chief, I have always said negotiation is

*preferable to confrontation. And yes, it would be
better to work together on issues rather than imply
retribution to the AFN or other first nations groups.
(AFN National Chief Phil Fontaine's open letter to the
Globe and Mail, March 30, 2007)*

While these two leaders exchanged barbs via open letters
in the lead-up to the National Day of Action, Treaty 1
strategists issued the following proclamation to mobilize
the rank and file:

Emergency!!
Treaties 1-11
Gathering:

*Request that each Treaty First Nation bring their
written list of grievances and Treaty violations to
put forth in a document to be presented to Canada.
... Chiefs encouraged to bring headdresses.*

Tuesday, April 10, 2007

Treaty No.1-Winnipeg, Manitoba

**"For as long as the sun shines, the grass grows
and the waters flow."**

Then on April 20, 2007 another 'sympathy' rail blockade
near Belleville coincided with the first anniversary of the
OPP's botched attempt at Caledonia to remove the native
occupiers from Douglas Creek Estates. CN quickly moved
for an injunction to which Shawn Brant, the blockade
organizer responded: "If (police) want a disaster on the

Deseronto boundary road, then they should consider enforcing (the court order)." The London Free Press on April 23, 2007 reported: "CN Rail spokesperson Mark Hallman said the injunction requires the protestors to 'dismantle the blockade forthwith'." Yet the blockade ran its course and was only dismantled after 30 hours. Two weeks later, CN sued Shawn Brant for damages and a permanent injunction was issued. Editorialists saw through Brant's protest and called him out, as follows:

Suing over the blockades: ... Shawn Brant, a protest leader who was named in the CN lawsuit, had this to say when the Ontario Provincial Police charged him with mischief and other offences: "Right now, I'm the voice. They think if they take away the people's voice, the people will stop."...

Who elected Mr. Brant the voice? Did the people? No. He is self-appointed. No doubt, natives have some genuine grievances. ... But of course, native peoples aren't the only ones with genuine grievances. ...

Good for CN for standing up for the banal fabric of law on which the dull peace and prosperity of this country rests. (excerpts: Globe and Mail editorial, May 11, 2007).

Then with just six weeks to go before the National Day of Action, AFN National Chief, Phil Fontaine, took direct aim at CN, as follows:

"I was really disturbed recently when I heard CN was going to start suing the people who were responsible for the obstruction in their ability to make money. But what the CN spokesman didn't say is that they occupy and possess all sorts of First Nations land."

Mr. Fontaine also sent a shot across the bow of governments talking tough on dealing with native protests.

"Any intimidation or threats will be met with similar threats. Any suggestion that governments are prepared to engage in a fight is so misguided, completely misguided. What should be happening is that government should be reaching out to us." (excerpts: reporter Paul Samyn, quoting AFN national chief Phil Fontaine, National Post, May 16, 2007)

One week later, the AFN officially proclaimed the National Day of Action:

FIRST NATIONS CALL ON ALL CANADIANS TO STAND WITH US ON JUNE 29th, 2007 issued at Gatineau, Quebec May 23, 2007

The Assembly of First Nations calls on First Nations, Canadian citizens and corporations, to stand together to insist that the Government of Canada respond to the crisis in First Nations communities.

*Since Confederation in 1867, First Nations have been subject to repeated attempts by the Government of Canada to forcibly assimilate us and erase our identities. Still, we survive today as distinct peoples. ... **It is time for action.***

The Globe and Mail's editorial board again criticized the AFN's handling of the issue:

The AFN's rash call: ... Mr. Fontaine either is being disingenuous or is willfully naive. By endorsing the day of action, his mainstream organization has signed on to the militant agenda of Chief Terrance Nelson of Manitoba's Roseau River Anishinabe First Nation. Last week, Mr. Nelson told The Globe and Mail's Joe Friesen "There's only one way to deal with a white man. You either pick up a gun or you stand between him and his money." It was Mr. Nelson's resolution "acknowledging" the planned blockade and mandating the AFN's national executive to seek the railways' voluntary compliance that was adopted by the AFN. On June 29th, then, the AFN hopes to stand between the white man and his money.

The AFN is playing an irresponsible game. A widely respected national organization, it has in effect chosen to fly the warriors' flag by legitimizing what in all likelihood will end in illegal acts as native hot heads don military apparel and roll the old school buses onto the tracks. ... (excerpts: Globe and Mail editorial, May 26, 2007)

June's arrival heralded the perfect storm of native protests. Three separate native rights disputes were leading towards a critical convergence that would propel the rise of native empowerment to new heights. First, the Ipperwash Inquiry report was issued to intense media coverage; second, Platinex won access to traditional lands on the strength of a Superior Court ruling that held that there indeed had been adequate corporate - native consultation to enable preliminary drilling; and third, Grassy Narrows activists took their clear-cut protest (along with a massive teepee) to the front-lawn of

Queen's Park. Tensions were clearly rising in the run-up to the National Day of Action.

New Land Claims Legislation

It was at this juncture, that Minister Prentice made back-to-back announcements designed to defuse the situation. In his words, he "accelerated" legislation for resolving specific claims "which now number 793" while at the same time warning "those who act outside the law must bear the consequences of their actions." Then he authorized a last minute settlement for Roseau River's treaty land entitlement, offering 30 hectares for urban reserve land in northwest Winnipeg. Indeed, it looked like the natives' pressure-cooker tactics to address these long-festering issues were working. Notwithstanding, here's what Chief Terrance Nelson said at the time:

> *"The worst thing that could happen is for June 29th to fizzle, because then people will look at that and say, 'See? The Indians just run away. All they do is threaten. All we have to do is show them who is boss'."*

> ... *"I'm not Ghandi," Mr. Nelson says. "I've known violence all my life. I grew up with it. And one thing I know is that you do not run from it." (excerpts: reporter Sarah Hampson quoting Chief Terrance Nelson, Globe and Mail, June 18, 2007)*

Now with less than ten days to go, it was CN's turn to publish a full-page open letter in national newspapers directed to the AFN National Chief:

June 21, 2007

National Chief Phil Fontaine
Assembly of First Nations
Ottawa, Ontario

Dear Chief Fontaine,

National Aboriginal Day is a time to recognize the important contribution of First Nations to making Canada the great country it is. We, at CN, join with all Canadians in welcoming the day as a time to celebrate First Nations people and their achievements. However, it is also a time for all of us to rededicate ourselves to working together to address the many problems that exist.

We are concerned that issues of poverty, lack of economic development, education and opportunity persist in many First Nations communities.

CN is a company that does business across Canada. In the eight provinces where we operate, we have a longstanding relationship with the First Nations people who reside along our rail lines. We are committed to working with the First Nations community and playing a part in addressing the unacceptable levels of unemployment and lack of opportunity in many communities. To do so is not only good for the First Nations, it is good for CN and good for Canada.

While some parts of the country are suffering a serious labour shortage, there are many First Nations people who want and need good jobs but lack the necessary skills or training to fully participate in the opportunities that exist. CN is committed to working with First Nations to ensure their members have the skills necessary to benefit from the employment opportunities, which exist in our company today and in the future.

We congratulate you and the Assembly of First Nations for establishing the Corporate Challenge Program. It makes great sense for Canada's leading companies to become partners with the First Nations and play a constructive role in addressing the serious issues that face your communities. We, at CN, intend to accept your challenge. We will work with you to enhance our existing programs and explore new avenues whereby First Nations communities can receive the appropriate training to gain meaningful employment.

Last year, I wrote to the Minister of Indian and Northern Affairs to encourage the Government of Canada to work to address your legitimate concerns regarding the pace of land claim settlements. We congratulate the Assembly of First Nations and the Government of Canada for the recent announcement of a plan to establish an independent land claims tribunal. We see this as a significant and positive development. We believe it is essential that these outstanding claims be dealt with in a more timely manner.

I hope a year from now we can look back and see a successful new partnership among First Nations people, government and business.

Sincerely,

E Hunter Harrison
President and Chief Executive Officer
CN

National Day of Action

When the big day finally arrived, rail lines in southern Manitoba weren't blockaded after all. Although, as reported below, they were in Ontario where Shawn Brant again caused major disruptions:

CN spokesman Mark Hallman expressed frustration that despite at least two court injunctions, illegal activity continues. ..."This is the third such blockade we've had to experience in the same general area in the last 15 months," he said. "It's of significant consequence to the company, a major irritant. It's really a difficult situation that we have people who just refuse to abide by the law." (excerpt: Allison Hanes, National Post, June 30, 2007)

CN, having just expressed wide-ranging support for native causes, was clearly still being targeted. Not coincidentally, the day before the National Day of Action, yet another full-page open letter appeared in national newspapers; this one was from organized labour and it offered wholehearted support for the National Chief:

The 80,000 members of the Laborers' International Union of North America (LIUNA) across Canada recognize the importance of this day to the people of your Nation. We join with all of you, not only today, but every day, in your struggle that is so deeply connected to our struggles.

The difficult conditions that exist among your people across this great country are a national tragedy. The lack of economic development and educational opportunities and the inherent poverty of the people of the First Nations are persistent burdens on our First Nations communities. ...

Congratulations to you and the people of the
Assembly of First Nations.

Sincerely yours in solidarity,

General President Terence M. O'Sullivan (excerpts
open letter of June 29, 2007)

It's likely that the negative editorial commentary the
AFN had garnered in the run-up to the National Day of
Action was behind this letter of support. Moreover,
labour often stands with natives at protests, providing
moral support for their shared social justice objectives.
That's because the labour movement itself had clarified
the legalities of exerting economic pressure on third
parties, in another major ruling by the Supreme Court of
Canada in 2002, as follows:

[45] ... Some economic harm to third parties is
anticipated by our labour relations system as a
necessary cost of resolving industrial conflict.

[72] Protection from economic harm is an important
value capable of justifying limitations on freedom of
expression. Yet to accord this value absolute or pre-
eminent importance over all other values, including
free expression, is to err. The law has never
recognized a sweeping right to protection from
economic harm. ... (excerpts: R.W.D.S.U., Local 558
v. Pepsi-Cola Canada Beverages (West) [2002] SCC
8) (author's underlining)

There's little doubt that LIUNA's open letter was
intended to augment native "freedom of expression" as
the National Day of Action approached; indeed their
respective agendas converged as if on cue. One month
later, CN announced in its June 23, 2007 press release,

its downward-revised economic forecast citing in part the effect of "two illegal blockades of our Toronto-Montreal main line". The company had paid a heavy price in spite of its public overture to the National Chief. Still, Shawn Brant's sentence for the National Day of Action blockade (and for the earlier one in April) was time-served (57 days), plus a 90-day conditional sentence to be served on reserve, and 1-year probation.

Pipeline Blockades

Yet the promotion of national rail blockades had its genesis in Treaty 1 where now these same chiefs were training their sights on major pipelines that were proposing to cross their traditional lands. Chief Terrance Nelson was threatening to do to pipelines what he had threatened to do to rail lines; and soon teepees marked the proposed right-of-ways and horse-mounted protests disrupted project planning and construction as far west as Saskatchewan.

Once again Chief Terrance Nelson was in the forefront, this time demanding concessions from the pipeline companies: "The only ones that are not included in the benefits are the First Nations, and we're saying that will no longer be the case," he said. "This is our wealth. The oil did not come on little wooden boats from Europe. It was here already." (excerpt: Paul Turenne quoting Chief Terrance Nelson, *Winnipeg Sun*, February 12, 2008)

On September 16, 2008 chiefs from across the prairies attended another strategic planning session in Edmonton where they threatened more blockades and lawsuits. Two weeks later they put their words into action by conducting rolling blockades along the proposed pipeline right-of-ways.

Now it was Manitoba's and Saskatchewan's turn to rush their *First Nations and Métis Consultation Guidelines* out the door. And once again, it looked like it had taken native protests to prod governments into action. The timing was critical, as the Federal Court was poised to rule on the adequacy of native consultation respecting three major pipelines: *Keystone, Southern Lights and Alberta Clipper*. And in a revealing turn of events, the federal court questioned the weight to be given to Chief Terrance Nelson's affidavit, specifically with respect to the crown's duty to consult:

[34] ... The Treaty One First Nations are simply not correct when they assert in their evidence that a duty to consult is engaged whenever the Government of Canada makes "any decision related to lands in our traditional territory inside the boundaries of Treaty 1." There is no at-large duty to consult that is triggered solely by the development of land for public purposes. There must be some unresolved non-negligible impact arising from such a development to engage the Crown's duty to consult. (excerpt: Brokenhead Ojibway First Nation et al. v. the Attorney General of Canada et al. 2009 FC 484)

Chief Terrance Nelson had advanced an incorrect treaty interpretation. Still this case represents a rare loss for the native side. Fittingly, the court applied common-sense observations citing the advance consultation work undertaken by the companies, and the fact that the pipelines were using existing corridors running almost entirely over private land and previously disturbed land. Moreover, the court "admonished" the natives for not fully engaging in the available regulatory procedures by saying: "There is a responsibility to use them."

CAPP's Strategy

Before leaving this litigation, there's a legal wrinkle that speaks volumes about how the game is played, strategically speaking. Notably as this case commenced, the main industry lobby, the Canadian Association of Petroleum Producers (CAPP), applied to be joined as a 'party' to the litigation. This raised the specter of having the entire weight of the oil and gas industry brought to bear against the smallest treaty region in the country. CAPP lost this motion in one of those 'first paragraph' judicial outcomes, as follows:

> *[1] ... CAPP is an industry association representing 150 companies which explore for, develop and produce natural gas and crude oil in Canada and it asserts that it "is adverse in interest" to the position taken by Treaty One First Nations in this proceeding. ... (excerpt: Brokenhead Ojibway First Nation et al. v. Attorney General of Canada et al. 2008 FC 735) (author's underlining)*

Now there's a legal sound bite that native strategists would be quick to pounce upon! It's the ultimate (David vs. Goliath) expression of one-sided courtroom optics. Shortly thereafter and likely in reprisal, four Treaty 1 chiefs were part of a larger delegation that met with President-elect Obama's key administration officials:

> *"We did get into the president-elect's office and we did meet with some of his advisors," (Peguis Chief Glenn) Hudson said. "We asked the U.S. government to respect our treaty rights in Canada and our indigenous rights. It was cordial. They were very accommodating." (excerpt: Alexandra Paul quoting Chief Hudson, Winnipeg Free Press, January 8, 2009)*

The new president's handlers were reminded that Obama had used the phrase 'dirty oil' while campaigning. Here were Treaty 1 strategists showing CAPP how the native empowerment game is really played. Moreover, the seeds of opposition to Alberta's oil exports were being planted at Keystone's expense before the president-elect was even sworn in. And there would be much more to come ...

CN's Litigation

CN had endured three blockades all of which took place in Ontario. The first two were sympathy blockades over the Caledonia land reclamation; the third, was over the National Day of Action. There's no doubt that the railway had been illegally targeted in all three. CN now announced that it was going to compete head-to-head with the pipeline industry, transporting oilsands output to wherever markets were best: "We have the capacity to move crude oil products on our network today. You can start with as few as 1,000 barrels a day. We can grow together to as many as 200,000 barrels per day or more." (excerpt: CN's webpage PipelineOnRail™) With this as a priority, CN now fast-tracked the resolution of native litigation and outstanding grievances. It paid restitution for the derailments that had impacted traditional lands, and it settled environmental charges over derailments that saw oil leak into Lake Wabamun, Alberta, and caustic soda spill into B.C.'s Cheakamus River:

> *CN settles all charges related to 2005 derailments in Alta. and B.C.: ... CN achieved fair and reasonable out-of-court financial settlements with parties affected by the derailment and spill, including Lake Wabamun residents and the Paul Band First Nation.*

In total, CN and its insurers spent in excess of $132 million to remediate the effects of the Wabamun derailment and spill, and to compensate affected stakeholders. ...

"These programs show that CN has lived up to the commitments it made at the time of these unfortunate incidents," said Harrison. "We said we would repair any damage done and fairly compensate those affected. We have done what we said we would do." (excerpts: CN press release, May 25, 2009)

In a concurrent move, CN sued Shawn Brant personally. Only this time CN didn't have to explain itself given his unrepentant public profile:

"They can sue me until the cows come home, but it isn't going to stop until the issues of First Nations people are dealt with respectfully, with honour and integrity," Brant said outside court. (excerpt: The Canadian Press, April 7, 2009)

The two sides were soon enmeshed in David v. Goliath type litigation. The saber rattling escalated as Brant countersued for $10 million based on allegations that CN's lines were "on land granted to the Mohawks [which had been] wrongfully expropriated." That Mohawks had been subject to "exploitation and mistreatment and were generally impoverished." And further that the "blockades (are) a healthy reaction to the history of exploitation." In response, CN contested Brant's allegations and had 20 of his 21 pleadings struck. That legal housecleaning underscored the reality that native firebrands typically excel only when playing by their own rules. (And there's a lesson in this for 'gee-whiz' media coverage that often accompanies their antics).

Manitoba Métis

Of course, southern Manitoba is also homeland to a significant historic Métis population. As reflected in the following excerpt, they, too, have won important legal precedents that add to the native legal winning streak:

[46] *The Métis community of Western Canada has its own distinctive identity. As the Métis of the region were a creature of the fur trade and as they were compelled to be mobile in order to maintain their collective livelihood, the Métis "community' was more extensive than, for instance, the Métis community described in Sault Ste. Marie in Powley. The Métis created a large inter-related community that included numerous settlements located in present-day southwestern Manitoba, into Saskatchewan and including the northern Midwest United States. (excerpt: R. v. Goodon 2008 MBPC 59)*

However, the Métis legal winning streak really started in 2001 with the Supreme Court of Canada's Powley case, which identified a distinct, culturally intact, Métis community near Sault St. Marie. Powley, a moose hunter, was a member of this Métis community that could trace its distinct lineage and identity back to the establishment of the colonial government. As a result, the Supreme Court of Canada held that he was exercising his constitutionally-protected Métis right to hunt for subsistence. In the aftermath of this historic ruling, the Métis National Council defined its geographic area of influence, as follows:

"Historic Métis Nation Homeland" means the area of land in west central North America used and occupied as the traditional territory of the Métis or Half-Breeds as they were then known. (excerpt: MNC

*'national definition of Métis' ratified September 27,
2002)*

Yet this definition excludes Metis living in other regions.
In fact, the Labrador Metis Nation changed its name to
NunatuKavut to reflect its Inuit heritage (as opposed to
Indian heritage). What's important to note is that over
the last few years, Métis have won key validating rulings
in Alberta, Manitoba, Ontario and Labrador, meaning
that their rights are expanding on a regional basis.

Thus, the rise of native empowerment on the prairies
is far from over, and it would be seriously short-sighted
to think that future rail, pipeline, potash and hydro-
transmission projects will escape close scrutiny. Native
demonstrations during the Saskatchewan provincial
election in Fall 2011 saw 1,000 marchers demand
resource-revenue sharing.

Furthermore, it's a fair question to ask: Just how
many chiefs are 'out there' that would back firebrands
like Chief Terrance Nelson? That question can be
accurately answered since he campaigned for National
Chief (to replace Phil Fontaine) in mid-2009. His single-
issue platform was more of the same: "*Natives control
resources and their resources are making others
wealthy.*" He won 57 of 552 votes cast by the chiefs on
the first ballot (10% of the total). That's one-in-ten chiefs
who saw things his way.

Ironically, these are the same odds as the resource
sector's chances of winning in court today.

6

ALBERTA: *GROUPTHINK*

Alberta represents the most status quo of all the resource-dependent jurisdictions. It's not about to legislate half of its northern territory into an anti-development deep-freeze as per Ontario's Far North Act. Nor is it likely to share its operational resource management policies with natives as per Quebec's Les Paix des Braves. Rather, its emphasis is on maintaining the status quo as established by regulatory outcomes that have long served the resource sector and the public interest. Thus, it's against this background that Alberta finds itself defending the status quo in an intense public relations battle being fought over the environmental integrity of its oilsands operations.

The stakes are very high as Alberta's economic future lies in maximizing the oilsands' resource potential. Yet its open pit mines are being demonized by eco-activists internationally. Compounding this problem is the fact that these activists have aligned with native communities located downstream on the Athabasca River. Hence, they have merged their agendas to the extent that the saga of the tailings ponds has evolved into the foremost David vs. Goliath match-up worldwide. Notwithstanding this intense corporate social responsibility struggle, closer to home in Fort McMurray, both Suncor and Syncrude have won industry honours when it comes to corporate - native relations with neighboring native communities.

Status Quo

Spring 2001 sets the stage. For it was that April, which saw a newly re-elected Prime Minister Jean Chrétien deliver a keynote speech to the Canadian Association of Petroleum Producers (CAPP) touting the oilsands. Its message is all the more remarkable given how native and environmental tensions in the oilsands have since unfolded. An excerpt from a Saturday Night Magazine article describing Chrétien's speech is provided below:

> *"The United States needs Canadian energy. ... The potential is enormous, and it will take massive investments to realize it. ..." (He) closed with three caveats, ... "a commitment to include aboriginal Canadians in the expanding opportunity;" by "high standards of environmental protection and enforcement" and by "an unswerving commitment to competitive markets and fair regulation, ..."*
> *(excerpt: Paul Wells, Bushwhacked, Saturday Night Magazine, June 9, 2001)*

Here was the prime minister telling CAPP to get going on maximizing aboriginal and environmental priorities. Prescient advice, because one month later, the Federal Court of Appeal supported the downstream natives in a lawsuit respecting the environmental integrity of their watersheds. The Athabasca Chipewyan had just won its challenge against the National Energy Board over power exports that B.C. Hydro wanted to sell into U.S. markets. The ruling addressed the environmental degradation caused by the W.A.C. Bennett Dam situated 1,000 kilometers to the west, with its fluctuating output impacting the Peace River's flow intensity and water levels as it traversed northern Alberta towards its delta. Here's the court setting the stage for what would be an embarrassing loss for the NEB, as follows:

[4] The Athabasca Chipewyan First Nation (ACFN) concentrated their opposition on the effects of the permits on the operation of the W.A.C. Bennett Dam, located in the Peace River Basin in north-eastern British Columbia. The Bennett Dam and its associated generating station is British Columbia Hydro's largest hydro electric facility. It controls the province's largest reservoir and accounts for roughly one-quarter of the utility's annual electricity production. Since its completion in 1967, the Dam has altered the natural flow of the Peace River. The ACFN submitted that this altered flow has resulted in significant changes to the ecosystem on its traditional and reserves lands, located approximately one thousand kilometers downstream in the Peace River Delta region of northern Alberta. Delta wetlands have dried out with grasslands being replaced by brush and shrubs. Wildlife populations, including fish, waterfowl and muskrat have declined. The ACFN says that the granting of the impugned permits exacerbated these already existing effects. (excerpt: Athabasca Chipewyan First Nation v. BC Hydro 2001 FCA 62)

The court took aim at the NEB's handling of the power export approvals:

[21] Moreover, the National Energy Board has not explained in its reasons, what changes, if any, the granting of the permits will have on the operation of

B.C. Hydro's dams and in particular, the Bennett
Dam, and whether any such changes would have
adverse environmental downstream effects. ... (Ibid.)

The court addressed the shortcomings of B.C. Hydro:

[27] B.C. Hydro's submission to the Board does not
assist in explaining in any coherent manner why the
Board would have concluded that there would be no
significant adverse environmental effects from the
granting of the permits ... the Board's decision cannot
stand. (Ibid.)

Obviously this ruling is notable for its 1,000-kilometer
cause-and-effect factor, which should have been a legal
wake-up call for the oilsands. For comparison purposes,
the Bennett Dam on the Peace River is four times farther
away from Fort Chipewyan than is Fort McMurray from
those downstream native communities on the Athabasca
River. Clearly, the courts were signaling that when it
comes to impacts on native communities, they were
prepared to take an expansive view of geography. Once
again the National Energy Board had been overruled in a
native legal challenge (first on the Maritimes and
Northeast Pipeline and now on B.C. Hydro's power
exports). And it was partly a reaction to this state of
affairs, as well as to the evolving case law on native
consultation, that it now moved to formalize aboriginal
consultation guidelines. After a series of start-stop half
measures, the NEB's guidelines for native consultation
stated, as follows:

Therefore in considering applications before it, the
Board will require applicants to provide evidence to
clearly identify the Aboriginal peoples that have an
interest in the area of the proposed project and to
provide evidence that there has been adequate Crown

consultation where rights pursuant to section 35 of
the Constitution Act, 1982 may be infringed if the
Board approves the applied for facilities. ...

Notwithstanding such Crown consultation activities,
the Board will continue to examine the efforts made
directly by the applicants to contact potentially
affected Aboriginal peoples to advise them of the
project and to involve them in meaningful discussions
regarding potential project impacts and appropriate
mitigation as set out in the Board's Guidelines for
Filing Requirements (excerpt: NEB press release.
March 2002)

So starting with the prime minister's speech to CAPP, followed by the federal Court of Appeal's overturning of B.C. Hydro's power export permits, and finally by the issuing of the National Energy Board's consultation guidelines in response; here were three hard-to-ignore benchmarks for the energy sector - as to how native and environmental issues would be addressed in the future. Put another way, these messages were delivered a full decade before the Copenhagen Conference on Climate Change which convened year-end 2010. Yet throughout this decade, Alberta appeared to be more intent on maintaining the status quo than working collaboratively with natives and environmentalists.

'Friends of the Lubicon'

Two decades earlier, Alberta's resource sector had been mesmerized by another joint native / eco-activist campaign that had played out in downtown Toronto. In fact, it was the 'Friends of the Lubicon' campaign that set the tone for subsequent events in the oilsands by demonstrating that these strategists knew when and where to strike.

Because in 1998, the Ontario court had sided with the 'Friends of the Lubicon' in a multifaceted lawsuit initiated by Daishowa, an integrated forest products manufacturing company. Daishowa's legal challenge had backfired; effectively sterilizing 10,000 square kilometers of prime logging rights in northern Alberta. The necessary context is provided by the court, as follows:

> *[a] For three years, from late 1991 to late 1994, the Friends continued their boycott campaign. They approached about 50 companies which purchased Daishowa paper products. The pattern for engaging customers was consistent, with minor variations for some customers. ... (excerpt: Daishowa Inc. v. Friends of the Lubicon [1998] 39 O.R. 620, p. 633)*

> *[g/h] Essentially, the Friends campaign against Daishowa was a simple two-stage campaign. The first stage was an approach to the direct customers of Daishowa with a request, coupled with the threat of a boycott, that they stop using Daishowa products. If this approach did not obtain the desired response, the Friends moved to the second stage, namely informational picketing at the stores of those Daishowa customers with a view to 'educating the customers of the customers' of Daishowa about the Lubicon Cree situation and the perceived connection of Daishowa to that situation, and with a view to enlisting their support to persuade Daishowa's direct customers to change their minds. ... (Ibid., p. 633)*

> *[c/d] The results of the Friend's campaign against Daishowa from 1991 to 1994 were, in a word, stunning. Approximately 50 companies which purchased paper products (mostly paper bags) from Daishowa were approached by the Friends. The list of these companies reads like a Who's Who of the retail*

*and fast food industries in Ontario - Pizza Pizza, the
Liquor Control Board of Ontario, Cultures, Country
Style Donuts, Mr. Submarine, Bootlegger, A&W,
Kentucky Fried Chicken, Woolworth's, Roots, Club
Monaco, Movenpick Restaurants, and Holt Renfrew,
to name but a few. 'Every one' of the companies
approached by the Friends joined the boycott of
Daishowa products. ... (Ibid., p. 634)*

*[f/g] ... Two companies, Pizza Pizza and Woolworth's,
did not join the boycott at the first stage of the
campaign. Pizza Pizza was subjected to picketing
outside its stores on two occasions: Woolworth's had
a single store picketed on two occasions. On the
second occasion most of the small group of picketers
dressed as trees; one picketer dressed as a chainsaw
and moved among the trees. Both Pizza Pizza and
Woolworth's joined the boycott. (Ibid., p. 634)*

The comprehensive remedies that Daishowa was seeking
are listed below; clearly, it was out to teach its protagonists a serious lesson in corporate legal clout:

*[f/g/h] The plaintiff claims an entitlement to
permanent injunctive relief on six bases:
1. the tort of interference with economic and
contractual relations, including breach of contract;
2. the tort of intimidation;
3. the tort of conspiracy;
4. the tort of misrepresentation;
5. the tort of defamation; and
6. the use and threatened use of unlawful means,
including unlawful secondary picketing, watching
and besetting, nuisance, injurious falsehood, as well
as the aforementioned torts. (Ibid., 636)*

Here was 'everything but the kitchen sink' type litigation. The trouble being, however, that if the court didn't support Daishowa on these facts, then these remedies could forever be lost to industry in future litigation. Indeed, that's exactly what happened. Daishowa won a token $1 for defamation due to the 'Friends' having invoked the genocide reference. But on all the other counts, the court decided in favour of the 'Friends of the Lubicon'. The court's logic was premised upon the issue of free speech, as follows:

> *[h] The Friends say that their picketing activities at the business locations of Daishowa's consumers is speech concerning public affairs. I agree. ...*
> *(Ibid., p. 645)*

> *[a/b] ...The loss of a traditional economy of hunting, trapping and gathering, the negative effect of industrial development on a communal spirituality anchored in nature, the disintegration of a social structure grounded in families led by successful hunters and trappers, alcoholism, serious community health problems such as tuberculosis, and poor relations with governments and corporations engaged in oil and gas and forest operations on land the Lubicon regard as theirs - all these have contributed to a current state of affairs for the Lubicon Cree which deserves the adjectives tragic, desperate, and intolerable. ... (Ibid., p. 646)*

The court even went so far as to refer to the 'Friends' tactics as being not only legal but also a model protest, as follows:

> *(g)... In short, an important part of the 'Friends' message, and certainly the most effective part, is the attempt, through speech in a picketing context, to*

*enlist consumers in a boycott of Daishowa products.
(Ibid., p. 647)*

*(h) Is there anything unlawful about such a
consumer boycott? And do those who conceive and
organize it violate any law? I think not. (Ibid., p. 647)*

*(h) In short, the manner in which the Friends have
performed their picketing and boycott activities is a
model of how such activities should be conducted in a
democratic society. (Ibid., p. 649) (author's
underlining)*

The ruling garnered such heavy media coverage that in
the aftermath, Daishowa voluntarily agreed not to log a
10,000-square-kilometer area. It's not every day that a
major resource company walks away from a massive
crown grant in one of the most accommodating resource
jurisdictions in the country. The litigation was settled
with formal settlement papers being filed in court. In the
end, here was a no nonsense legal preview for the
oilsands; because the rise of native empowerment had
already made itself felt right in the neighbourhood.

Sour Gas

In Alberta, surface access for oil and gas exploration
has long been governed by fairly straightforward rules of
entry. The unique thing about most of the province's
petroleum rights is that the crown owns them outright -
not the surface landowner. As a result, the subsurface
rights from the government's disposition process carry
the express right of surface entry.

Typically there are just two points of contention: 1)
which landowners are entitled to standing as interveners
before either of two tribunals, and 2) what amount of

compensation should be paid for the consequential surface disruption? Only landowners who gained official standing would be heard, and those who didn't were simply left out of the process. This regulatory process ran uninterrupted for years, and was managed by two quasi-judicial boards operating at arms-length from ministers.

That was the way it was and the way it was meant to be until 1980, when Amoco's Lodgepole well near Drayton Valley 'blew-out' creating a toxic plume of gas that spewed out of control for months. Initially it roared out of the ground as hydrogen sulphide (H_2S) one of the most lethal gases in nature. Odourless in small concentrations and heavier than air, it migrates to topographical depressions where it awaits unwary passers-by, dead before they hit the ground, purple-looking, the oxygen stripped out of their bloodstream.

Fortunately that didn't happen, but two rig workers had succumbed at the scene. Unsubstantiated rumours circulated that a local might have discharged a shotgun shell into the deadly plume turning it into a giant fireball; the combustion process transforming the H2S into a less lethal gas, sulphur dioxide (SO2), which is still a serious health hazard. So it was the dank smell of rotten eggs that wafted south over Calgary and environs. Household silver tarnished overnight. Everyone knew that there was a serious problem somewhere in the northern gas fields. Moreover, the raging inferno greatly complicated the capping effort. In due course, provincial regulators would convene a special inquiry - the Lodgepole Inquiry - on how to better safeguard sour gas drilling and production.

That inquiry heard from a host of interveners who, in the normal course of regulatory events, would have been on the outside looking in. More than anything, the inquiry launched the Pembina Institute, which is staffed by home-grown environmental watchdogs based in Drayton Valley, which would go on to become the oil-sands' nemesis 30 years later. At the time, the Lodgepole

Inquiry made a series of recommendations pertaining to the drilling of sour gas wells that were adopted by regulators and embraced by industry. Thereafter, sour gas receded from the front pages, reappearing intermittingly usually only when tragedy struck (typically involving oil field workers). But 'home on the range' it was not. Landowner tensions had become more and more heated when in 1998, an executive of a junior oil company died not from sour gas - but from gunshot wounds - while overseeing a botched oil well remediation on a farm near the small rural community of Olds.

Vice President Patrick Kent was shot point-blank in front of his stunned work crew by landowner Wayne Roberts. Roberts had been complaining to regulatory authorities for over two years before he took the law into his own hands. When he was arraigned on murder charges, Wiebo Ludwig (a local activist) attended court in order to get his anti-industry message out. His warnings likewise were starting to make headlines across the province, as follows:

Wiebo Ludwig, a Peace River-area rancher who recently had charges dropped in connection with an oil well bombing this summer, said enough is not being done and violence was inevitable. (excerpt: Nova Pierson. Calgary Sun. October 6, 1998)

Andrew Nikiforuk, who wrote a Governor General award-winning book profiling industry protagonist Wiebo Ludwig, caustically referred to these escalating tensions as a modern day 'range war'. His observation was not only accurate, it was prescient. And it was against this tumultuous backdrop that Alberta natives made their first moves in asserting their treaty rights. They targeted seismic operators who cast a very large footprint over their traditional lands. Natives had long insisted on being consulted before the crown issued seismic permits. They were upset with the government's line that they didn't have special rights; only the right, like everyone else, to participate in the regulatory process (assuming they could gain standing). The natives asked why the treaty said one thing and the government said another.

Traditional Lands

Treaty 7, which includes Calgary the home base of oil-patch power, appears to support the native position. The key clause right from the Treaty is provided below:

> *And Her Majesty the Queen hereby agrees with her said Indians, that they shall have the right to pursue their vocations of hunting <u>throughout the Tract surrendered</u> as heretofore described, subject to such regulations as may, from time to time, be made by the Government of the country, acting under the authority of Her Majesty; and saving and excepting such tracts as may be required or taken up from time to time for settlement, mining, trading or other purposes by Her Government of Canada, or by any of Her Majesty's subjects duly authorized therefore by the said Government. (excerpt: The Treaty with the Blackfeet, No. 7, 1877) (author's underlining)*

Natives maintained that they had an implied right to have a say in the crown's seismic permitting process. But Alberta wasn't accepting this interpretation, even though just three years earlier the Supreme Court of Canada upheld a treaty right for subsistence hunting on their traditional lands in northern Alberta, as follows:

> *[82] ... The rights granted to Indians by treaties usually form an integral part of the consideration for*

the surrender of their lands. For example, it is clear
that the maintenance of as much of their hunting
rights as possible was of paramount concern to the
Indians who signed Treaty No. 8. This was, in effect,
an aboriginal right recognized in a somewhat limited
form by the treaty and later modified by the NRTA
[Natural Resources Transfer Agreement 1930]. To the
Indians, it was an essential element of this solemn
agreement. (excerpt: R. v. Badger [1996] 1 S.C.R., p.
771)

Native strategists believed that they were up against a de
facto industry-government-regulatory alliance in the oil
patch, and now they wanted their treaty rights recognized. But they had serious competition for the public's
attention, because Wiebo Ludwig, a local farmer and self-
styled oil patch reformer, believed that he was up against
the same alliance. His battle against Encana (then called
Alberta Energy Corp) soon eclipsed all other issues.
That's because a two-year spate of oil patch vandalism
swept the region around Ludwig's Trickle Creek farm
before he was finally incarcerated as a convicted oilfield
saboteur. Once the maker of non-stop head-lines, it was
ironic that Ludwig was released from jail to little or no
fanfare except for a tiny article in the National Post, as
follows:

"Convicted oilpatch vandal Wiebo Ludwig will be
released on parole on Nov. 14," officials said. Ludwig
was convicted of bombings and vandalism near his
home in Hythe, Alta., in April 2000, and sentenced to
28 months in jail. An official said Ludwig's test results
on a recidivism questionnaire indicated he was
unlikely to reoffend. (excerpt: National Post,
November 21, 2001) (author's underlining)

Soon the focus shifted away from the range war and onto the greatest challenge in Alberta's energy history - unlocking the economic potential of the oilsands. It was at this critical juncture, just when native empowerment in Alberta was at its lowest ebb, that inexplicably the Alberta government handed natives the legal wins that they needed to reboot their treaty rights campaign.

On July 1, 2000 (Canada Day) provincial wildlife officers broke-up a native community's fishing derby held near St. Paul on Whitefish Lake right on the reserve's waterfront. Here's how the appeal judge framed the incident at the start of the ruling:

> *[11] ... the Appellants were participating in an event billed in the community as its "Annual Family Fish Derby Whitefish Lake." Participants were restricted to Nation members and fishing had to be in the Reserve area of the Lake. (excerpt: Houle v. Canada, 2005 ABQB, 127)*

> *[12] ... this event, Family Fun Day, had been hosted annually at the Reserve on July 1st for at least two previous decades. Its purpose was "to provide members of the Reserve's community - families, parents, children and Elders - with the opportunity to socialize and have fun as a community in a way that was free of drug and alcohol use." (Ibid.)*

With such an introduction, it doesn't take a legal scholar to predict who's going to win this case. The judge quite properly admonished the authorities, as follows:

> *[96] It is well known that to accommodate European settlement, treaties were made which accorded certain rights to First Peoples in perpetuity. Considering the extent of the lands which were opened up to settlement, courts, in my opinion, should*

*be extremely cautious in allowing anything to
infringe on the constitutionally-protected rights of
First Peoples. Those rights as the Supreme Court of
Canada said in Sparrow at page 1119, should be
respected by the government, courts, and "indeed all
Canadians." (Ibid.)*

Worse, the crown even admitted in open court that
mistakes had been made, raising the obvious question:
Then why proceed? Here was a treaty win served-up 'on a
platter'! Perhaps the hard line that Alberta and industry
officials had been concurrently taking in the media had
something to do with it, as follows:

*"We do not recognize traditional lands, as a
province," says Pearl Calahasen, Alberta's Minister
for Aboriginal Affairs and Northern Development. ....
In terms of royalties, that's off the table at the
moment."*

*"If there is compensation paid ... the oil industry
doesn't want any payments coming out of its pockets,
said CAPP's Mr. Pryce, "As far as we're concerned, it's
not our obligation." (excerpt: reporter Patrick
Brethour, Globe and Mail, February 22, 2003)*

These public utterances reflected the status quo tenor of
the crown / industry / native dialogue one year before
the fishing derby ruling. Indeed it certainly looked as if
government and industry were 'singing from the same
songbook'. Yet this treaty win, combined with the
political fallout from the Ipperwash tragedy, appeared to
have momentarily forced the government to abandon its
status quo stance.

Consultations Guidelines for Industry

For without a doubt, Premier Ralph Klein would have taken a personal interest in the mounting troubles that former Ontario Premier Mike Harris was experiencing over recently released OPP communications that had occurred late in the day of the fateful shooting of Dudley George (ten years earlier). But now the airwaves were full of media innuendo swirling around Harris and Ipperwash, with reports of an OPP superintendent calling his administration a "redneck government" ..."barrel suckers"... in love with guns."

This was the context that immediately preceded the posting of Alberta's draft "First Nations Consultation Policy on Land Management and Resource Development" to a government website (literally overnight). It was likely that the Alberta premier saw how Ipperwash had ensnared Premier Harris in personal litigation, and daily in question period with calls for a formal inquiry to examine his role. Premier Klein would have realized that any similar police misstep on his watch would likewise land squarely on his desk and remain there for years. Disconcertingly, the same result would occur in the event of an industry misstep, which was something over which he had little or no control. Hence, the rushed posting of the native consultation guidelines, with no accompanying announcement or fanfare; as there were few votes to be won in Alberta for this initiative.

Just one week later at an energy conference in Calgary, Aboriginal Affairs Minister Pearl Calahasen spelled it out for industry as to why the 'times were a-changin' as follows:

> *"Alberta wanted to take full advantage of its resources and now this unique consultation climate would mean political stability. Alberta's status as [a] treaty province was formally acknowledged - the*

*timely development of land and resources was
paramount - the province has 200,000 Aboriginal
People who were tired of looking-in all the time.*

*Cabinet had approved the draft guidelines (as did
several departments) and all craved certainty.
Alberta was being proactive - though the law remains
unclear - quoting the Supreme Court of Canada that
'Treaty rights are sacred.'*

*It's a clear message to industry that we will not
shrink from our role to oversee this process in order
to create certainty for all parties - and economic
certainty. First Nations have rights - they are rights
holders. We started this process and are not
motivated by the courts - in fact the courts have
helped us!" (excerpts: Minister Calahasen's speaking-
notes, Calgary, May 31, 2005 paraphrased by author
in attendance)*

With these remarks, Calahasen, a Métis from Grouard,
put her stamp of approval on a government policy that
she hoped would launch Alberta into a new era of native
legal rights awareness. A lone voice in cabinet, she
understood the causal connection between native rights
and economic certainty. Indeed, her pronouncements
were just in the nick of time, because natives in northern
Alberta were poised to win yet another major treaty
ruling.

Now the Supreme Court of Canada added its weight as
to how the issues relating to the communities located
downstream from the oilsands should be addressed. The
court took direct aim at the federal crown, which up to
this point had been 'missing in action' in the consultation
department with respect to the impacted natives:

[52]   It is not as though the Treaty 8 First Nations did not pay dearly for their entitlement to honourable conduct on the part of the Crown; surrender of the aboriginal interest in an area larger than France is a hefty purchase price. (excerpt: Mikisew Cree First Nation v. Canada et al. [2005] SCC 69)

[54] ... The contemplated process (i.e. consultation) is not simply one of giving the Mikisew an opportunity to blow off steam before the Minister proceeds to do what she intended to do all along. ... (Ibid.)

[57]   As stated at the outset, the honour of the Crown infuses every treaty and the performance of every treaty obligation. Treaty 8 therefore gives rise to Mikisew procedural rights (e.g. consultation) as well as substantive rights (e.g. hunting, fishing and trapping rights). Were the Crown to have barrelled ahead with implementation of the winter road without adequate consultation, it would have been in violation of its 'procedural' obligations, quite apart from whether or not the Mikisew could have established that the winter road breached the Crown's 'substantive' treaty obligations as well. (Ibid.)

This was a huge win because it spread the blame around; now the federal government likewise was on a steep learning curve.

Dene Tha' and Mackenzie Gas Pipeline

At this point, native legal wins in Treaty 8 were starting to mount: Badger, Friends of the Lubicon, Athabasca Chipewyan, and Mikisew Cree. All of these were high level rulings and two of them affected traditional lands located downstream from the oilsands. Indeed, there would soon be another ruling; this one having the potential to halt the proposed Mackenzie Gas Pipeline environmental review. This time it was the Dene Tha' who were arguing that they had been frozen-out of that project's environmental review process, as follows:

> *"They were never even told about the process," said Robert Freedman, the lawyer who filed an application for a judicial review of the regulatory process yesterday. ... Freedman said his clients have written Imperial Oil, federal ministries, the National Energy Board and the Canadian Environmental Assessment Agency to say, "What about us?" (excerpt: Canadian Press & London Free Press, May 18, 2005)*

Six weeks after filing the legal challenge, Imperial Oil's senior executive on the Mackenzie Gas Pipeline project relocated to Houston. There may or may not be a link between the pipeline project having drawn a native lawsuit and the reassignment of its senior executive, but there are indeed several instances in the native legal winning streak where lawyers, project heads, and even entire executive teams have been replaced - soon after their project hits a legal speed-bump!

The Dene Tha' legal challenge arose because they had been left out of the environmental review process most likely because they were situated just below the NWT border in Alberta. Hoping not to lose project momentum, the proponents now argued in court that the Dene Tha' should instead 'wait it out' and see what the environmental review ultimately said about native impacts. The proponents also warned that should the case go forward, that held the potential to trigger other native challenges. But for the Dene Tha' the issue was straightforward: the regulatory process was already well underway and they hadn't been consulted or involved. The Federal Court's response to the proponent's arguments was terse and to the point:

> *[11] The issue is solely whether this litigation should be held off until a later day. (excerpt: Dene Tha' First Nation v. Canada 2006 FC 307)*

> *[27] In my view, it is fairer and more efficient, and potentially more effective, to the parties and all persons interested in this project that any legal infirmities with the creation of the mechanisms to approve this project be dealt with fully and expeditiously. …. Whether other native groups have similar claims which could produce multiple proceedings is speculative and not a basis for granting this stay. (Ibid.)*

> *[28] Lastly, the Court must be reluctant to tell an applicant/plaintiff that they cannot come to this Court and cannot determine the issues, venue and remedies to which they say they are entitled because it is more convenient for their opponent that they litigate elsewhere and at a different time. A party generally has a right to invoke the applicable jurisdiction in which to seek redress. (Ibid.)*

Really! It's hard to imagine the court coming to any other conclusion. As a result, this misguided attempt to block the natives was now added to that Treaty 8 cluster of legal wins. Moreover, the court again admonished the crown on its handling of events as follows:

> *[4] Quite remarkably, when the Ministers did decide to 'consult' with the Dene Tha' , upon the establishment of the process for the Joint Review Panel, the Dene Tha' were given 24 hours to respond to a process which had taken many months and years*

*to establish and had involved substantial consultation
with everyone potentially affected but for the Dene
Tha'. This last gasp effort at "consultation" was a case
of too little, too late. (excerpts: Dene Tha' First Nation
v. Canada 2006 FC 1354)*

*[12]   That the pipeline does not run through a
reserve, contrary to the Ministers' implied
submission, is insignificant. A reserve does not have
to be affected to engage a Treaty 8 right as held in
Mikisew Cree. ... What is important is that the
pipeline and the regulatory process, including most
particularly environmental issues, are said to affect
the Dene Tha'. (Ibid.)*

Imagine the boardroom consternation when the resulting
project delay caught the attention of the Wall Street
Journal:

*"The decision adds an additional level of uncertainty
to the regulatory process," says Pius Rolheiser, a
spokesman for Imperial Oil Ltd., the lead partner in
the project. (excerpt: Christopher J. Chipello. Wall
Street Journal, November 17, 2006)*

For those keeping score, it was the Dene Tha' win that
caused the first wheel to fall off the Mackenzie Gas
Pipeline project. That win was followed by intense negotiations as to how the review process might respond and
resume. Finally in mid-2007, a $25 million cheque was
forwarded to the Dene Tha' by the federal government to
compensate them for Ottawa's regulatory oversight. Then
as fate would have it, the Alberta government served-up
yet another native win that likewise was decided in the
opening paragraphs. That's because the judge clearly felt
that the charge in question put both the court and the
administration of justice itself on trial, as follows:

[3] In December of 2004, the Appellant was teaching his children how to trap wildlife (snaring squirrels) just outside of Hinton. He was charged with hunting without a license. (excerpt: R. v. Kelly 2007 ABQB, 41)

Instead the court used the strongest legal language to admonish the crown's approach, as follows:

[75]... The Appellant has been seriously prejudiced by the actions of the Government. (Ibid.)

[78] ... a conviction for an offense relating to activity described in art. 6 can only be characterized as abusive. In my view, to hold otherwise would reflect very poorly on the administration of justice in this Province ... (Ibid.)

[86] ... I find a conviction would shock the conscience of the community and bring the administration of justice into disrepute. ... (Ibid.)

It's clear that this Métis ruling is a serious condemnation of the prosecutorial process, as the words "shock the conscience of the community" are not often used by the courts. It's hard to believe that cases involving such trivial issues propel the native legal winning streak; and now a win over the trapping of squirrels was added to the fishing derby win. Such that by mid-2007, the oilsands were encircled by a native legal win cluster that seemingly owed its existence to the crown's blind adherence to the status quo.

West Fraser Pulp Mill

It's not as if the citizens of Hinton didn't have more serious real-life issues to worry about than the resident squirrel population. That's because eco-activists had successfully targeted its pulp mill as a destructive force in the boreal forest that threatened the survival of the local woodland caribou population. The highlight of the anti-clear cut campaign featured an advertisement in the New York Times of a chainsaw-wielding model in a snug-fitting bodice with angel wings standing amid clear cuts extending for as far as the eye could see - with the caption - "Victoria had a dirty secret." This marketing ambush so profoundly resonated that the publisher of Victoria's Secret catalogues (Limited Brands) agreed at once to stop buying paper from West Fraser's pulp mill in Hinton. The loss of the catalogue supply contract was a major economic blow given the catalogue's massive circulation. The catalogue company's media-savvy reaction is reflected in the following statement by its senior vice president:

> *"The growing controversy about logging in caribou range is of serious concern to us, and we want to ensure that our paper consumption does not contribute to the demise of endangered species," said Tom Katzenmayer, senior vice-president of community and philanthropy for the company (Limited Brands). ...*

But for pulp workers in Hinton the damage was done. The ForestEthics' campaign had been so effective that now Limited Brands expressly agreed to a host of conditions. The first of which was aimed directly at the Hinton pulp mill operation:

> - *Eliminating suppliers sourcing from logging company West Fraser, ...*

> - *Shifting their flagship catalogue to 10% PCW content beginning in 2007*

- *A commitment to Forest Stewardship Council certification (FSC) ...*

- *Overall catalogue paper reduction*

- *Annual independent audit of environmental progress*

- *A commitment to phase out of Endangered Forests*

- *One million dollars committed to research and advocacy to protect Endangered Forests and ensure leadership in the catalogue industry.*

By 2008, eco-activists had once again brought the Alberta forest industry to heel in a well-executed campaign; its campaigns against Daishowa and West Fraser had been hugely successful with the result that now, the eco-activists also had their own strategic winning streak.

Target Oilsands

It was at this juncture that ForestEthics turned on the oilsands with back-to-back advertisements in U.S. media; only this time they were aligned with downstream native communities who had both won recent court challenges. The first advertisement ran February 17, 2009 with an unmistakable message for the new president, as follows:

The Mikisew Cree and Athabasca Chipewyan First Nations and environmental group ForestEthics have placed a full-page ad in USA Today highlighting the human and environmental damage wrought by Canada's Tar Sands. The unprecedented advertisement, which features an oil splatted map

*of North America with oil oozing down from Canada
into the United States, comes just two days before
President Obama's first trip to Canada, and it makes
an impassioned address to the new President.
(excerpt: ForestEthics press release, 2009)*

The second advertisement ran on June 24, 2009 and
targeted Hillary Clinton, Secretary of State, as follows:

*Secretary of State Clinton's likeness appeared in a
full-page political cartoon-based ad run today in Roll
Call by ForestEthics and Sierra Club. In the cartoon,
a young girl anxious about a huge pipeline labeled
'World's Dirtiest Oil' asks Secretary Clinton: "Is this
my clean energy future?" (excerpt: ForestEthics press
release, 2009)*

The oilsands were now being branded as 'dirty oil'.
Moreover, downstream natives were being welcomed
into the open arms of eco-activists and litigators intent
on confronting the prime economic engine of the Alberta
economy. Soon legal challenges alleging out-of-control
oilsands development were launched by the: Woodland
Cree, Beaver Lake Cree, Chipewyan Prairie Dene, and the
Athabasca Chipewyan. The rise of native empowerment
was now poised to oppose the oilsands in tandem with
eco-activists' campaigns. And of course, the natives were
now armed with that major legal winning streak served-
up by an unwitting industry and a government de facto
alliance intent on preserving the regulatory status quo.

Premier Stelmach

Indeed, it was this flurry of native litigation that greeted
Premier Ed Stelmach just as he took his turn at the
provincial helm. Tellingly, in one of his first moves, he

collapsed the fledgling, Aboriginal Affairs department into the much larger Sustainable Development department in a move that native strategists rightly interpreted as a political downgrading.

Soon troublesome landowner issues would likewise preoccupy the new premier. He experienced major credibility problems due to the fact that the main industry regulator, the Energy Utilities Board (EUB), had allowed undercover operatives to attend local community meetings and listen-in on landowner conference calls so as to elicit anti-NIMBY intelligence with respect to a major north / south hydro transmission line upon which the EUB was poised to rule. In response, the premier was being publicly mocked on the steps of the legislature by protestors dressed as spies. As a result, the power line hearing was aborted, legislative changes were proposed, and the EUB was split into two separate agencies all in an attempt to denote greater regulatory transparency and accountability. A last minute legislative amendment now gave landowners expanded access to the board review processes. This outcome was something that aggrieved landowners had long demanded.

It was in this charged climate of landowner-rights, regulatory-repackaging, and political turmoil that none other than Wiebo Ludwig stumbled back into the headlines. He was involved in a 'dust up' with oil field workers at an installation located near his farm and was charged with assault. He pleaded not guilty. If there was one Albertan who couldn't sit idly by while sweeping regulatory reforms were occurring for which others were getting the credit, it was Wiebo Ludwig. Whatever his reasons for the alleged punch-out, he was now back in the news and would stay there for some considerable time. The following excerpt from a CTV interview that took place two months later is insightful:

CTV's Lisa Rossington asked Ludwig whether he thought the violence attacking the pipeline would escalate in light of the two recent bombings in northeastern B.C.

"You still want to go there where you shouldn't be going," said Ludwig from his home in Hythe Alberta - about 70 kilometers southeast of Dawson Creek.

"... the industry is escalating its developments - that's the escalating that you should be concerned about. That's where the violence is. That's where the dangers are. ... Yeah but I think we should stop yakking about that, frankly, because the industry is killing lots of people ... They're serial killers." (excerpts: CTV B.C. reporters Darcy Wintonyk / Lisa Rossington, October 20, 2008)

The good news for Ludwig was that, on the very day he was calling the energy industry "serial killers", the RCMP was clearing him of being a bombing suspect, as follows:

RCMP also ruled out Wiebo Ludwig, who was convicted of vandalizing oil and gas wells in Alberta in the late 1990s and spent almost two years in prison, as a suspect in the pipeline bombing. (excerpt: CBC News, October 20, 2008)

However, less than three months later, there was another serious bombing. But this time it was in an affluent Edmonton suburb, at the private residence of former Syncrude President, Jim Carter. He was an oilsands visionary notable for having implemented some of the most progressive native employment and business programs in the oil patch (if not all of Canada) but now his home had been torched by Molotov cocktails! Since his home had been burned to the ground, the crime appeared to be unsolvable; although a possible clue was that his car had been previously vandalized. Its vanity plate read DRT 2 OIL (a common bumper sticker and hard hat adornment for oilsands boosters). Theories abounded as to whether this was a related event with experts now expounding on the possibility of domestic terrorism. The oil patch soon posted a $500,000 reward.

More public relations trouble for the oilsands surfaced in February 2009, when a British bank announced that it would help fund the legal costs of the Beaver Lake Cree's court challenge as part of its 'toxic fuels' corporate social responsibility campaign. The Manchester-based, Cooperative Financial Services had pledged 50,000 pounds; and with that, native opposition to the oilsands went international. Here was support from within the financial sector itself no doubt intended as a backhanded shot at Canadian banks; some of which were taking heat at their AGMs for bankrolling massive oilsands expansions. Now the oilsands were increasingly profiled as an international social justice issue: so the protection of the native subsistence lifestyle and, consequentially, community health downstream were just two issues that were not about to go away. They would soon be presented in even starker terms to parliamentarians. In May 2009, the Commons Standing Committee on Environment and Sustainable Development travelled to Edmonton, where it heard directly from impacted natives, as follows:

"We are simply not prepared to watch more and more of our territory being infringed, nor are we prepared to accept the just-trust-us approach of government and industry while our health is impaired and cancer rates continue to rise in Fort Chipewyan," said George Poitras, of the Mikisew Cree First Nation.

..."The federal government has both the legal tools and the legal obligation to protect our rights and our

health." (excerpt: reporter Hanneke Brooymans, The Edmonton Journal, May 13, 2009)

Mining-Watch Win

Given that these same communities had already won major legal rulings against the crown, regulatory boards and industry, their concerns should have ignited decisive action. But it was precisely at this juncture that a legal bombshell, served up by the eco-activists, landed dead center in the oilsands tailings ponds.

The Federal Court of Canada now "directed" the Federal Minister of the Environment to collect and report "tailings and waste rock disposal information from mines in Canada" with respect to the establishment and operation of an automated pollution data bank that was required under federal statute. The court did not mince words, as follows:

> *[207] It seems to me that the reason <u>the Minister has issued Notices and Guides under sections 46 and 47 telling mining facilities not to report</u> such information is because, if it is reported, then the Minister is obliged to publish it under section 48 in the established NPRI. But this approach amounts to <u>turning a blind eye to relevant information</u> that all stakeholders agree should appear in a national inventory. I see nothing in section 46 or the general scheme of CEPA that allows the Minister to do this. (excerpt: Great Lakes United and Mining Watch Canada v. M.O.E. [2009] FC 408) (author's underlining)*

> *[208] <u>Section 48 obliges the Minister to establish a national inventory of releases of pollutants</u> using the information collected under section 46 "and any other*

information to which the Minister has access ...." The record shows that the Minister is well-aware that information is readily available (indeed the Minister may already possess it) that should be collected and placed in a national inventory of releases of pollutants. Indeed, the only thing that would appear to be preventing this from occurring is that not all stakeholders want the relevant information to appear under NPRI; ... (Ibid.) (author's underlining)

[209]... Meanwhile, the Canadian public is deprived of information concerning a significant source of pollution in Canada and concerning the environmental and the health risks that releases of such pollutants pose for Canadians. ... (Ibid.)

[225] <u>Instead of adhering to these objectives and duties in the present case,</u> the Minister has chosen not to publish information in a national inventory of releases of pollutants about mining facilities to which he has ready access while, at the same time, publishing similar information accessed from other sectors. The result is that the people of Canada do not have a national inventory of releases of pollutants that will allow them to assess the state of the Canadian environment and take whatever measures they feel are appropriate to protect the environment and facilitate the protection of human health. (Ibid.) (author's underlining)

The fact that the court's several admonitions were aimed directly at the federal minister implies serious political foot-dragging in Ottawa. For the impacted native communities downstream from the oilsands, seeing the court so emphatically order the minister to make this data public, essentially legitimized what they had been saying all along. As a direct result, the native / eco-activist merger was now stronger than ever. Moreover respected scientists, whose scientific findings had previously been questioned and at times vilified, stepped-up in support. The reaction of one eminent scientist is reflected below:

> *"The magnitude of the numbers is going to really*
> *shock people," David Schindler said. "... It's huge*
> *compared to any other mining development*
> *anywhere on the planet."*
> *(excerpts: CBC News, June 18, 2009)*

Soon the oilsands were once again in the news for all the wrong reasons; this time migrating ducks had landed in Syncrude's vast tailings ponds. After first publicly apologizing, Syncrude then chose to fight the charges. Meanwhile, Suncor incurred back-to-back fines: $675,000 for failing to install pollution control equipment and for failing to provide information to Alberta Environment; and (along with the Compass Group) a further $400,000 for various non-compliance offences. The provincial government, under mounting pressure from the public's condemnation of its lackadaisical approach, now announced that henceforth it would be more open and transparent in the laying and prosecution of environmental charges. Once again, it appeared that this series of unfortunate events strongly validated what the downstream native communities had just told the Commons Standing Committee.

Terrorist Threat-level

On the saboteur front, the July 2009 long weekend saw back-to-back oilfield detonations on July 1 (Canada Day) and on July 4 (Independence Day). These were bombings nos. 5 and 6 occurring within sight of each other. In fact, bombing no. 6 happened while safety crews were still working to repair the damage from bombing no. 5. As a direct result, the RCMP started using the term "domestic terrorism" in their investigation; notable since bombing no. 6 involved the release of potentially lethal sour gas.

Then in the ultimate case of bad timing, it was at this juncture that the energy industry released a special report on oil patch terrorism entitled: *Resource Issues and Security Issues in Northern Alberta.* It was a collaborative effort to quantify the risks facing the oil patch, funded by Nexen, authored by Dr. Tom Flanagan and issued by The Canadian Defence and Foreign Affairs Institute. This report would send the corporate / native dialogue off in another direction entirely; because it equated the threat level posed by Treaty 8 natives living downstream from the oilsands to that posed by oil patch saboteur(s). Key excerpts from this report, which Treaty 8 natives found highly offensive, were set forth in its conclusion, as follows:

CONCLUSION

6.1 Risk Assessment: *Resource industries in northern Alberta will undoubtedly face both violent and non-violent obstruction in the future, as they have in the past. Below is a qualitative risk assessment of the various groups that have offered or might offer obstruction:*

Saboteurs: <u>Medium</u> overall - *high risk of individual incidents, but low risk of sufficient coordination to disrupt operations on a wide scale. ...*

Treaty 8 First Nations: <u>Medium</u> overall - *long history of past blockades. Mikisew decision gives an enhanced legal platform, but there is no history of successful coordinated action that could impede*

*industry on a large scale, and First Nations in the
area have generally refrained from violence.
Overall, the most likely scenario is a continuation of
isolated and uncoordinated obstructive activities,
both violent and non-violent, which may occasionally
slow down or hold up particular projects, but which
will probably not threaten the ability of resource
industries to continue their operations in the region.
However, this relatively optimistic assessment would
have to be reexamined if evidence emerges of
collaboration among the various threat groups.
(excerpts: Dr. Tom Flanagan, from Resource
Industries and Securities Issues in Northern Alberta,
prepared for the Canadian Defense and Foreign
Affairs Institute, funded by Nexen Inc. June 2009, 11)*

This equating of Treaty 8 activism with oil patch
saboteur(s) drew a swift reaction from the same native
leaders who had just taken their case before the Commons
Standing Committee, as follows:

*"We would never collaborate with saboteurs or people
who are blowing up pipelines," said George Poitras,
strategist, Mikisew Cree. (excerpt: reporter Kelly
Cryderman, National Post, July 15, 2009)*

*"... It's very disappointing that a study done by the
CDFAI which was sponsored by an oil company is
claiming that we are a high risk threat to the oil
industry by assuming scenarios of First Nations
acting as eco-terrorists." ... (excerpt: Athabasca
Chipewyan First Nation, Press release, July 27, 2009,
quoting Chief Allan Adam of the ACFN)*

*"First Nations object to 'threat' label: We're being
branded,... Especially when we have never been
consulted on the matter, there needs to be room for*

*correction and that's why we're here to make sure
something is done about it," quoting Dene National
Chief Bill Erasmus. (excerpt: reporter Katie May,
Northern News Services, July 30, 2009)*

Even northern editorialists felt compelled to add their voice in support. Wasn't industry concurrently trying to win native support for the proposed Mackenzie Valley Pipeline? So this would hardly be perceived as helping that effort. Here's an excerpt from the pertinent northern editorial:

*Ignorance is the real threat: One of the simplest
things to do in life is label somebody. Political science
professor Tom Flanagan of the University of Calgary,
did just that last month by referring to First Nations
as a threat to oil sands expansion. ... Aboriginal
people have every right to oppose development that
fails to involve them and harms the environment.
That doesn't make them a threat. Instead it proves
what many First Nations people have said all along:
they are the true stewards of the land. (excerpt:
Editorial, NWT News North. August 10, 2009)*

In point of fact, the Mackenzie Gas Pipeline project was still hitting legal speed bumps and more wheels were falling off; since by now both the Dene Tha' and the Deh Cho had won important court rulings. So here was a northern media outlet telling the energy industry to start properly connecting the native empowerment dots if that key energy project was ever to see the light of day.

Colomac Mine

There's another reason why northerners would be offended over this dubious security report, because the north has had a long and unsatisfactory experience with tailings ponds. One tragic vignette drives home a host of environmental and safety issues.

Native hunters had long complained that caribou killed in the vicinity of the Colomac gold mine (NWT) didn't appear normal when gutted. Eventually taxpayers paid to fence the tailings pond ($500,000) in order to keep animals from licking the salt-rich but pollution-laced environs. That toxic brew was now Ottawa's responsibility and it had in turn given a remediation contract to a northern company that was undertaking monitoring work - when tragedy struck:

> *David Le Gros was by himself when he went through the frozen pond. His co-workers called for help when they found his camera beside a hole in the ice. The RCMP are investigating the man's death but say they do not suspect foul play. (excerpt: CBC News, March 3, 2009)*

No doubt northern editorialists had this tailings pond fatality in the back of their minds when they rebuked industry's saboteur comparison. That's because tailings ponds are potentially dangerous in all respects, extending from the native food chain to mine remediation attempts. In any event, the key issue here was the sustainability of the native subsistence lifestyle, which was why the fence at Colomac was installed in the first place. More to the point, this was precisely the same health and livelihood issue repeatedly raised by Treaty 8 native communities downstream from the oilsands.

Wiebo Ludwig

Paradoxically on the same day that Treaty 8 natives rejected the saboteur comparison, industry doubled its reward; putting Treaty 8 natives on the same terrorist threat-level as saboteur(s) with a million dollar bounty.

Soon the Manchester Cooperative Group was back on the scene with another major donation; and this time they had a BBC documentary team in tow. The Beaver Lake Cree were now going international backed by the Cooperative Group and the World Wildlife Fund's 'toxic fuels' campaign. Was there any doubt that the saboteur misstep caused these stars to align thereby giving this international campaign a strategic public relations boost?

Then, in mid-September 2009, Wiebo Ludwig penned an open letter to the *Globe and Mail* imploring the "Person(s) responsible" to stop; he even went so far as to assert that the bombing campaign had borne fruit! Having just been branded a 'medium level' security threat, Ludwig now appeared to be taking credit as a concerned fellow citizen, as follows:

> *To the Person(s) responsible for the bombings at Tomslake: An open letter!*
>
> *... I did offer to help stop the bombing and that is the only reason I am writing this open letter to you now. So, whoever you are and whatever your objectives, you need to know that you have already set a lot of good things in motion ...*
>
> *It is apparent that you have exercised some thoughtful restraint up to this point, not only by making sure that the explosions you set were "minor" and "controlled", but also your decision to call for a three month truce ...*
>
> *The industry as well as the RCMP are not oblivious to your concerns.*
> *(excerpts: Wiebo Ludwig's open letter, Globe and Mail, September 13, 2009)*

Of course, Ludwig didn't credit the native legal winning streak as a major factor driving (his) sour gas reforms. However more than any other factor, it was natives who were showing the way to achieve expanded landowner standing before the regulators. In fact, just one month later, the Alberta Court of Appeal applied the Dene Tha' test (for standing) in a major ruling that significantly expanded the scope of landowner interventions in sour gas drilling applications. Ostensibly, the credit for these reforms goes to three women in southern Alberta, as follows:

[2] The Appellants each own land and reside near the wells which are the subject of Grizzly's applications. Ms. McGinn lives approximately 2.91 km from the wells, Ms. Duperron lives approximately 5 km from the wells, and Ms. Kelly lives approximately 6 km from the wells. (excerpt: Kelly v. Alberta (ERCB) 2009 ABCA 349)

[3] ... The wells contain H_2S, a gas which is life threatening at very low concentrations. If gas escapes from one of the wells and ignites, it could convert to SO2 which is also a hazardous substance. Together H_2S and SO2 are sometimes referred to as "sour gas." (Ibid.)

[29] In the decision under appeal, the ERCB failed to address the first aspect of the <u>Dene Tha' test for standing.</u> ... Had those errors not occurred, it would have concluded that the Appellants had met the first requirement of standing. (Ibid.) (author's underlining)

[30] Other errors were made in relation to the second branch of the test [i.e. the Dene Tha' test] as to whether the Board had information which showed

> *that the application before it might "directly and*
> *adversely affect those interests or rights. ..." (Ibid.)*

This ruling, by the highest court in the province, made business headlines as the Energy Resources Conservation Board (ERCB) immediately suspended its processing of sour gas drilling applications until it digested all the implications of what was clearly an embarrassing rebuke to its regulatory purview. Indeed it had lost on all six grounds of appeal; then after a two-week hiatus, the board issued a key press release along with expanded criteria for enabling landowner standing, as follows:

> *... The Court determined that residents within a*
> *Protective Action Zone (PAZ) could be directly and*
> *adversely affected by applications to which a PAZ*
> *relates. The Court also stated that applicants <u>must</u>*
> *<u>include these residents</u> in their participant*
> *involvement programs. (excerpts: ERCB press*
> *release. November 13, 2009) (author's underlining)*

Really it was the Dene Tha' legal test that initiated these long-overdue regulatory reforms; meaning it was Treaty 8 natives (not saboteurs) who ultimately expanded regulatory access and standing for impacted landowners.

So that industry-funded terrorism report completely missed the fundamental political science aspect of: how these reforms materialized; how Treaty 8 natives lawfully expanded landowner access and standing before the regulatory process; and how as a direct result, 'range-war' tensions were eased throughout the province.

Instead the report was an exercise in industry 'groupthink' which single-handedly set corporate / native relations back just at the very moment when the oilsands were about to face their most embarrassing legal test - both in a court of law and in the court of public opinion.

'Ducks on a Platter'

Le Gros's tragic death at Colomac preceded Syncrude's public apology by 30 days; although it was the ducks that would garner international headlines over the next two years with graphic media images of dead and dying waterfowl. The trial would examine the steps Syncrude had taken (or should have taken) to warn the ducks off. Although in its first court appearance, Syncrude raised the prospect of mounting a constitutional challenge to the federal Migratory Birds Convention Act, which it elaborated upon on the courthouse steps, as follows:

> *Outside the courthouse, Syncrude spokesperson Allan Moore said a challenge, questioning the right of the federal government to lay the charge, is only one option the company has at its disposal.*
>
> *"There's still a lot of analysis [to be done]: understanding what the charges entail, what the implications are. And we need to analyze that to understand what they involved before making a plea," Moore said. (excerpts: CBC News, June 10, 2009)*

Perhaps unbeknownst to Syncrude, just one year earlier, a similar constitutional challenge had already been presented in a New Brunswick courtroom. J.D. Irving Ltd. had been logging on its private landholdings when it inadvertently destroyed a number of great blue heron nests. Its lawyers, hoping to head off a prosecution, argued in a preliminary legal round that aspects of the federal Migratory Birds Convention Act were unconstitutional due to vagueness and overly-broad wording. However that application was unsuccessful and the constitutional challenge failed. The presiding judge didn't mince words in describing the purpose of the legislation, as follows:

> *(Provincial Court Judge) Cumming said the wording of the act is clear and the intention 'remains conservation and protection.' ... 'The subject matter of the legislation is the protection of migratory birds that travel and are found internationally, requiring a single and unified approach to fulfill Canada's obligations under an international treaty'. 'This is not hunting legislation ... this is environmental legislation.' (excerpt: CBC News, June 9, 2008)*

Four months later J.D. Irving Ltd. admitted guilt, paid a $10,000 fine and made a court-ordered $50,000 contribution to avian environmental research and installed a court-mandated buffer zone around the heron colony. Their goal was to put the event behind them. They even reconstructed some of the destroyed nests.

But in Syncrude's case, the events leading up to the charges are particularly instructive, because these charges weren't laid in the normal fashion. In fact, they were precipitated by a Sierra Club private prosecution filed against Syncrude nine months after the incident; in effect publically embarrassing the provincial and federal governments into laying their formal charges one month later. It looked like they were forced into doing their job.

One month later, Syncrude apologized admitting that the death toll was three times the initial estimate. Then with the apology behind them, Syncrude turned around and entered 'not guilty' pleas!

Yet there had been no such delay in the fishing derby or squirrel trapping prosecutions. The former went ahead in spite of a candid crown admission that "mistakes were made" (para.84); while the latter proceeded in spite of an expressed "uncertainty in the law relating to Métis harvesting" (para.9). Was this not an apparent double standard in the administration of wildlife legislation?

In the ultimate irony, this lengthy delay meant that the start of the duck trial coincided with the Copenhagen Conference on Climate Change and thus became a high profile prop for embarrassing Canada on the world stage. Billboards in the U.S. portrayed images of oil-soaked ducks and targeted Alberta as a tourist no-go zone. Premier Stelmach belatedly realized that his province's main economic driver was front and center on the international stage. Worse was to come, since British Petroleum's blowout in the Gulf of Mexico was now into its third month, and the casualty list there - both in human and marine life - was fast becoming an industry 'game changer'. There the director of the U.S. Mineral Management Services was forced to resign over the agency's mishandling of the catastrophe. In turn, the priority status of the Migratory Birds Convention Act was elevated and quickly made its way to President Obama's office where he publicly insisted upon its full application.

As reflected in the statute itself, the whole point of the original 1917 convention was that both countries would safeguard migrating birds:

[4] The purpose of this Act is to implement the Convention by protecting and conserving migratory birds - as populations and individual birds - and their nests. (excerpt: Migratory Birds Convention Act, 1994)

Now events came in quick succession: on June 2, 2010 President Obama publically swore "to bring those responsible to justice"; and on June 25, convictions were entered against Syncrude in the duck trial. Yet that's the moment when two of Stelmach's senior cabinet ministers publically criticized the latter process:

Liepert [energy] told reporters that the trial was over-publicized and that Alberta had bigger issues to deal with. Danyluk [infrastructure] suggested that Syncrude wasn't to blame in the incident. (excerpt: CBC News, July 6, 2010)

Instead of the more appropriate 'no comment' before sentencing, here were two senior ministers potentially (and no doubt unwittingly) influencing the outcome. Stelmach called these remarks "Unfortunate" and said "They're not speaking for what we want to achieve as a government." Then on the very day that the convictions were entered, Syncrude again mused publicly about whether it needed to appeal the verdicts, as follows:

... Our decision to go through a lengthy and difficult trial wasn't about the fine. As we said in court, we are deeply concerned that the judge's decision on these charges sets a precedent that could have serious ramifications on Canada's mining industry. (excerpt: Syncrude press release, June 25, 2010 quoting Syncrude's president and CEO)

Instead, the following month saw Syncrude fixate on coming up with a "creative sentence" in the duck trial. Having been convicted on both counts and now armed with a new legal team, the resulting $3 million fine mirrored the payout profile of the J.D. Irving Ltd. penalty. Canada and Alberta extracted maximum fines ($300k and $500k, respectively) with the court-approved balance ($2.2 million) going to various avian preserves and research institutes. The next day's Globe and Mail headline touted "$3-million fine a drop in the barrel for Syncrude" and quoted Syncrude spokesperson Cheryl Robb as she publicly pleaded for forgiveness: "From our perspective at Syncrude, we're eager to move forward. The incident haunted us and we regret that it ever happened." (excerpt: reporter Josh Wingrove, *Globe and Mail*, October 23, 2010)

So ended a public relations marathon of two and half years duration, all the while with the specter of dead and dying ducks haunting the airwaves, during which the oilsands garnered unmitigated international notoriety. Because it was during this very time-span that opposition to the oilsands really coalesced, with the duck trial providing weekly fodder to 'dirty oil' opponents who were now also challenging pipelines proposing to access export markets in the U.S. and China. From a public relations viewpoint, Syncrude's media and legal strategy achieved the near impossible; in effect serving the ducks up on a platter to ever increasing international disdain!

More Native Litigation

The next time eco-activists and natives would team up was when Nancy Pelosi, the U.S. house speaker, visited Canada in early September 2010. While native leaders were having a private session with her in Ottawa, the downstream chiefs and eco-activists filed yet another legal action citing the Species at Risk Act. According to the chiefs, the issue was protection of critical caribou habitat:

> *"Today is kind of historic for us, because we have finally come to the realization that enough is enough,"* said Chief Al Lameman of the Beaver Lake Cree Nation. *"Our animals are suffering because of the oil exploration that's going on." (excerpt: CBC News, September 8, 2010)*

That sentiment was supported by the AFN's press release issuing immediately after the Pelosi meeting, as follows:

*The health impacts of the oil sands have been raised
in recent studies such as the one by David Schindler of
the University of Alberta, which is very critical of the
Province of Alberta and the oil sands industry for
failing to effectively monitor the Athabasca River. The
study found that in the summer months the oil sands
industry releases all thirteen of the U.S.
Environmental Agency's 'priority pollutants'. These
include mercury, lead, cadmium, and nickel among
others, in concentrations that exceed those
recommended by either Alberta or Canada for the
protection of aquatic life. (excerpt: AFN press release,
September 9, 2010)*

Three weeks later, in a speech at an Alaskan energy
conference, Alberta's Energy Minister Ron Liepert
defended the oilsands in geopolitical terms, as follows:

*Which brings us to one of the other reasons we're here
in Alaska. We need to get the truth out about the
oilsands because their development is critically
important, not just to Alberta, but to both our
countries.*

*Its origin is from a safe democratic country, which
respects human rights and develops its resources in
an environmentally responsible way. The U.S. is
likely to be importing oil for many years into the
future. Legislation that restricts oil from Canada is
not in the best interests of either the U.S. or our
country. (excerpts: Minister's speaking-notes.
September 28, 2010)*

Here was Alberta now in 'ethical oil' mode; notable after
all those eco-activist sit-ins and public relations embar-
rassments that were now regularly inflicted upon the
oilsands at home and abroad. Also of interest, oilsands

output seems 100% destined for U.S. markets in this late-2010 oilsands sales pitch. Nevertheless, it took back-to-back visits by James Cameron and Nancy Pelosi (plus a Species at Risk legal challenge) to finally convince industry, Ottawa and Alberta to establish an independent panel of experts to oversee the monitoring of water-related pollution issues. This move also came in the immediate aftermath of photos of fish with huge tumors caught in Lake Athabasca and an ornithological report stating that the duck death count in the tailings ponds was more likely thirty times higher.

Downstream Water Monitoring:

The environmental and health issues demanded nothing less than a state-of-art methodology for assessing all the potentially negative environmental impacts. The federal commissioner of the environment had just issued his report profiling (in an actual oilsands case study) the very situation that governments were now trying to get a handle on. That report revealed serious federal inattentiveness and ineptness, as follows:

Environment Canada has insufficient data to monitor oil sands development:

Alberta's oil sands cover roughly 140,200 square kilometres in the Athabasca River, Cold Lake, and Peace River regions in the province. The first large-scale oil sands commercial operation began in 1967. Studies have suggested that oil sands mining has environmental impacts as a result of freshwater use and pollutant releases. Environment Canada recently identified the oil sands region as a priority ecosystem and hotspot for further assessment and intervention. At the time of our audit, the Department had one

*long-term water quality monitoring station located
on the Athabasca River in Wood Buffalo National
Park, about 150 kilometres downstream from the oil
sands. The provincial government and private sector
monitor water quality in this region, but their data is
not available in the Department's regional long-term
water quality database.*

*Environment Canada's water quality monitoring
station in Wood Buffalo National Park has been in
place upstream from the First Nations community of
Fort Chipewyan since 1989. The station was
originally established to track the long-term status
and trends of nutrients in the river that could be
affected by pulp and paper production.*

*In 2009, the Department issued a report on water
quality status and trends in Wood Buffalo National
Park. The report recommended expanding the
monitoring parameters to include pollutants related
to oil sands development. At the time of our audit, the
Department was still considering their
recommendation. Consequently, the Department's
Fresh Water Quality Monitoring program has no
baseline measures or long-term data to track changes
in water quality and aquatic ecosystem health in the
river associated with oil sands development.
With regard to water quantity, the Department has
not determined whether it currently has an adequate
number of stations to monitor water flow related to
oil sands development. ... As a consequence, there
may be significant risks to the quality and quantity of
fresh water that have not been assessed and are not
being monitored in areas of federal jurisdiction.
(excerpts: 2010 Fall Report of the Commissioner of
the Environment and Sustainable Development,*

chapter 2.38, Office of the Auditor General of Canada)
(www.oag-bvg.gc.ca) (author's underlining)

With this, the federal environment commissioner's report gave credence to what the downstream natives had been saying all along. CBC described the findings as a "stunning revelation" in a "scathing" report with the "bizarre" outcome that the testing was "for just about everything but oilsands pollutants" (Greg Weston, CBC News, December 7, 2011). However, the CBC's reporting standards would soon be called into question because - industry was fighting back!

CBC's Reporting Standards

As it turned out, the CBC Ombudsman would now receive back-to-back complaints about how it reported on the oilsands. The first, came from an oilsands major producer; and the second from a leading scientific researcher. For readers who question the CBC's object-tivity in its coverage of the oilsands, the following two reviews are instructive. In order to facilitate the analysis of these the two scenarios, the CBC coverage is related first, followed by the ombudsman's adjudication. The first CBC news report that brought complaints aired three weeks after Syncrude's sentencing in the duck trial and is reproduced below in its entirety:

Alta. oilsands pond sludge oozes into bush
Last Updated: Monday, November 15, 2010 | 5:32 AM
MT files from the CBC's Michael Dick & James Hees

A northern Alberta tailings pond appears to have
toxic sludge flowing into the muskeg from an
uncontained western edge, a situation uncovered by a
CBC News investigation.

The pond, located in a remote area about 70 kilometres northwest of Fort McMurray, contains toxic waste from the Horizon oilsands project operated by Calgary-based Canadian Natural Resources Ltd. (CNRL). It has been in operation for about a year.

The pond has containing berms on all but its western side. According to documents obtained by CBC News, the company is relying on topography and clay beneath the surface to contain the tailings on that section of the pond. CNRL is legally permitted to have this setup. The plan was approved six years ago by Alberta's Energy Resources Conservation Board (ERCB).

But members of the Fort McKay First Nation are worried animals they traditionally hunt and trap may be drinking the water flowing from the tailings pond because there isn't a barrier to keep them away. "I feel like I want to cry," said band councillor Mike Orr. "I grew up on the land. That's the way I was brought up - to live off the land."

Band worries about toxins in food chain

CBC News was invited onto the traditional traplines by members of the Fort McKay First Nation. Dikes surround the pond on all but the western side. The land rises slightly at that point and the natural rise in elevation appears to be used to contain the tailings. Streams appear to flow toward and away from the tailings pond. Fresh deer and moose tracks are seen going towards the water. Muskrat dams are visible nearby.

The sight upsets Orr, a hunter and trapper who was raised on a trapline. Orr is concerned that toxins in the tailings may get into the food chain. "They should have a gate or something right around there and no creeks coming to it," he said. "Divert the creeks or something because we have all that water flowing into here, good clean water with the animals and the beavers. ... it's got to stop."

CNRL did not make anyone available for an interview on the weekend, despite several requests for comment from CBC News. Environment Canada declined comment. A spokesman indicated in an email to CBC News that his department will assess the tailings pond to ensure it complies with federal laws.

Clay not always reliable, expert says

CBC News shot video of the tailings pond and screened it for the world-renowned water expert and ecologist from the University of Alberta, David Schindler.

"This is such a big area," Schindler said as he watched the video. "Some of those chemicals have to be seeping into groundwater and Environment Canada should step in."

Some scientists believe that using the land to contain tailings might be better at keeping toxins out of the water than dikes, which are usually made of sand. The land beneath the forest floor is made of clay, which is believed to be a natural sealant. But Schindler says clay isn't completely reliable and engineering tests often don't account for holes created by tree roots or burrowing rodents.

"I'd be concerned that there might be some tree root holes that, after the trees die and the roots decay, that there are channels that material could follow either into groundwater or into other surface waters that are lower elevation," he said.

Orr hopes the federal government moves quickly to make sure toxins aren't contaminating the area's food and water. For his part, Schindler expressed disbelief that regulators would approve this type of tailings pond. "[I] wonder if the people who approved this have ever gone back for a look," he said.

This story caused a political storm, landing later the same day on the floors of both Parliament and the Alberta Legislature; thereby putting intense pressure on governments and Canadian Natural Resources Limited. In due course, the latter's general counsel was one of three who asked the CBC Ombudsman for a review. What follows are the ombudsman's conclusions, significant in that his critical assessment focused on one key issue - the sustainability of the native food chain:

Conclusion: CBC News performed an important public service in gathering the facts first-hand. It visited the affected region. It used credible sources - the First Nation of the area and an authoritative scientist - to raise important questions about the habitat for wildlife and impact on the food chain. Its efforts questioned the wisdom of a licensing process that permits a possibly porous shoreline to contain toxins in an area inhabited by wildlife and a source of food.

I concluded the stories themselves were fair in their description of the sprawl of tailings to avoid drawing a conclusion that could not be scientifically supported.

CBC sufficiently established that the tailings pond was not violating its licence, and it drew upon a scientist and residents to raise concerns there might be an unexpected consequence.

While the stories demonstrated restraint, the categorical tone of the online headline ("Alta. oilsands sludge oozes into bush") was insufficiently supported. The fears of the ecologist and of First Nations were important to discuss. Without an independent test of the muskeg or of wildlife to furnish proof to those fears, the headline asserts damage; it would have been better phrased were it attributed as a concern of a relevant party.

The more significant matter here, though, involves the inclusiveness and balance of the first report. With its investment in the story, CBC News was concerned about losing the competitive advantage if it further delayed publication. It attempted unsuccessfully to reach a CNRL representative for comment on the weekend before publishing. It did not violate CBC Journalistic Standards and Practices in attempting to include CNRL and noting it was not available. But it was difficult to fault CNRL for not providing a spokesperson on what appeared to be a non-urgent matter on a weekend. Waiting to include the company perspective from the outset would have served the audience better, defused potential criticism, and been more reflective of the standards and practices.

That being said, CBC News was fair-minded in following the reaction to the initial reporting. As the day progressed, and in the days that followed, it gave voice to all parties in the controversy.

Kirk LaPointe CBC Ombudsman

(excerpts: Reports about the environmental condition of an oilsands tailings pond, issued March 1, 2011)

CNRL had a legitimate point with respect to the headline, but the overarching reference to CBC News having fulfilled an "important public service" gave the clear advantage to the CBC. Notably, it was the sustainability of the native food chain that ultimately decided the merits of the newsworthiness of the story. In this key respect, the Ombudsman's ruling stands in the court of public opinion as a native win.

However, just six weeks after the CNRL report aired, CBC's 'The Current' ran a radio segment examining the causality between purported contaminants in the water and cancer clusters in downstream communities. On the program, Dr. Steve Hrudey, an eminent scientist and medical authority, concluded that the Royal Society's independent research had not established scientific causality. Afterwards he faulted the program for implying that he had urged the need for further studies when instead it was his view that the research bore "*ample evidence*" to reach the conclusion that it did.

Hrudey charged in a letter to the CBC dated January 6, 2011 that 'The Current': "knowingly skewed the message of this story to fit their invalid and unsubstantiated view of the circumstances surrounding the existence of an unusual cancer cluster in the largely aboriginal community of Fort Chipewyan which they would attribute to oil sands contaminants." One week later, Hrudey received a written apology from the show's producer stating that indeed "the program misstated your position" but called the error "inadvertent." Hrudey considered that aspect of the apology to be "not credible" and wrote the CBC Ombudsman requesting a review. This time the Ombudsman sided with the complainant:

Conclusion: The inaccuracy about the panel's views on the need for further studies did not meet CBC standards and practices, nor did the on-air treatment of the complaint. The correspondence with the complainant acknowledged that with a fulsome personal apology. Of course, there is also a wider obligation to the audience.

The audience would have benefited from background on the College of Physicians and Surgeons of Alberta's findings about O'Connor's controversial 2006 diagnoses. As it stood, the statement of Hrudey and not O'Connor was challenged.

It also would have been more helpful to the audience if, in the second broadcast, the program clearly identified the earlier information concerning further studies as inaccurate.

The Current has a strong tradition of thoughtful, varied and challenging discussions that seek diverse opinions and demonstrate consistent, impartial curiosity. In recent times it has featured extensive interviews with the Alberta premier and environment minister, the president of the Association of Canadian Petroleum Producers, the chief executive officer of Suncor, the chief energy economist of ARC Financial, and entrepreneur T. Boone Pickens on matters concerning the oil sands. Indeed, the discussion that followed the complainant's audio clip articulated the scientific challenge of causality.

Kirk LaPointe CBC Ombudsman. (excerpt: Proving Causality in Cancer, The Current, April 11, 2011)

When this review issued, both Canada and Alberta were in full publicity mode announcing their downstream water monitoring proposals; which in due course will form the scientific baseline data for measuring purported linkages and causalities. The obvious inference being, that until such time that this baseline data exists, questions surrounding water toxicity and cancer clusters will likely remain an unsettled issue - at least in the public's mind. In any event, the federal and provincial governments were finally moving in tandem to address the critical issue of whatever might be in the water.

Then to underscore the greening of the oilsands, Alberta announced to great fanfare, the Draft Lower Athabasca Integrated Regional Plan that earmarked two million hectares of (industry held) land that would now become conservation areas "*supporting wildlife mobility and habitat stability.*" Yet the same downstream natives once again registered objections citing their "*lack of involvement*" and claiming that this was just one more example of Alberta's approach to their "*economic assimilation*", as follows:

> *Alberta is doing more of the same thing and expecting a different result. The provincial government consistently fails to meet even our basic needs when it comes to air, land and water within the region and fails to meaningfully engage First Nations in land management decisions in accordance with our aboriginal and treaty rights. Until Alberta makes meaningful efforts to protect land, regulate industry and ensure that First Nations are at the table <u>as full partners</u> to develop solutions to the serious environmental challenges that government and industry are creating, they can count on our opposition to further development within the region. (excerpt: Chief Allan Adam, Athabasca Chipewyan First Nation press release April 8, 2011) (author's underlining)*

WikiLeaks and Bruce Carson

Two other events coincided in spring 2011 that offered behind-the-scenes glimpses of what was motivating the oilsands' dynamics federally. We now know from Wiki-Leaks that Environment Minister Prentice had returned from Europe shocked over Canada's international black-eye as a result of the 'dirty oil' branding:

> *As Prentice relayed it, the public sentiment in Norway shocked him and has heightened his awareness of the negative consequences to Canada's historically 'green' standing on the world stage, ... he felt the Government of Canada's reaction to the dirty oil label was 'too slow' and failed to grasp the magnitude of the situation. (excerpt: reporter Steven Chase, Globe and Mail, January 8, 2011, quoting from U.S. Ambassador's David Jacobson's cable - released by WikiLeaks in December 2010)*

We also now know that Prentice at the time was being advised on oilsands reputational-management issues by the ultimate Ottawa political 'fixer' - Bruce Carson - who had even attended a meeting at the highest levels in Washington as an 'unpaid advisor'. The meeting in question also involved Canada's ambassador and the U.S. Secretary of Energy, and inconveniently occurred just five days after that federal court ruling ordering: "that the Minister is directed to publish pollutant release information to the public through the National Pollution Release Inventory."

Bruce Carson had just settled-in to the federally-funded Canadian School of Energy and Environment (CSEE) based in Calgary as its inaugural executive director, having left the PMO a few months previous. When Carson's role imploded just over a year later, becoming the subject of an alleged RCMP lobbying investigation (unrelated to oilsands issues) he took leave from the CSEE, and likewise stepped-down from the specialist water panel that had just been created to monitor downstream water issues. Controversially, getting on this panel in the first place underscored his political usefulness, as his was not a scientific role; but now his clouded departure reflected negatively on that critically important process. Moreover, his was the second panel departure in as many months; the first being that of an eminent U.S. water scientist who left immediately upon ascertaining that the panel lacked native representation. Soon it was the provincial government's selection process itself, which was in damage control mode on the floor of the Alberta legislature:

Ms. Blakeman: Thanks very much, Mr. Speaker. The Environment minister insists that the appointment to the water panel of a self-described best friend of the Prime Minister was based on expertise, not political connections, but it is difficult to find confirmation that this individual had specific expertise on water beyond his part in helping to create the Canada School of Energy and Environment and his subsequent appointment as head of that school. ... He has no direct water experience. ...

Mr. Renner: Mr. Speaker, I beg to differ. I believe that the people that are on this panel were brought into the panel for different expertise in different areas. Some have a scientific background, some have a business background, and some have a background in being able to liaise and bring forward complementary research in other areas. So I disagree with the premise that the member brings forward. (excerpts: Alberta Hansard, March 23, 2011)

There's more than a hint of 'groupthink' in the Alberta government's defense of Carson's appointment. Indeed, just one month later the Globe and Mail ran an editorial on the travails of the climate change debate that used a similar term - "tuning out" - in what was intended as an indictment of the joint government / industry approach:

> *Tuning out is also an option, the one Stephen Harper has pursued for most of his two mandates. It's also a tried and tested strategy employed by many of our companies engaged in oilsands development - they have effectively ceded the rhetorical terrain to international NGOs. The Liberals too are guilty. ... (Both) have helped to marginalize Canada on the world stage. (excerpt: Globe and Mail editorial, April 23, 2011) (author's underlining)*

This editorial is completely accurate in explaining how groupthink ceded the rhetorical terrain to eco-activists. Groupthink likewise ceded the legal terrain to natives. Call it 'tuning out' - or call it 'groupthink' - either way, that is what's preventing the oilsands from realizing their full economic potential. And until that fundamentally changes, the future of Canada's energy economy hangs in the balance.

When the Penny Dropped

The first tangible sign of progress on the oilsands occurred July 4th 2011 when the province's specialist water panel cited native concerns; using wording that was 180 degrees opposite from the wording employed in that 'groupthink' security threat level report, as follows:

> *The aboriginal groups that participated in the Panel's engagement sessions expressed a keen desire to*

participate in a credible and transparent regional monitoring process - one that would involve them in all aspects of monitoring, from the collection of data to interpretation and evaluation of data and information, identification of knowledge gaps, and governance and planning. <u>These groups displayed a highly sophisticated understanding of their legal rights, the industrial processes that are being carried out on their traditional lands, and environmental monitoring science and policy.</u> However, the Panel also noted a high level of cynicism about government and industry-led monitoring and regulatory processes with which aboriginal groups have interacted in the past. To varying degrees aboriginal participants expressed deep frustration with these processes; they felt the processes had not given credence to their concerns about cumulative impacts of oil sands development, were highly adversarial, and did not engage or empower them to participate as equals in the management of their Treaty Lands, rights for which they cited certain constitutional protections. (author's underlining)

Representatives from Fort McKay and Fort Chipewyan felt that an open and transparent system that engaged the community and provided gainful employment opportunities for young people in activities centered on environmental stewardship would be well received. The Panel is aware of a Canada-First Nation Joint Action Plan to which Canada and the Assembly of First Nations recently agreed. This recognition by Canada to pursue enhanced cooperation between government and native leaders may signal a major shift in both leadership and attitudes toward joint initiatives. As such, it would be consistent with those initiatives to carefully examine the potential advantages of

community-based monitoring programs in the
aboriginal communities and lands in the Lower
Athabasca region. (excerpt: p. 45/46 Report of the
Alberta Environment Monitoring Panel, section 5.7
Aboriginal Participation June 2011)

In the media roll out, Alberta's Environment Minister conceded on all the points long in contention, even citing the "ad hoc, inadequate, piecemeal system" currently in use. Yet it remains to be seen if the Alberta government adopts Recommendation 16:

Aboriginal Participation: The Panel recommends that
the Commission establish a mechanism, in
consultation with representatives from Treaties 6, 7
and 8 and the Métis Nation of Alberta, to enable
aboriginal communities to develop a proposal for
their participation in Commission activities, including
community-based monitoring programs. (Ibid p. 46)

CBC News described the report as "remarkably blunt" (reporter Terry Reith CBC news July 5, 2011) no doubt to underscore its prior (challenged) treatment of the contentious subject matter. But now with the benefit of the panel's own commentary, it would appear that what the downstream natives had been saying all along was, in the main, accurately reported. Indeed, they didn't have to wait long to be vindicated over their oft-voiced concerns respecting habitat protection for woodland caribou. By the end of July 2011, the Federal Court was again ordering the federal Minister of the Environment to do his job - giving him one month to develop a Recovery Strategy for woodland caribou, as follows:

[68] ... the basis for the overall conclusion reached by
the Minister, particularly the evidentiary basis, was
not meaningfully discussed ... and the record does not

otherwise explain the Minister's decision in a satisfactory manner. In the context of the Decision as a whole, this conclusion essentially came "<u>out of the blue</u>". ... (author's underlining)

[69] Accordingly, the Decision cannot stand and must be set aside. (excerpts: Athabasca Chipewyan First Nation, Beaver Lake Cree Nation, Enoch Cree Nation v. Minister of the Environment and Attorney General of Canada 2011 FC 962)

Seven months later the same natives were back urging the judge to order the minister to provide meaningful reasons as to his refusal to issue an emergency order to protect woodland caribou in northeastern Alberta. Thus it's abundantly clear that natives have momentum on their side, given their strategic ability to access the legal process and see it through to force a judicial conclusion.

Then media reports surfaced in early 2012 of a previous high level strategy meeting with CAPP, federal and provincial officials and Bruce Carson, wherein lists were discussed that profiled natives as oilsands 'adversaries' - in a classic case of mutual groupthink!

And if the oilsands hornet's nest of public relations missteps needed more agitation, it arrived with an open letter from the native leadership of Fort McKay, right after the local MP implied that natives were being funded to oppose the oilsands by eco-activists. The reply from the most impacted oilsands native community speaks volumes of how groupthink is squelching native goodwill:

As a First Nation in the heart of Alberta's Athabasca oilsands region, we felt it necessary to respond to disparaging assertions by Brian Jean, MP for Fort McMurray-Athabasca. He has called for federal legislation to block foreign funding of environmental opposition to major oil and gas projects such as the Northern Gateway pipeline.

He alludes to the possibility of First Nations chiefs being paid directly by such environmental interest groups to oppose these projects.

These uninformed opinions and insinuations that question our people's integrity are profoundly insulting not only to us as a First Nation but also to all aboriginal people across the country. We take issue with the suggestion that we are not a people of integrity.

We also believe that it is inappropriate for him to speak on behalf of First Nations in Canada. He may represent the region in which our particular First Nation resides; however based on our experiences, he has failed to make the effort to become adequately familiar with the region and its people at a deeper level - not just with First Nations but with all community stakeholders.

With regards to our First Nation and community, we have cultivated and maintained strong and effective long-term relationships with industry. Our land is close to a number of oilsands projects, and we make our concerns known to industry in a spirit of open dialogue.

For example, our community has been working closely with industry, the Wood Buffalo Environmental Association and scientific experts on air-quality monitoring and reporting for Fort McKay. We have made important strides, with industry taking steps to reduce emissions, the environmental association installing air-monitoring instruments,

*and our First Nation developing an air-quality index
for Fort McKay.*

*Our First Nation also created a working group with a
local oil and gas company for sharing information on
industrial odours.*

*While our issues may not always be addressed to our
satisfaction, we are committed to working with
industry with the aim of reaching acceptable
solutions for all. Our relationship with industry is
something we will continue to work at. It is premised
on openness and transparency.*

*We welcome Jean to meet with Fort McKay's chief
and council to become better informed about the
relationship between First Nations and industry and
the issues related to oil and gas development in the
Wood Buffalo region.*

*Chief Jim Boucher, Councillors David Bouchier,
Gerald Gladue and Raymond Powder, Fort McKay
First Nation
(open letter printed in the Edmonton Journal
February 17, 2012 – under the headline - 'Tory MP
insults First Nations")*

Canada's prime minister was back from China barely a
week when this letter appeared; he had led a large trade
delegation (on energy) that was criticized for lacking
native representation. This letter makes that omission
look like a missed opportunity. Chief Jim Boucher is the
recipient of the Canadian Council of Aboriginal Business
highest honours for his business acumen with oilsands
projects.

Yet this key example of constructive dialogue on the
oilsands from the native leadership at ground-zero,

stands in stark contrast to native pipeline opposition that increases exponentially as the right-of-way approaches tidewater. One month later the coastal leadership issued a warning to the Joint Panel Review on the Northern Gateway project: "We know the Governments of Canada and B.C. .... think we're not prepared to go to battle ... We are." (Chief Elmer Moody, Gitxaala Nation JRP transcript March 14 2012 para 17841).

In simplistic terms - bitumen, tankers, groupthink - are the three factors that are impeding Canada's future economic prosperity. With proper safeguards, the first two can be scientifically and technologically regulated to bring oilsands production and bitumen transportation risks to within acceptable limits. Whatever those limits will be, it's a safe bet that natives will have a major voice in deciding and potentially controlling. This is what Quebec achieved in 2002 with Les Paix des Braves.

'Groupthink'

'Groupthink' continues to cloud Alberta's vision for winning international acceptance of the oilsands; yet the controversy has a clear and readily identifiable fix. Get natives onside! To do that, the traditional food chain has to be protected in a holistic manner and native rights and entitlements have to be accorded full partnership status.

Today, natives and eco-activists are joined on a number of fronts with the common goal of holding Alberta and Canada to account. But it was 'groupthink' that created misstep after misstep on the native file, making the merger of native and eco-activists agendas inevitable. While there are many embarrassing examples, nothing represents industry 'groupthink' better than the follies of the duck trial.

What if the oilsands were situated in the vicinity of St. Paul / Minneapolis and drained 1800 kilometers down the Mississippi? Native voices would barely be heard in the general public outcry. Yet downstream from the oilsands it's a different story; there natives apparently can only be heard through their legal winning streak and via international joint eco-activist campaigns.

That's what Le Gros' death at Colomac, Syncrude's duck trial, and the CNRL Ombudsman's challenge all have in common: each is a site-specific indicator along the extended watershed as to what potentially threatens native subsistence. And as long as these threats persist, the full economic potential of the oilsands will never be realized. Today, only natives can green the oilsands and thereby imbue Canada's bitumen with a measure of international respectability. The paradox is simple: only natives can ensure the oilsands economic prosperity as a key export; and only groupthink stands in the way of getting them onside to further our mutual economic interests.

7

BRITISH COLUMBIA: *OLYMPIC BACK-FLIP*

No province has experienced the power of the native legal winning streak quite like British Columbia where, although it's been a significant force for incremental change, it actually has been an impediment to fundamental change. Why negotiate a political settlement when you can always do better in court? An excerpt from an article citing Chief Jacob's response to the 'The New Relationship', the major legislated overhaul proposed by Premier Gordon Campbell at the end of his second term, echoes this sentiment:

> *"There are too many unanswered questions at this point," (Chief Gibby) Jacob said. "If they are not answered, we will come out all guns blazing against it. ... First Nations have right and title. You can't bicker with that and set up rules and constitutions to stop it."*
>
> *Jacob argues that aboriginal groups are faring better in court than in the premier's office and the proposed legislation is mostly about stability for government*

*and industry. (excerpt: reporter Kim Vanlochem
quoting Chief Jacob, The Squamish Chief, June 19, 2009)*

There are a number of key messages in Chief Jacob's remarks that help explain what's been happening in B.C.'s troubled resource sector. It's clear that the province has paid a high price for failing to address legitimate native concerns respecting resource projects impacting traditional lands. To natives it appeared that government and industry were 'in cahoots'; so they turned to the courts and are now filling the political void with pro-native judgments. It's little wonder then that natives are reluctant to turn away from the courts, just when major rulings are going their way on such fundamental issues as aboriginal title.

Native Militancy

Furthermore, no province has experienced the thrust of native militancy to the same degree as has British Columbia. By 1973, the American Indian Movement (AIM) had already made inroads into the B.C. interior (just as hostilities were poised to erupt at Wounded Knee, South Dakota). In August 1974, armed B.C. natives manned a blockade near Cache Creek protesting socio-economic conditions on the Bonaparte Indian reserve. However, the main event occurred two decades later in 1995, in a shootout with police during which 60,000 to 70,000 rounds of (police) ammunition were expended bringing the 31-day standoff at Gustafsen Lake to its climactic end. Ostensibly the dispute was over access to a sun dance site on a privately owned ranch.

Internal government documents have recently come to light that help explain how this firefight came about. Months before, an RCMP officer had been shot at by a warrior with the bullet whizzing by his head. Also there

were native firearms seizures including an AK47 and a
semi-automatic pistol. Now as the RCMP prepared to
make their move they clearly had run out of patience, as
the tone of this high-level interoffice memorandum
makes clear:

> *I spoke with RCMP Sgt Peter Montague this morning
> (Aug 22/95). The RCMP is continuing its strategic
> planning and it seems that will continue for the next
> 24 hours.*
>
> *Montague remains pleased with overall messaging
> from the AG, however he says there is concern with
> one item. Apparently Minister Dosanjh said in one of
> his (sic) radio interviews that "force should only be
> used as a last option." Montague is cautioning
> against any softening on the law enforcement line. In
> Montague's words, "we are at the last option." The
> RCMP feel that they have made every attempt to
> negotiate an end to this situation.*
>
> *The Gustafson Lake natives have been invited to tell
> their side at RCMP news conferences. The natives
> have also indicated that talks with the police, the
> Province, or the federal government, is not an option.
> They are only interested in taking up their issues with
> the Governor General or the Queen.*
>
> *Montague does not want there to be any
> misunderstanding about the current thinking on
> Gustafson Lake. The current planning being
> undertaken by the RCMP is not an effort to establish
> talks. The RCMP is planning to bring this "situation to
> an end."*

If violence is to be avoided, the natives on site remain free to lay down their arms and walk out. Presumably the timing on this option is running out.

The most recent language from the native camp indicates that, given a fight with the RCMP, the only way the militants are prepared to leave is in body bags.

The most recent messaging from the Cariboo Tribal Council and the Canoe Creek band has strengthened their condemnation of the militant group. Canoe Creek band Chief Agnes Snow told CBC radio this morning, she feels the RCMP have been very patient in dealing with this matter. That's all to this point. (Interoffice Memorandum dated Aug. 21 1995, Paul Corns author, Government Communications Office memo to five recipients (PREM, AG, AAF offices et al.)

It's likely this recently unclassified memorandum paved the way for the firefight that would occur less than a month later. It's all the more remarkable for the RCMP's sideswipe of the Attorney General's public messaging.

Coincidentally, the hostilities at Gustafsen Lake were cresting just as the policing action at Ontario's Ipperwash Park was reaching its own point of no return. Indeed, the OPP had a senior observer posted onsite at Gustafsen Lake whose role was to report back on operational strategy and tactics to the Ipperwash command post. As it transpired, Dudley George would be shot by a police marksman on September 5, 1995 - with the shootout at Gustafsen Lake exploding the following week.

Ten years later in 2005, there would be another significant and scary policing action. It involved the 'takedown' of B.C. native activist, David Dennis, founder of the Westcoast Warrior Society, in downtown Vancouver. The country's elite anti-terrorism unit transformed the urban landscape (Burrard Bridge) into a mid-level conflict 'no-go' zone. Dennis was transporting 14 guns and 10,000 rounds of ammunition; but when questioned by police, he explained that it was destined for his youth wilderness survival camp instruction program. Apparently the paperwork checked out as he was subsequently released. It made for a dramatic day of police and media news clips, as the downtown seemingly turned into a Hollywood movie set - only this was the real thing!

The extensive publicity surrounding these troubling incidents, not to mention the public's apprehension as to what was going on behind the scenes, set the stage for the remarkable native legal winning streak that was about to be unleashed in B.C. courtrooms. Perhaps too, the judges felt that a new way forward was long overdue.

Wake-Up Call

As in the other provinces, the B.C. native legal winning streak started with a somewhat poetic wake-up call for all concerned; in a 1985 ruling that halted clear-cutting on Meares Island. Natives had declared Meares Island to be a "tribal park" and opposed clear-cutting on the basis that it was an intrusion that interfered with their aboriginal title. Here's the court's wake-up call:

> *[48] Meares Island is important to MacMillan Bloedel not because of its trees, but because it is where the line has been drawn. It has become a symbol.*
> *(excerpt: MacMillan Bloedel v. Mullin [1985] BCCA 3 W.W.R. 577)*
>
> *[52] The evidence shows that the Indians still use Meares Island, including the Heelboom Bay area, and that logging is not compatible with that use. (Ibid.)*

*[54] The Indians wish to retain their culture on
Meares Island as well as in urban museums. (Ibid.)*

*[55] The Indians have pressed their land claims in
various ways for generations. The claims have not
been dealt with and found invalid. They have not been
dealt with at all. Meanwhile, the logger continues his
steady march and the Indians see themselves
retreating into a smaller and smaller area. They too
have drawn the line at Meares Island. The Island has
become a symbol of their claim to rights in the land.
(Ibid.)*

*[78] It has also been suggested that a decision
favourable to the Indians will cast doubt on the tenure
that is the basis for the huge investment that has been
and is being made. I am not influenced by the
argument. Logging will continue on this coast even if
some parts are found to be subject to certain Indian
rights. It may be that in some areas the Indians will
be entitled to share in one way or another, and it may
be that in other areas there will be restrictions on the
type of logging. <u>There is a problem about tenure that
has not been attended to in the past. We are being
asked to ignore the problem as others have ignored it.
I am not willing to do that</u>. (Ibid.) (author's
underlining)*

This wake-up call for social justice emanated from B.C.'s
highest court over 25 years ago, and its human rights
component is unmistakable. The court set out the stark
choice that it faced when industry wanted to clear cut
'traditional lands'. Following this pattern, similar judicial
wake-up calls launched the native legal winning streak in
other regions of the country: mining in Labrador, logging
in New Brunswick, hydropower in Quebec, burial grounds

in Ontario, hunting and trapping in the prairies, and oil field access in Alberta.

Courts as Referee

Since many of the B.C. cases demanded all-or-nothing outcomes, the courts were put squarely in the role of referee. The Court of Appeal's opening paragraph in a major ruling some 15 years later (2001) provides a prime example of how judges defined the evolving landscape:

> *[1] <u>Doing business in British Columbia in the 1990's was fraught with uncertainties.</u> In some instances, businesses sought to develop land over which aboriginal people asserted rights. The provincial government found itself in the middle, encouraging economic development while attempting to resolve the competing claims. (excerpt: Apex Mountain Resort Ltd. v. British Columbia 2001 BCCA 479) (author's underlining)*

> *[2] In this case, the appellants claimed they lost their ski resort because the respondent Province failed to advise them of its position concerning aboriginal blockades on an access road leading to the resort, or alternatively failed to take the action it was contractually obligated to take to ensure the access road remained unimpeded by blockades. The trial judge dismissed their claims, and they appeal from that decision. (Ibid.)*

It is obvious from the matter-of-fact tone of the opening paragraph that the courts will play referee if required to do so. In this instance, the court reviewed all the risks facing the proponent and specifically addressed them, as follows:

[51] The trial judge considered the evidence of <u>what Apex "knew, and when it knew it"</u> and concluded: "I find that it appreciated the access risks it faced before it acquired control of the resort and again immediately after it initially announced its expansion plans. I find that nothing the government did or said misled the plaintiff or caused it to make an investment which it would not otherwise have made." (Ibid.) (author's underlining)

[77] In my view, the trial judge considered this issue in the context of the entire relationship between the Province and Apex, and there are no grounds on which to find he erred. (Ibid.)

Here's a ruling that should have put resource proponents on notice that the rise of native of empowerment was starting to make itself felt.

Citizen Campbell

In 2000, Gordon Campbell personally launched a legal challenge questioning some of the major components of the historic Nisga'a land claim settlement. This was especially notable since this was the first B.C. treaty settlement to come along in 100 years. Campbell lost in the opening paragraph, as follows:

[1] The plaintiffs seek an order declaring that the Nisga'a Treaty recently concluded between Canada, British Columbia and the Nisga'a Nation is in part inconsistent with the Constitution of Canada and therefore in part of no force and effect. For the reasons which follow, I conclude the application should be dismissed. (excerpt: Campbell et al. v. AG BC/AG Cda & Nisga'a Nation et al. 2000 BCSC 1123)

Gordon Campbell had attempted to diminish the first
real of sign of treaty progress in a province that had been
in denial with respect to native rights since its entry into
Confederation. Did he really believe that the court would
upend the Nisga'a self-government components of the
treaty, or was he simply playing to his right-wing political
base? Ostensibly, Campbell was troubled by the extent of
the self-government powers that the treaty held for
native land management policies and practices. And he
wasn't alone in thinking this way. Three years earlier,
during closing arguments before the Supreme Court of
Canada in the Delgamuukw case (June 18, 1997) the
province had argued against aboriginal title, as follows:

> *All intervenors fail to tell you the meaning and*
> *consequences of aboriginal title. ...*
> *This case is a moving target ...*
> *The courts are setting policy not law ...*
> *The province is negotiating out of a moral duty - a*
> *political duty - but not a constitutional duty to*
> *negotiate....*
> *Don't crystallize that as a duty or as a constitutional*
> *right. (author's notes paraphrased, having attended*
> *closing arguments)*

However, the Supreme Court of Canada was not
persuaded, and the Delgamuukw ruling set forth the
court's new legal test for establishing aboriginal title. The
outcome was 180 degrees from that for which the
province had argued. A long period of political denial
now set in as was reflected in Campbell's decision to
challenge the Nisga'a Treaty. Thus, it's more than a little
ironic that Gordon Campbell was first in line to lose to
natives. The court, in refuting his argument, found the
Nisga'a Treaty to be 100% constitutionally compliant in
empowering natives to make decisions with respect to
land use, as follows:

*[135] ... First, it is "aboriginal law" which is part of
the source of aboriginal title. Second, <u>the right to
decide how to use that land</u> is also a part of the right -
part of aboriginal title "in its full form." (Ibid.)
(author's underlining)*

What the court was saying is this: since the treaty
granted a land base, natives have the ability to direct the
use that land - denoting self-government powers to that
end. Thus, the outcome saw the court upholding the self-
government component of the treaty, even imbuing it
with a high degree of judicial validity. This was precisely
the outcome Gordon Campbell had wanted to avoid. Yet
paradoxically, in his polarizing attempt to score political
points, Campbell instead ended up winning a powerful
ruling for the native side.

Delgamuukw

The seminal Delgamuukw ruling, which was handed
down in late-1997, specifically addressed B.C.'s future
resource development prospects. Judge La Forest, a
resource law expert in his own right, was fully cognizant
of the potential for trouble ahead (economically speaking)
when he sagely provided a road map for B.C., as follows:

*[202] ... the general economic development of the
interior of British Columbia, through agriculture,
mining, forestry, and hydro-electric power, as well as
the related building of infrastructure and settlement
of foreign populations are valid legislative objectives
... (excerpt: Delgamuukw v. British Columbia [1997]
3 S.C.R. 1010)*

*[203] ... [But] these legislative objectives are subject to
<u>accommodation</u> of the aboriginal peoples' interests.*

This accommodation must always be in accordance with the <u>honour and good faith of the Crown</u>. Moreover, when dealing with a generalized claim over vast tracts of land, accommodation is not a simple matter of asking whether licences have been fairly allocated in one industry, or whether conservation measures have been properly implemented for a specific resource. Rather, the question of accommodation of "aboriginal title" is much broader than this. Certainly, one aspect of accommodation in this context entails <u>notifying and consulting</u> aboriginal peoples with respect to the development of the affected territory. Another aspect of accommodation is <u>fair compensation</u>. ... (Ibid.) (author's underlining)

La Forest's ruling identified all the benchmarks of the native legal winning streak and heralded more than a decade of legal controversy in B.C.'s resource sector. That's because natives would be forced to litigate and win on every one of these principles before they finally would be taken seriously.

Council of Forest Industries

The forest industry would likewise pay a high price for opposing the Nisga'a Treaty. The Council of Forest Industries (COFI) submissions to government stressed the advisability of making cash payments to natives in lieu of a land base; and ensuring that any treaties negotiated did not portend special rights, as follows:

Members of the forest industry conclude that the most practical, and least disruptive, way to provide treaty benefits to aboriginal people is to negotiate a one-time exchange of undefined aboriginal rights for a *settlement package which consists <u>primarily of cash</u>. The effect would be to provide aboriginal people with the means to purchase interests in whatever commercial enterprises they choose. (excerpt: COFI overview of Nisga'a AIP to B.C. Select Standing Committee on Aboriginal Affairs. October, 1996) (author's underlining)*

Though we agree with the general support for negotiating treaties, we feel too little attention has been paid to another of the poll's findings. I refer to the finding which concluded that: "Once land claims are settled, the public does not like the general idea of any ongoing special rights for natives. In fact, the vast majority of respondents agree with the statement "after the issues are settled, <u>native people should have the same rights as everybody else, no more and no less.</u>" (excerpt: COFI speaking notes to B.C. Select Standing Committee on Aboriginal Affairs committee December 1996) (author's underlining)

Did COFI not realize that the treaty process was all about settling the issue of economic uncertainty for industry? Clearly, the forest industry association in its advice to government was on the wrong page. And it wouldn't be long before it bore the brunt of the rise of native empowerment for which it was obviously unprepared.

Campbell's First Term

The June 2001 election that swept Premier Campbell into power, with the largest majority in B.C. history, was in no small measure fought over his strategy to contain the rise of native empowerment in the resource sector. Native protesters had regularly picketed his campaign bus and native angst escalated significantly once he assumed office. Relevant headlines for 2001 provide an overview of the rising tensions:

Skiers' resort plans put on ice by native land claims
(Financial Post, Dec. 19, 2000)

Ruling threatens B.C. power exports
(Globe and Mail, Mar. 16, 2001)

Natives' 'war council' threatens to shut B.C.
(National Post, Jul. 24, 2001)

B.C. natives threaten to cap massive gas field development; Industry urges B.C. to resolve native issues (Financial Post, Aug. 7, 2001)

Resort Owners Lose Appeal
(National Post, Aug. 09, 2001)

B.C. natives blockade Petro-Can pipeline site
(National Post, Aug. 14, 2001)

Indian bands lay claim to site of B.C. legislature
(National Post, Aug. 28, 2001)

Petro-Canada CEO fears native activism threat
(Financial Post, Sept. 6, 2001)

Apologize to B.C. aboriginals, Premier urged
(National Post, Dec. 1, 2001)

Natives arrested in resort blockade bid
(National Post, Dec. 29, 2001)

Because of his legal challenge on the Nisga'a treaty, the premier had unwittingly become his own lightning rod. Maintaining the status quo had worked only so far as to get him elected; but could he now contain the rising storm of native anger? Even his Select Committee on Aboriginal Affairs was urging a more conciliatory stance; ironically, just when the National Post ran a timely editorial praising Campbell's strategy to conduct a provincial referendum on native land rights. The editor's play on words hit the mark, as follows:

> <u>*No more Mr. Nisga'a*</u>*: ... In the spring, British Columbians will be sent mail-in ballots seeking their opinions on 16 treaty and land claim questions. ...*
>
> *British Columbians were denied the crucial right to have their say during the Nisga'a fight, and Mr. Campbell's referendum plan is a welcome restorative. There is no reason to believe its conclusions and suggestions about the treaties will be less than fair, much less racist. (excerpts: National Post editorial, December 6, 2001) (author's underlining)*

But racist was exactly how natives saw it; where the majority would be given carte-blanche to delimit minority rights. Native strategists were united in their opposition:

> *"We will do harm to this province if you are going to do harm to us. ... That's not a threat. That's a promise. If you want a fight, you're going to get it. We will go to the markets of the world and tell them what you are doing to this province." (excerpt: reporter Rod Mickleburgh, quoting native strategist George Watts speaking <u>pre</u>-referendum. National Post, March 9, 2001)*
>
> *The referendum results will lead to "more litigation and more conflict on the land."*

(excerpt: reporter Robert Matas, quoting native
strategist Stewart Phillip speaking <u>post</u>-referendum.
Globe and Mail, July 4, 2002)

In fact, the majority of the public 'took a pass' on participating in the referendum. Church groups, human rights groups, even professional pollsters (the latter being especially scathing in their criticism) all discredited the premier's referendum process. The result left the province more polarized than ever over how best to address the mounting rise of native empowerment.

Ironically, it was at this moment that same-day headlines sounded a dire economic warning that couldn't be ignored: "Broke B.C. joins the 'have-nots': Eligible for about $30 M in federal equalization." (National Post, February 8, 2002). In contrast, the economic news in Quebec was quite different. "Crees sign historic deal with Quebec - Natives to receive $3.5-billion over 50 years and share in benefits of natural resources." (Globe and Mail, February 8, 2002). Here were two resource-dependent jurisdictions pursuing radically different strategies. With the one difference being: whatever Quebec was doing was working. Now Campbell had reached the point of no return. Chastened, he would soon apologize to natives in a throne speech that denoted a historic turning point in the crown / native relationship:

Errors have been made in the past. Our institutions
have failed Aboriginal people across our province.
Your government deeply regrets the mistakes that
were made by governments of every political stripe
over the course of our province's history. It regrets
the tragic experiences visited upon First Nations
through years of paternalistic policies that fostered
inequity, intolerance, isolation and indifference.
Inadequate education, health care and housing;
rampant unemployment, alcoholism and drug abuse;

unconscionably high rates of physical and sexual abuse, incarceration, infant mortality and suicide are the hallmarks of despair and have disproportionately afflicted First Nations families on and off reserve....

The place to meet is at the negotiating tables, not in the courts or on opposite sides of new barriers to understanding.

Your government will take another bold step to forge a new era of reconciliation with First Nations. Starting this year, funding will be earmarked in the budget for revenue-sharing arrangements with First Nations that wish to help revitalize the forest industry in their traditional territories. The distribution of that revenue will be negotiated with the First Nations <u>in exchange for legal certainty that allows all regions and all British Columbians to more fairly prosper from their resource industries.</u> (excerpts: Throne Speech Hansard, February 11, 2003) (author's underlining)

Turning Point

This speech marked the moment when the province started on the long road back to economic recovery. It is unfortunate that it came so late in the day, because the native legal winning streak was just ramping-up. Jeffrey Simpson was the first national columnist to postulate that B.C. natives now had a de facto veto to stop projects they didn't like, as follows:

A right that walks, talks, and smells like a veto is probably a veto, even if the courts did not use the word. ... No consent, no mine. ... (excerpt: columnist Jeffrey Simpson, Globe and Mail, May 1, 2002)

Simpson was on to something as native legal wins were coming down the judicial pipeline that saw the courts wrestling with the veto concept in one ruling after another. Native strategists were successfully contesting a series of commercial closings and it now looked like they had found the 'Achilles heel' for fostering even more economic uncertainty in all sectors of the economy.

Almost overnight, B.C. became the only jurisdiction in the country that saw a series of major commercial closings thwarted as a result of successful native legal challenges. More bad news arrived in the form of unflattering headlines respecting its overall dismal economic performance nationally: *"Quebec passes B.C. as 3rd richest province: 2003 provincial rankings"* (*Globe and Mail*, May 3, 2004).

By year-end 2004, the forest industry itself was reeling from an impugned corporate / commercial transaction. In this case, the Supreme Court of Canada blocked a forestry transaction (the otherwise routine transfer of a Tree Farm License) making it obvious to all that 'business as usual' in crown woodlots was no longer. And the reason why the status quo was upended had everything to do with the rise of native empowerment:

> *The Supreme Court of Canada released its decision today in a case that the Haida Nation launched to protect its old-growth forests of Haida Gwaii. The Court held in favour of the Haida, holding that <u>the Province has a legal duty to consult</u> with the Haida about timber harvesting in Weyerhaeuser's Tree Farm License 39. (excerpt: Haida press release. November 18, 2004) (author's underlining)*

The impugned license transfer from MacMillan Bloedel to Weyerhaeuser was struck down over the lack of meaningful crown consultation with impacted natives. Here were the two biggest names in B.C. forestry now at the center of a native legal win that had caught the powers that be totally off guard. The court specifically ruled on the native veto, as follows:

> *[48] This process <u>does not give Aboriginal groups a veto</u> over what can be done with land pending final proof of the claim. The Aboriginal "consent" spoken of in Delgamuukw is appropriate only in cases of established rights, and then by no means in every case. Rather, what is required is a process of balancing interests, of give and take. (excerpt: Haida Nation v. British Columbia 2004 SCC 73) (author's underlining)*

Clearly, the province was at a crossroads and its economic recovery was far from certain. Natives had delivered on their warnings to create uncertainty with protests and litigation. The high-water mark of which was the Point Grey golf course litigation where, in an extraordinary step, the highest court in the province went so far as to order that the transaction be undone:

> *[71] ... the University should be ordered, if the lands have been conveyed to it, to <u>re-convey the lands</u> to the Crown and if the purchase price has been paid, the <u>purchase price should be repaid</u>. ... (excerpt: Musqueam Indian Band v. British Columbia, et al. 2005 BCCA 128) (author's underlining)*

Quebec had turned this corner. But could B.C.? To his credit, the premier now set out to remedy the problem in a major province-wide overture to natives, which he called "The New Relationship." He would lead his province out of the native empowerment vortex one way or another. The only question was - did he have support?

Campbell's Second Term

Finally, there was some good economic news coming out of the northeast oilfields, which was enough to fuel Campbell's re-election in May 2005. After delivering two balanced budgets, B.C. was finally poised to shed its 'have-not' fiscal status. That June he announced The New Relationship: his goal was to find a way to implement the Supreme Court of Canada directives and all the other superior court rulings resulting from the native legal winning streak. But the problem now was that natives were so empowered through their recent court wins that The New Relationship announcement was met with considerable skepticism. These feelings are reflected in the remarks of Chief Stewart Phillip, at a Calgary resource conference, as follows:

> *"The issue is about justice - not law. The province is still seen as remote and untamed, representing a colonial view of the world, which is essentially the essence of the problem. Rather there should be a collective responsibility to share the land. ... The situation in B.C. was much more racist with its colonial legacy, the residential schools and terrible injustices. (We're hearing a greatly sanitized version of recent events from B.C. forestry officials.)*

> *All progress to date has been made in the courts; as of June 1, 2005 there are another 34 cases before the courts, the majority are resource-related, and the government is consistently losing! It's been a protracted struggle and even though the economy is rebounding - it's based on false drivers of growth. However, a 'tip of the hat' is due to the premier, after Delgamuukw the government's unilateral attempts to maintain the status quo have failed, so now we have a new process [The New Relationship] that's a joint*

undertaking from the outset and it's the right thing to do. However, if that fails we'll be back in court and at the barricades. We have the 7 best legal minds in B.C. on our side.

In the recent provincial election the NDP grew from 2 to 34 seats, so the legislature is more balanced than before. The treaty process has been an abject failure and that racist referendum was boycotted by the majority - with only 26% participation by the public." (excerpts: BCUIC Stewart Phillip paraphrased by author in attendance. Calgary, June 1, 2005)

With these caveats, B.C. natives agreed to unite in order to give The New Relationship a chance to develop. According to provincial press releases, it was to be "a new government-to-government relationship based on respect, recognition and accommodation of Aboriginal title cases," and supported by a separate Ministry of Aboriginal Relations and Reconciliation. That November, Premier Campbell heralded the Kelowna Accord at a federal / provincial premiers' conference specifically convened to focus on national native issues. His words spoke volumes about the tough lessons he had personally learned from the rise of native empowerment, as follows:

It's that we are a nation of nations, defined not just by two solitudes that have preoccupied the history of Canada but by a third solitude as well, a forgotten solitude. It's a third solitude that exists, that has been ignored, dismissed through most of our history; a third solitude that has been discounted by governments at every level and of all political stripes. ...

For me, this meeting is about facing up to the failings of the past and the real needs of the present. [It's] not

*to find fault or to cast blame but to find new paths to
a brighter future. ...*

*In British Columbia we are breaking new ground in
areas like revenue sharing and cooperative decision-
making that will hopefully move us beyond the roots
of narrow mindedness. (excerpts: Premier's opening
remarks, Kelowna Conference, November 2005)*

Thus, after all the grief that Campbell had inflicted on the
native file - his failed Nisga'a legal challenge, his misguided general referendum, his government's legal losing
streak, and the recent "impoverished vision" admonition
from the Supreme Court of Canada - he had finally come
to realize that natives were the critical link between
access to resources and economic certainty. Now he was
on the right page and in a rush to make up for lost time.

However, reconciliation was not to be. That's because
the political winds had abruptly changed with the
election of Prime Minister Stephen Harper in January
2006. Harper had made it clear from the outset that he
viewed the promised $4.5 billion in native funding for
the Kelowna Accord as an unfocused and uncommitted
expenditure that his government could not support.
Premier Campbell expressed dismay and fought for the
Accord's reinstatement; he also started working with
industry and natives like never before. Yet in spite of
making one-off deals in the energy, forestry and hydro
sectors, the negative fallout from the Kelowna Accord's
demise provided a steady stream of native empowerment
headlines throughout 2007, as follows:

*Natives won't allow port (National Post, Apr. 26,
2007)*

*Get the Shell out! (Financial Times, U.K. ad
campaign, Aug. 21, 2007)*

First Nations leaders oppose mine proposal
(Prince George Free Press, Aug. 31, 2007)

Shell backs away from court showdown - sacred
headwaters (NationTalk, Sept. 1, 2007)

Native veto new reality in B.C.'s resources sector
(Globe and Mail, Sept. 21, 2007)

Chastened B.C. miner abandons open-pit plan
(Globe and Mail, Sept. 26, 2007)

Musqueam band halts sale of B.C. office towers
(Globe and Mail, Sept. 29, 2007)

First Nations in B.C. to fight construction of new dam
(CBC News, Oct. 2, 2007)

These were the very protests and lawsuits that Chief Stewart Phillip had warned about. In response, the premier reasserted his commitment to making diplomatic and substantive reforms as native pressure built on the eve of the June 29, 2007 National Day of Action, as follows:

For instance, this year, we set in motion removal
from the B.C. legislature of murals that have long
offended First Nations by depicting Aboriginal people
in passive, subservient roles. And after decades of
impact from flooding of the Williston Reservoir
during construction of the WAC Bennett Dam in the
1960s, the Province and BC Hydro signed agreements
with Kwadacha and Tsay Keh Dene to compensate
them for the destruction of their communities. Our
government also settled a long-standing claim with
the Songhees and Esquimalt First Nations related to

the land where the legislature now sits. (excerpt: premier's statement re National Day of Action, June 28, 2007).

Premier Campbell had even started his high-level diplomacy by petitioning Prime Minister Harper to bestow 'nation-status' upon natives (as Harper had just done for Quebec). Now a year later, he appointed Sto:lo leader and jurist, Steven Point, as Lieutenant Governor, who's first formal act was to usher in the long-awaited Tsawwassen Treaty. And while the native legal winning streak had predominantly impacted the resource sector, there were now two high profile wins in urban areas: blocking the sale of the Point Grey golf course, and the sale of two federally-owned buildings in the heart of Vancouver's commercial district. Indeed the rise of native empowerment was even making itself felt in the neighbourhood of the proposed Olympic Village!

Aboriginal Title

Then came the biggest native win of all. It took the form of a major (albeit non-binding) ruling on aboriginal title by the British Columbia Supreme Court that impacted 45% of the Nemaiah Valley in the Chilcotin district. Named after Chief Roger William, the ruling came 10 years to the day after the Delgamuukw decision. Thus, it had taken a full decade to have the Supreme Court of Canada's 'aboriginal title' test finally apply. Its impact was immediate and heralded a potential game-changer for all parties involved. Native strategists trumpeted the fact that they had just won ownership of 45% of their traditional territory. Hypothetically, and based on mathematical extrapolation, this win fundamentally redrew the map of B.C. in terms of native land rights.

Native strategists proclaimed their new-found legal clout, as follows:

> *... Why would any First Nation be foolish enough to ratify any BCTC (treaty) settlement for less than 5% of their territory when the Xeni Gwet'in has achieved recognition of their aboriginal title to 50% of their territory? (excerpt: UBCIC press release, Nov. 21, 07)*

The B.C. government was at a loss for words and seized upon the non-binding aspect of the ruling: "What did they get? Sorry - they got an opinion," was all Aboriginal Affairs Minister de Jong could say at the time (reporter Justine Hunter, Globe and Mail, November 24, 2007). That's because the aboriginal title aspect had been declared by the judge to be 'non-binding' due to a technicality in the natives' pleadings. Instead, he urged the parties to negotiate a land claim settlement based on his findings, given that he had presided over 339 days of proceedings making it one of the longest trials in B.C. history. Even though the ruling was non-binding, it was the first time that any court had quantified aboriginal title in land percentage terms. Thus, the ruling represented a 'crossing of the Rubicon' for native strategists; from this point forward, treaty negotiations could only start once the government recognized the existence of aboriginal title (in order for natives to engage). Clearly, the 45% factor outpaced the government's ability to respond; thus the ruling required appellate review.

The Iceman

Just a few months later, B.C. natives received another opinion - one that didn't come from a judge - rather it came from a team of geneticists who, in a remarkable

DNA analysis, linked an iceman to his present-day native descendants residing in northern B.C. The iceman had been discovered in a glacier a decade earlier (robed in furs and found with his hunting gear) and was believed to have lived in the early 1700's. Now DNA analysis could positively link natives to their lands, as follows:

> ... *241 native people from B.C., the Yukon, and Alaska... gave DNA samples for testing and the results produced 17 positive matches. "All of those 17 people, and potentially their families, have the same common female ancestor as Kwaday himself [the iceman]." Chief Diane Strand said ...*

> *"The blood sample proved it that through mitochondrial DNA that the long-ago person and myself and my sister ... we're related. It was moving and overwhelming," Pearl Callaghan said ... (excerpt: CBC News, April 25, 2008)*

Here was a native ancestor that Captain Cook might have recognized during his mapping expedition along the B.C. coast. Because coincidentally, just as the iceman's DNA results were announced in Victoria, Captain Cook's expedition journals were undergoing rigorous legal examination in a Vancouver courtroom. Since he had provisioned his ships in Nootka Sound, natives argued that that event gave credence to the existence of commercial trade. Expert testimony analyzed the accuracy of several early explorer journals; and indeed, some of the reconstructed historical events and scenes were not unlike those portrayed in the B.C. Legislature's controversial murals. Thus, for a brief moment in the spring of 2008, all these 'back to the future' factors converged and revealed an extraordinary historical inter-connectedness to issues that were making the news daily: the 45% aboriginal title ruling, the minister's "just an opinion" quip, the Iceman's DNA results, Captain Cook's journals, and the Eurocentric 1932 murals. All facets of B.C.'s history seemed to be on trial in one way or another. This was the backdrop for the launching of the premier's third election campaign where once again the rise of native empowerment would be front and center.

Now the premier headed off a brewing controversy over the staging of the 2010 Olympics - on native land - by agreeing to share mining revenues on future mines. He then appointed another noted native leader as head of the British Columbia Treaty Commission, as follows:

> *The province has authorized its provincial negotiators to include revenue sharing with First Nations on new mining projects. .... British Columbia is the first province in Canada to share direct revenue generated from mining. (excerpt: premier's press release, October 23, 2008)*

> *Michael de Jong, Minister of Aboriginal Relations and Reconciliation, announced today that the new chief commissioner of the British Columbia Treaty Commission will be Chief Sophie Pierre of the Ktunaxa Nation ... replacing Grand Chief Stephen Point who left in 2007 (to become Lieutenant Governor). (excerpt: minister's press release, December 15, 2008)*

The Recognition and Reconciliation Act

The main plank in the premier's re-election platform was his promise in the Throne Speech of February 16, 2009 to introduce legislation to recognize aboriginal rights and title in a proposed Recognition and Reconciliation Act. And while he was confident enough to make this the centerpiece of his campaign platform, media pundits didn't miss the political irony: "If someone 10 years ago had said Gordon Campbell would one day stand up and promise to recognize aboriginal title, he would have been laughed off as a crank!" (columnist Les Leyne, Victoria Times Colonist, February 17, 2009).

If the premier needed more credibility to sell his native reforms to industry, it came the very next day in a double ruling from the province's highest court striking down two regulatory board decisions, which was due yet again to the lack of proper native consultation and missed native impacts. Here was the native legal winning streak reasserting itself as if on cue. Surely now the premier could count on industry to support his re-election platform to legislatively reconcile aboriginal title and thereby attain economic certainty for all parties right across the province. The moment to do so had arrived.

Of course industry wanted to know what the proposed Recognition and Reconciliation Act would mean going forward. And that's where the government's and the native council's (jointly produced) 5-page *Discussion Paper on Instructions for Implementing the New Relationship* came into play. It laid out the dozen or so key legal principles and premises that would guide the drafting of the legislation that was intended to serve as the basis for a new crown / native relationship. Instead, the Discussion Paper itself immediately became the target of a highly charged war of opposing legal opinions (industry *v.* native) that reached a crescendo just as the premier headed out on the campaign trail. Excerpts from the Discussion Paper's introduction are provided below:

> *Scope: The Act will apply to all ministries and provincial agencies, in particular those that have any direct or indirect role in the management of lands and resources in the province and will take priority over all the other statutes dealing with these subject matters.*

Proclamation: The Proclamation would describe how we are at a point in our collective history where there is huge opportunity to <u>turn the page of history</u> and establish a new relationship of respect and recognition.

Ratification of Instructions: This Discussion Paper on Instructions for Implementing the New Relationship is the result of work undertaken by representatives of First Nations political organizations and senior representatives of the Government of British Columbia. The two parties must now take it to their Principals for review and consideration. (Discussion Paper on Instructions for Implementing the New Relationship. February 19, 2009) (<u>author's underlining</u>)

Yet after all the expense, lost opportunity and economic strife visited upon the resource sector during the rise of native empowerment, it was industry lawyers who raised strenuous objections by issuing a withering public legal critique of the Discussion Paper. According to their analysis, the Discussion Paper was not only replete with legal defects, it also took liberties with the judicial directives pertaining to aboriginal title. Their main criticisms were, as follows:

1. *The legislation will give First Nations a veto.*
2. *The legislation will recognize aboriginal title throughout all of B.C., potentially giving enormous power and control to First Nations and inconsistent with current law relating to aboriginal title.*
3. *The legislation proposes power and control to the First Nations well beyond what has been established by the Supreme Court of Canada.*

4. The legislation has core legal defects.

*The [Discussion] Paper asserts that the legislation
will contribute to certainty for third parties. The only
certainty arising from this legislation may be the
certainty that resource development will be
dramatically reduced in B.C. as potential investors
look elsewhere, including other Canadian provinces
where resource development requires approval only
from Federal and Provincial governments. (excerpt:
Legal Observations Concerning the 'Discussion
Paper', March 9, 2009)*

This last point implied that industry would soon have to
seek project approval from natives. So here was a hard-
hitting industry response that made the premier look as
if he was capitulating to the native empowerment agenda.
And, if their aim had been to draw the native strategists
out, it worked. Stung by the overwhelmingly negative
industry reaction, lawyers for the native side launched a
counterattack against the industry lawyers:

*... This dismissive approach is disappointing coming
from two lawyers who specialize in Aboriginal law
and must be familiar with the jurisprudence of the
Supreme Court of Canada.*

*... The statement about First Nations having a veto is
obviously intended to raise alarm among the industry
clients of the authors ... (excerpt: native side legal
critique, March 12, 2009)*

The public was soon overwhelmed with legal warnings
and legal arguments, such that the premier's campaign
became mired in a propaganda war of competing legal
briefs. Moreover, the intensity of the legal criticism now
made it appear that Campbell might be losing the

backing of both sides. Liberal MLAs were reporting negative grassroots feedback that soon boiled over in caucus. Predictably, the political brakes were applied and the proposed legislation was put on hold. It would not see the light of day again.

On May 12, 2009, Premier Campbell was returned to office winning 49 of 85 seats. He took the high road saying that he still wanted to forge ahead with his New Relationship reforms, and native strategists likewise responded in kind: *"We applaud the Premier for his vision and commitment, as this is much needed and positive legislation"* (First Nations Leadership Council press release. May 13, 2009). However, the political landscape had fundamentally shifted. Now fourteen native-side lawyers (in a 22-page commentary) asserted that the premier's reforms didn't go nearly far enough; and one by one the native leadership withdrew from the premier's reform process. So what had happened post-election to destroy The New Relationship? Chief Stewart Phillip's explanation of events at a subsequent Vancouver resource conference is especially revealing, as follows:

"In the Fall of 2008 we (the B.C. Union of Indian Chiefs) passed a resolution to shut down the province - which was also subsequently passed by the B.C. Native Summit - all this happened just prior to the release of the government's infamous Discussion Paper.

Their own Discussion Paper created a near mutiny within their MLA ranks and fearing an MLA backlash everything was put on hold.

Then the business sector's legal critique was issued, which was inflammatory and that set the tone for what followed. In our ranks things quickly deteriorated. It was the opposition from business that

*inflamed the native fundamentalists by creating
'Armageddon' in our ranks. It quickly became clear
that the grassroots were not comfortable and so the
whole thing was rejected by our side.*

*Business and industry killed the Recognition and
Reconciliation Act by giving rise to fundamentalist
forces. Indeed there is fear of reform!" (excerpts:
UBCIC Chief Stewart Phillip, Vancouver conference,
December 7, 2009, paraphrased by author in
attendance)*

According to this explanation by a key native strategist, it
was industry opposition, which stoked their own "fear of
reform", that combined to kill the proposed Recognition
and Reconciliation Act. But it's not as if the premier
hadn't set the stage for all the parties to embrace the
historic opportunity. The Lieutenant Governor was an
esteemed native leader, as was the head of the B.C.
Treaty Commission; moreover, the leaders of the Four
Host Nations were designated as heads-of-state for the
2010 Winter Olympics. To his credit, Gordon Campbell
had succeeded in diplomatically getting the native
leadership onside to engage in a constructive dialogue.

Perhaps there's a simpler explanation for understanding why the biggest missed opportunity in recent
B.C. history played out in the unfortunate manner that it
did. The overriding reality was that strategists on all
sides had presumed and prejudged the proposed reforms
without giving the process a chance to bear fruit. As it
turned out, all that Premier Campbell derived from his
principled and conciliatory stand by proposing The New
Relationship was across-the-board ingratitude; an
incomprehensible result for a politician who had just
gambled his political career to bring all sides together in
an attempt to legislate 'certainty' in the resources sector.

As a result, the usual postures were soon adopted: with government pretending that it could muster sufficient land tenure certainty to promote orderly resource development; with industry forever hoping and waiting for project clarity from pending court rulings, and with native strategists more opposed than ever. They wouldn't have to wait long to learn where their respective strategies were heading.

On October 28, 2010 the Supreme Court of Canada issued yet another major ruling broadening the scope of native consultation and accommodation. If industry was now hoping for the courts to stem the rise of native empowerment - it was clearly mistaken.

Four days later, Taseko's Prosperity Mine proposal, which had faced sustained and escalating native opposition for well over a year, was overruled by Ottawa on environmental grounds in what was a major blow to the province's (and the premier's) hoped-for mining renaissance. In fact, the province had already issued its mining license. Taseko stock valuations fell 25% in the immediate aftermath.

The very next day Premier Campbell announced his resignation. He gave no reasons. "Something happened" blared front-page coverage in the November 4, 2010 *National Post* (the HST fiasco was singled out as the most likely culprit). Clearly, being overruled by Ottawa on the Prosperity Mine was a major embarrassment, not to mention a personal rebuke, for the one provincial leader who had tried more than any other to promote crown / industry / native reconciliation in the hope of fostering legal certainty in the resource sector. He had promoted the Kelowna Accord, petitioned the prime minister to grant natives nation-status, and had even offered to jointly draft key legislation addressing the implications of aboriginal title. Yet for this progressive premier it was typically one step forward and two steps backward; such that, by the time of the Prosperity Mine's regulatory demise, Campbell's political career itself had become just another casualty in the rise of native empowerment.

In March 2011, the premiership passed to Christy Clark who had adeptly moved into the private sector while the New Relationship train-wreck took its toll on the crown / native relationship. Only now she reaped the whirlwind of native angst playing out daily over the Northern Gateway pipeline. How different might her return to politics have been if her predecessor's initiative had carried on and progress was being made on the crown / native relationship?

For his part, Gordon Campbell accepted the position of Canadian High Commissioner to the UK where one of the issues was oilsands reputational-management. While he was attending a Canada-Europe Round Table in London, a pair of youthful eco-activists interrupted the proceedings to perform an 'oil orgy' on top of a table front and center. Also front and center were her maple-leaf undies and his Union Jack briefs. It was a faux courtship: Canada's charms were oil, the UK's were markets, and each smeared oil to stoke the other's desire. The assembly adjourned and the event was on You-Tube in a matter of hours, closing out with Campbell smiling wistfully as he gazed at the mess. He likely realized that eco-activists will never come onside; yet he knew that natives were waiting to come aboard. He also knew that he had strategically set the stage for that to happen and had almost pulled it off.

Therein lies the explanation to BC's ongoing resources predicament - total frustration all around. Today that sentiment is the defining public relations feature of the Northern Gateway pipeline environmental review. By now native strategists had blocked the Sable Gas pipeline and killed the Mackenzie Valley Gas Project by winning a total of 4 legal wins (on review processes alone).

Throughout, the native playbook was there for all to study - who knew?

Yet Premier Gordon Campbell, like Minister Robert Nault, will over time be vindicated. Both paid the political price for doing what had to be done and both were shortchanged by short-sighted establishment vested interests. But the trouble with missed opportunities of these magnitudes - means that now as a direct result - the cost of reconciliation increases exponentially. Resource revenue sharing by itself will no longer suffice. That will now be but one component that will have to be augmented by substantial power sharing in the management of resources on native traditional lands.

Perversely, both Nault and Campbell were out of office just when they were needed most. But Campbell's premiership was truly unique, in the sense that he ended up 180 degrees from where he had started, the highlight being his amazing Olympic back-flip on the native file.

8

NORTHWEST TERRITORIES: *BOARDED-UP*

At an arctic energy conference in the spring of 2005, former Sahtu Chief and long-time northern reporter, Cece MacCauley, provided attendees with a one-page primer on the NWT's evolution. She intentionally made it politically incorrect in order to incite action on energy:

> ... we in the N.W.T. have only been introduced to a government since 1960. We went from a nomadic people, who had to plan their lives to survive. Our only government in those days were: the Hudson's Bay Company who taught us debit and credit: the RCMP who only looked out for the odd brew pot: and the missionaries, Catholic and Anglicans, who taught us religion and how to read and write.

> Our population in the N.W. T. is 42,000 of which 2/3 live in or around our capital city of Yellowknife. ... the 1/3 of the N.W.T. with the three regions, Deh Cho, Sahtu, and the Beaufort Delta, are scattered in twenty-three towns and communities. They have been hanging on for 45 years, with a wish and a prayer, waiting for the government to look at the northern

part of the territory. (excerpts: Cece MacCauley's
media handout, Calgary. March 7, 2005)

Today, the north is still 'hanging on with a wish and a
prayer' and it certainly doesn't have to worry about
having an overheated energy economy. The Mackenzie
Gas Pipeline project is further away now than when it
was first proposed, and the resumption of offshore
drilling in the Beaufort Sea is likely even further away.
Over the past 20 years, only the central barrens diamond
miners have made any real economic difference; and
those operations are now well past the mid-point of their
productive lives. Historically speaking, the northern
treaties came first: Treaty 8 in 1898 paved the way for
overland access to the Klondike gold fields; Treaty 11 in
1921 staked out the oil riches at Norman Wells.
Negotiated in considerable haste, neither treaty was
successful in settling the native land title question.

Berger Commission

Northerners have seen this movie before with the initial
pipeline postponement of 1977. Often overlooked is the
fact that the Berger Commission concluded that the
construction of the pipeline itself was viable; however
land claim settlements were now the priority. Thus, a 10-
year project postponement was deemed to be in order as
per the commissioner's recommendation, as follows:

I have concluded that it is feasible, from an
environmental point of view, to build a pipeline and
to establish an energy corridor along the Mackenzie
Valley, running south from the Mackenzie Delta to the
Alberta border. ...

*Native people desire a settlement of native claims
before a pipeline is built. They do not want a
settlement - in the tradition of the treaties - that will
extinguish their rights to the land. They want a
settlement that will entrench their rights to the land
and that will lay the foundations of native self-
determination under the Constitution of Canada.*

*... a Mackenzie Valley pipeline should be postponed
for ten years. If it were built now, it would bring
limited economic benefits, its social impact would be
devastating, and it would frustrate the goals of native
claims. Postponement will allow sufficient time for
native claims to be settled, and for new programs and
new institutions to be established.*
*(excerpts: Commissioner Berger's covering letter to
Minister Allmand, April 15, 1977)*

Hence, the project was postponed in 1977 to allow
sufficient time for the negotiation of native land claim
settlements. But another factor driving the process was
that one of the very first native legal wins emanated from
the Mackenzie Valley around the same time - the
Paulette case. The presiding judge, a renowned northern
jurist, upheld the legality of a native claim caveat filed
with respect to their traditional lands; whereby 16
northern chiefs claimed almost 45,000 square miles.
Three years later the caveat was struck-down by the
Supreme Court of Canada. However, while it wended its
way through the appeal process, public opinion rallied
strongly to the native side. The groundswell of northern
support backed the spirit of Justice Morrow's ruling and
propelled the issue onto the floor of Parliament. The
critical question was whether the northern treaties had
truly settled the matter of native land rights; or was it
necessary to negotiate land claims settlements in order to
provide legal certainty? Prime Minister Chrétien opted

for the latter course of action and the era of northern land claims negotiations was launched.

But it was Morrow's initial ruling that had legitimized the political necessity of reaching land claim settlements in the north. And Chrétien's response meant that Ottawa could no longer rely on the northern treaties to settle the issue of native land ownership and, by implication, access to resources. Morrow took delight in the political outcome claiming in his memoirs that the natives had "lost the battle but had won the war." Indeed, while the caveat was struck down on technical grounds, the 16 chiefs hadn't left court empty-handed. Because land claim settlements were now essential to clear the way for northern energy exploration. Moreover, the OPEC oil cartel was in its ascendency and Ottawa had ambitions of opening up the north in part to counteract its reliance on foreign crude. However, an unforeseen era of protracted land-claim negotiations had started, and most of them would last considerably longer than the 10-year temporary postponement that Berger had recommended.

Committee of Original Peoples' Entitlement

It is of particular note that the most important northern land claim settlement of all had already been reached - right next door in Alaska. And access to oil was the reason why. The Prudhoe Bay oilfields were discovered in 1968. In order to secure industry access, the Alaskan Inupiat were granted 40 million acres and $700 million - a monumental land claim settlement. The distance between the Inupiat villages on the coast of Alaska and the Inuvialuit villages on the coast of the NWT is fairly short. Hence, it is not difficult to trace the starting point from where the negotiating strategy of the Committee of Original Peoples' Entitlement (COPE) emanated. Their demands were driven by the fact that their Alaskan 'cousins' had just negotiated the largest land claim in U.S. history. Moreover, it had the backing of the U.S. energy industry. In reflecting on this period, Nellie Cournoyea, a 'larger than life' Inuvialuit leader long respected for her no-nonsense manner, recently commented: "COPE wasn't liked very much; we had to step on a lot of toes. The government didn't like it. They thought they were doing the best for everybody, and everybody should be happy about their programs and services - we should be grateful" (reporter Lauren McKeon quoting Nellie Cournoyea, Canadian Business Magazine, May 12, 2008). Still today, this 'Ottawa knows best' mantra drives northerners to distraction and many would claim that with respect to the Mackenzie Gas Pipeline project - nothing has changed.

Canada's first far north land claim settlement was reached with COPE in 1984 and was likewise driven by industry's need for access to resources. The COPE settlement then became the template for the next two settlements, which covered the northern two-thirds of the Mackenzie Valley: the Beaufort Sea (COPE territory), the Mackenzie Delta (COPE & Gwich'in territory), and Norman Wells (Sahtu territory). Reaching these three land claim settlements had been difficult, in part, because each region had its own suite of regulatory rules, procedures and boards. 'Balkanization' of the north is what the critics muttered under their breath.

But it was a different story entirely in the southern territories where achieving Deh Cho sign-off still remains problematic to this day. While Berger had surmised that 10 years would be sufficient, 35 years later, the Mackenzie Gas Pipeline project only had native support along the northern 60% of the right-of-way. The southern 40%, the Deh Cho, today remains *terra incognito* in terms of resource certainty and right of way access for pipelines.

"A Bad Deal for Canada"

Over in the central barrens, diamond explorers likewise had been pressing for resource access and economic certainty. As a result of the discovery of diamonds, land claim negotiations in that region were now fast-tracked. Nevertheless, when the Tlicho settlement was signed-off in late 2002, it still had to go before Parliament for official ratification. Imagine everyone's surprise when an open letter written by MP Jim Prentice cautioned parliamentarians to rethink its passage, as follows:

A bad deal for Canada:
by Jim Prentice (Conservative Party critic for Indian Affairs)

This agreement with the Tlicho, a First Nation of 3,500 in the Northwest Territories, may be the most significant Indian treaty negotiated in the past 100 years. It is the first modern treaty to combine a comprehensive land claim and a self-government agreement. It will create a Tlicho government, transfer 39,000 square kilometers of land to the band's ownership and provide Tlicho with $150 million. ...

Why has a nation of 32-million people accorded such rights to a community of 3,500? Will other First Nations with which Canada will be negotiating self-government win the same right? ...

My concerns, and those of my Conservative colleagues, relate to the failure of the federal Government to protect Canada's interests.
(excerpts: Jim Prentice's open letter to National Post, December 9, 2004)

Indeed, it was an inauspicious start for the one federal politician who would soon go on to guide the Mackenzie Gas Pipeline project as federal point man in the Conservative cabinet. Yet here he was, just two months after arriving on Parliament Hill in the fall of 2004, firing broadsides at the latest northern land claim settlement in his capacity as opposition critic. Less than a year later, Prentice would become the Minister of Indian Affairs! He then saw the link between land claim settlements and economic certainty; paradoxically, he now pressed for a similar settlement with the Deh Cho. That's because the Mackenzie Gas Pipeline project, based in his Calgary constituency, had started to gather momentum. The massive pipeline would connect the Beaufort Sea to Alberta's pipeline hub and it required legal certainty along the entire right-of-way. For starters, all those newly established regulatory boards (native, territorial, and federal) would have to align and cooperate in order to meet project timelines. Moreover, the project would require federal leadership, territorial cooperation, and native support from top to bottom. Could it be done?

Diamond Mines

The pipeliners could have learned a thing or two about mega-project approvals had they been paying attention as to how the diamond miners were faring. Those open pit mines were the first northern mega-projects and, as a result, they garnered serious native and eco-activist opposition; coincidentally, just as the federal environmental review process was undergoing a legislative sea-change. One of the numerous regulatory surprises for the miners was Ottawa's insistence on something beyond the scope of the governing legislation. In a precedent-setting press release Northern Development Minister, Ron Irwin, decreed that there would now have to be an

Environmental Agreement in order to address a host of recommendations that lay outside of the legislation:

> *... a number of recommendations of the EARP panel review which lie <u>outside the scope</u> of these regulatory permits. To address these recommendations, the federal government will seek to enter into an "Environmental Agreement" with BHP. ... To ensure full commitment to all conditions of the project and to assist monitoring, an environmental agreement with the company is seen as essential. ... The federal government, in discussion with the GNWT and Aboriginal groups, will negotiate the agreement with BHP. ... The project is therefore approved <u>subject to satisfactory progress</u> on the agreement with government,*
>
> *<u>Before issuing major licenses</u>, Mr. Irwin will review progress on the negotiation of an environmental agreement and the negotiation of impact benefit agreements between BHP Diamonds Inc. and the affected Aboriginal groups. ... final approval of the project by Cabinet will be <u>subject to satisfactory progress</u> being made on the environmental agreement with government and impact benefit agreements with Aboriginal groups affected by the project. ... (excerpts: Minister Irwin's 16-page press release of project conditions entitled: "Canada's First Diamond Mine One Step Closer," August 8, 1996) (author's underlining)*

It's abundantly clear from this expanded ministerial directive that the northern regulatory process facing the miners was 'political' from start to finish. Neither the Environmental Agreement nor the IBAs were legally required in the regulatory review process, the governing legislation or the pertinent regulations. Instead, the minister was invoking political pressure and moral suasion to force the miners into recognizing the legitimacy of the environmental and native agendas. This approach was greeted with industry misgivings for had he not just given the natives a veto? One thing was certain: the government was applying an ad hoc approach that verged on regulation by press release. Even the opening paragraph describing the 'purpose' of the Environmental Agreement stated that these measures were legally binding; thus cloaking the ad hoc process with a measure of regulatory legitimacy:

1.1   *Purpose: This Environmental Agreement is intended to be a <u>legally binding</u> agreement which provides for Project-related environmental matters <u>additional to such matters governed by legislation, regulations and Regulatory Instruments</u> and for the establishment of and identification of roles of the Monitoring Agency, in order to achieve the following purposes:*

    a) to respect and protect land, water and wildlife and the land based economy, essential to the way of life of the Aboriginal Peoples;

    d) to maximize the effectiveness and co-ordination of environmental monitoring and regulation of the Project;

    e) to facilitate effective participation of the Aboriginal Peoples and the general public in the achievement of the above purposes. (excerpt: Environmental Agreement, January 16, 1997) (author's underlining)

In hindsight, the Irwin approval process was just the start of an evolving northern regulatory regime that would remain in flux for well over a decade. It would result in such a proliferation of boards, mandates, causes and court challenges that the Northwest Territories has today become one the most complex regions in the country for gaining project approvals. All of this was in plain view for the architects of the Mackenzie Gas Pipeline project who proceeded to devise their right-of-way strategy as if the north would 'roll out the red carpet' up and down the valley.

'Caveat Emptor'

In June 2002, all the regulatory agencies involved in the pipeline project unveiled their environmental review 'Cooperation Plan' thereby merging the mandates of 8 public hearing boards, 6 agencies with direct regulatory interests, and 3 government observers, as follows:

> *The chairs of the boards and agencies responsible for assessing and regulating energy developments in the Northwest Territories have developed a Cooperation Plan describing how, in principle, they will coordinate their response to any proposals to build a natural gas pipeline through the Northwest Territories. (excerpt: Introduction to Cooperation Plan, June 2002)*

But no sooner had the hoped-for efficiencies in the regulatory process coalesced when storm clouds began to gather. The Deh Cho threatened to rock the regulatory boat by demanding that their land claim be settled before the environmental review started. Spring 2004 saw a headline in an industry trade journal that should have screamed 'caveat emptor' up and down the pipeline right-of-way. Anadarko was pulling out of the Northwest

Territories citing "political uncertainty"! It had a gas field in Deh Cho territory and the company needed to run a small pipeline 40 kilometers down into the B.C. grid to tie it in. Stonewalled on all fronts, Anadarko's press release garnered front-page coverage in *Far North Oil & Gas* magazine:

> *... Anadarko Canada Ltd. announced it was delaying a major oil and gas project in the Fort Liard area for at least one year due to <u>political and economic uncertainty</u> in the Deh Cho. ... Anadarko, which has invested $150 million in the Fort Liard area to date, proposed to lay pipe for a gathering system in winter 2004. (excerpt: Stephen Burnett, citing Anadarko's press release, Opportunities North, spring 2004) (author's underlining)*

Anadarko would not return and its costly experience should have been a 'canary in the coal mine' warning for the Mackenzie Gas Pipeline project. Moreover, Anadarko had fielded a highly capable native consultation team; hence, if Anadarko's mini-gas line couldn't make it to market (right next door to the North American grid) then perhaps the Mackenzie Gas Pipeline project needed to reassess its risk. Because by fall 2004 it would see its own regulatory process challenged by the Deh Cho who were hoping to invalidate the Cooperation Plan. Then, as if on cue, the eco-activists joined in. The pipeline project was now heading into a serious public relations storm:

> *CPAWS supports DehCho in pipeline action: The Dehcho First Nations have currently protected about 50% of the land in their territory through their interim measures agreement and the NWT Protected Area Strategy. They are now working on a land use plan to create a long term balance between land*

protection and resource development. (excerpt: CPAWS press release, September 13, 2004):

This prompted the pipeline's native partners to finally speak up. The Aboriginal Pipeline Group (APG) wanted the Deh Cho to know of its frustration, given that the delay and cost overruns were starting to take their toll on project momentum which they had bought into:

Nellie Cournoyea, who chairs the Inuvialuit Regional Corporation, says the purpose of the meeting was to tell (Herb) Norweigan where the other aboriginal groups stand. ... "These three groups feel offended that no consideration was taken by the Deh Cho as to how these actions are going to affect us," she says. (excerpt: CBC News, October 5, 2004)

Undeterred, the Deh Cho pressed ahead with their legal challenge as to the review of the panel's composition. They had asked for two seats and had been refused. Then six months later a low-level legal order was issued from the Prothonotary's Office in Vancouver. Before going to trial on the main issue, the federal government would have to turn over to the Deh Cho almost five years of internal government records; namely any document that addressed how the federal minister had weighed the selections to the Joint Review Panel. Here's the order's wording that would create bureaucratic chaos in Ottawa:

Reasons For Order:
[5] As I have already indicated the Minister of the Environment established the Joint Review Panel, by a decision of 3 August 2004. However the Applicants say they were excluded from the formal part of all of this ... only becoming aware that the agreement, the subject of this review, on 18 August 2004, when it was released to the public.

[8] ... the Applicants do not seek all of the material
which was generated over the past five years, but
only such drafts, minutes, notes of meetings, briefing
notes, drafts of agreements, drafts of correspondence,
and documents in the possession of the Minister,
including the Minister's copies of correspondence
received and draft and final news releases; ...

[13] ... In the present situation it is proper that the
Applicants have additional material, that is all
produceable relevant material produced by or which
may have been before the Minister up to the day that
the decision was in fact made. <u>This may go back four</u>
<u>or five years in order to include material leading to</u>
<u>the June 2002 Cooperation Plan.</u> However this should
not be looked upon as an impossibly onerous task ...
(Norwegian v. Minister of Environment FC
prothonotary, March 15, 2005) (author's underlining)

This was a huge procedural win for the Deh Cho. Imagine
having the opportunity to peruse all those notations
made by deputy ministers in the margins, not to mention
the minister's own comments on the candidate appointment process. The Deh Cho had struck at the government's most vital point, revealing the political decision-
making process. The dilemma for government was how
to respond. Compliance with the judgment appeared to
be a daunting task given the sensitivity of the issues and
the five-year time span involved. Thus the political
backstroke! Ottawa soon cut the Deh Cho two cheques:
one for $16.5 million for their participation in the pipe-
line review, and one for $15 million for economic
development - a total of $31.5 million. Yet this was a sig-
nificant win for the Deh Cho that emanated from just a
preliminary round of legal skirmishing. What would the
main event be like? Soon it was open season on the
project's lead proponent, with Elizabeth May penning an

open letter to the CEO of Exxon Mobil, Mr. Lee Raymond, warning of more trouble ahead:

Incompetence of Imperial Oil - Your Canadian subsidiary, Imperial Oil, has shown itself to be singularly inept in preparing the environmental impact statement and managing the public participatory process for the Mackenzie Gas Project. There are numerous environmental issues that Imperial Oil has failed to address satisfactorily in its environmental impact statement. The upcoming Joint Panel Review and National Energy Board hearings will provide an opportunity for full, public discussion of these issues before independent arbiters who are not subject to political direction by elected officials.

Uncertainties - Given the opposition of the many groups and First Nations in Canada to the Mackenzie Gas Project and the errors committed in the early stages, you and your shareholders should not discount the potential for litigation in Canada, which could result in project delays and additional costs. (excerpts: Elizabeth May Executive Director of Sierra Club of Canada and Carl Pope Sierra Club, Open letter dated October 31, 2005)

The eco-activists hit the mark as "project delays and additional costs" became the project's defining feature as it approached the start of the regulatory review process. Soon the Deh Cho joined the fray fuelling the mounting regulatory uncertainty, as follows:

Earlier today, Imperial Oil announced to the National Energy Board (NEB) that it was ready to proceed to the public hearing phase of the Mackenzie Gas Project (MGP) review process. Imperial Oil has made this decision despite the fact that Imperial and Dehcho

First Nation communities have only recently begun discussions on land access agreements.

Dehcho First Nations (DFN) Grand Chief Herb Norwegian responded to Imperial's announcement by saying: "We will not allow Imperial Oil, the NEB, or Canada to trample Dehcho rights simply for the sake of quickly building this pipeline. DFN will consider all of our options in responding to this aggressive action from Imperial."

Imperial Oil has been repeatedly warned that pushing the Dehcho communities into public hearings prior to the signing of project agreements would be a significant mistake. The Dehcho First Nations now have no choice but to aggressively defend the rights and interests of Dehcho people. (excerpts: Deh Cho Statement, November 23, 2005)

Thus, the stage was set. Eco-activists and native strategists had now put both the proponents and the Joint Review Panel on the defensive just as the hearings commenced.

De Beers

By way of counterpoint, over in the central barrens, De Beers had decided to challenge the principal regulator (the Mackenzie Valley Environmental Review Board) over how it proposed to review its Gahcho Kué diamond mine. De Beers was looking for regulatory certainty, yet the judge did not find fault with the regulatory process and the judgment was a major endorsement of the native and environmental priorities in the regulatory process:

[25]... Parliament intended the Review Board to be the main instrument in the assessment of projects for

*development in the region. Aboriginal people were
intended to have meaningful input in this process.
Parliament intended that potential environmental
impacts and public concern be important factors for
the Review Board in making decisions. Parliament
also intended that the preservation of social, cultural
and economic well-being of the residents of the region
and the importance of conservation to well-being and
way of life of aboriginal people be taken into account.
(excerpt: De Beers v. Mackenzie Valley et al. 2007
NWTSC 24)*

De Beers explained in its ensuing press release that the
company was primarily concerned with heading off
future legal challenges in the project permitting process:

*De Beers Canada welcomes clarity on the Gahcho Kué
environmental assessment process: ... "This is the first
time a mining project in the Northwest Territories
will be required to undergo an Environmental Impact
Review. De Beers was seeking confirmation that this
process is in compliance with the legislation, in order
to provide us with the security that any permits
granted would not be subject to future challenges. We
are pleased that we can now take the Gahcho Kué
Project forward with confidence in the environmental
assessment process and look forward to participating
in a thorough review of the project," said Jim
Gowans, President and CEO of De Beers Canada Inc.
(excerpt: De Beers press release, April 3, 2007)*

The fact that the De Beers legal challenge occurred at all
underscored the ongoing regulatory uncertainty surrounding major projects in the Northwest Territories.
Indeed, why would proponents spend billions of dollars
to extract resources in some of the most remote regions
on the planet, if the same forces that drove Anadarko out

("political and economic uncertainty") remained a serious project risk factor?

Dene Tha'

Then in July 2007, the Mackenzie Gas Pipeline project fell afoul of the Dene Tha's legal challenge in northern Alberta (profiled in Chapter 6). They had been left out of the review process, and now Ottawa, again in political backstroke mode, likewise cut them a $25 million cheque. When added to the Deh Cho payout, the total compensation paid to natives now rang-in at $56.5 million! Moreover, it seemed that both industry and government were oblivious to the regulatory and legal lessons that the Mi'kmaq had taught the Maritimes and Northeast Pipeline proponents a few years earlier. Tellingly, Jim Prentice was the federal minister sued in both the Deh Cho and Dene Tha' litigation; and both outcomes propelled the native legal winning streak forward ostensibly at the expense of his pipeline project. It can certainly be argued that these two native legal wins 'knocked the wheels off' the Mackenzie Gas Pipeline project; as each one portended delays, budgetary increases, media criticism and overall loss of regulatory momentum. Headlines soon profiled the pipeline project as if it were transiting through the three stages of death:

Pipeline in 'Nation's Interest': Prentice reacts to industry naysayers (National Post, Jun. 1, 2007)

Another year's wait for Mackenzie Valley Pipeline Report (CBC News, Dec. 5, 2008)

TransCanada pessimistic on Mackenzie go-ahead (National Post, Feb. 12, 2009)

Mackenzie Valley pipeline 'a national embarrassment'
MGM's Sykes (National Post, May 5, 2009)

Mackenzie uncertainty fills Inuvik with dread
(National Post, Jul. 2, 2009)

Pipeline dream in peril (National Post, Oct. 27, 2009)

By far the most vitriolic criticism was directed at the hapless Joint Review Panel, which was now years behind in concluding its environmental assessment; all the while operating totally independent of government supervision. Their delay in reporting their findings caused the panel to take heavy broadsides from northerners, industry analysts and business media who collectively came to view the panel's intransigence as an indication of the main regulatory dysfunction eroding the resources sector's ability to achieve 'political and economic certainty' in the north. How the panel's budget tripled from $6.3 to $18.7 million over a two to three year period was also cause for serious concern. All the while, TransCanada Pipelines had been picking up 100% of the costs of the Aboriginal Pipeline Group (APG) comprising those native groups who had bought-in to the project. As reflected in the following excerpt, even APG President Bob Reid had some matter-of-fact things to say about the project's troubled future, as follows:

> *The total has reached $140 million. TransCanada*
> *writes it off if the pipeline is not approved. APG*
> *doesn't have to pay a cent. That's a loan you could not*
> *negotiate in the commercial market. The JRP has*
> *totally dropped the ball. This delay might be taken as*
> *a symbol that the North is not ready for this project.*
> *(excerpt: Alberta Oil Magazine, June 1, 2009)*

This statement clearly echoes Anadarko's earlier warning about "political and economic uncertainty." Indeed, the Anadarko 'chickens had come home to roost'! The rise of native empowerment was without a doubt a main cause of political uncertainty and economic risk surrounding the achievement of major project approvals in the north. Having natives onside for 60% of the right-of-way does not a pipeline make; not when natives in the remaining 40% have racked-up impressive legal wins that confound the ability of government and industry to consult and accommodate. TransCanada's CEO, Hal Kvisle summed up the project's predicament in a Financial Post Magazine interview in late 2008, a month before the joint review panel reported-in, as follows:

> *"The Mackenzie has been an incredibly difficult*
> *project to move forward. We have real challenges on*
> *the regulatory front in Canada. Things just get*
> *bogged down. And no question we're bogged down in*
> *the Mackenzie. We're talking about a multi-billion-*
> *dollar impact on the cost of the Mackenzie project. It's*
> *the complexity of the regulatory process - and the fact*
> *that it's still not over - that has added something like*
> *$3 billion to the cost of the Mackenzie project."*
> *(excerpt: Brian Banks and Claudia Cattaneo quoting*
> *Hal Kvisle, Financial Post Magazine, November*
> *2008)*

Lost Opportunity Costs

Then in early 2009, AFN National Chief, Phil Fontaine, issued an economic alert to corporate Canada in response to the prime minister's infrastructure roll out. He was keeping score on those "lost opportunity costs" incurred by corporate Canada, and the Mackenzie Gas Pipeline project was high on his list, as follows:

*(The government) estimates between $350 Billion in
resource development projects over the next 10 years.
These will only take place with First Nations
cooperation. The Mackenzie Valley pipeline project
cost increased from $1B to $10B between 2001 and
2008 and has been delayed well over 20 years due to
a failure to ensure First Nation participation. Lost
opportunity costs on this project are immeasurable.
(excerpt: AFN press release, January 6, 2009)*

This is an important comment linking the rise of native
empowerment to the country's economic priorities, and
the resulting collateral damage from lost opportunity
costs. From his statement there's little doubt that natives
see themselves as a form of insurance for safeguarding
resource projects in the regulatory approval process.
Another important comment emerged when natives
publically castigated eco-activists over their interference
in economic development. When Ottawa announced its
June 2008 oil and gas lease auction for the Beaufort Sea,
it was welcome news to northerners who were grasping
at any sign of industry interest. Imagine their surprise
when the World Wildlife Fund moved to block the lease
auction by petitioning the prime minister, as follows:

*WWF-Canada today called on Prime Minister
Stephen Harper to postpone the proposed sale of oil
and gas rights in five large portions of the Beaufort
Sea, until a management plan is available for the
region that takes into account which industrial
activities may be appropriate for which areas. The
current areas up for lease overlap known key habitats
for ice-dependent species like polar bear, beluga and
bowhead whales, threatening their future.
(excerpt: WWF- Canada press release. May 27, 2008)*

Nellie Cournoyea, CEO of the Inuvialuit Regional Corporation, issued an immediate rebuttal that spoke volumes as to the real dynamics behind the native / eco-activist relationship, as follows:

> *The Inuvialuit are sick and tired of having their future economic well-being blindsided by southern based environmental organizations that poke their self-righteous noses into someone else's backyard without either having the decency to consult with the people that live there or offer any realistic alternatives to their economic challenges. ...*
>
> *The Inuvialuit do not need WWF-Canada or any other environmental organization, sitting in their Ottawa or Vancouver condos, telling the Government of Canada what is good for the Inuvialuit and their environment. The healthy polar bear population in the Beaufort Sea has been a testimony to sound management practices by the Inuvialuit and government for many years and we intend to keep it that way. WWF-Canada, try fixing up your own backyard for a change. (excerpts: IRC press release, May 27, 2008)*

Clearly, natives will challenge eco-activists who are standing in the way of their economic priorities; and fittingly, WWF-Canada immediately issued an apology. But by now the regulatory delay had caused such an outcry that it prompted Ottawa to create a one-man commission to investigate. The former head of the Alberta Energy Utilities Board was tasked to review and report on how to foster northern regulatory efficiencies. McCrank's report addressed many of the factors contributing to northern regulatory uncertainty, and even harkened back to the Irwin era of "ad hoc environmental agreements on a project-by-project basis." But on the subject of the plethora of regulatory boards, McCrank thought that perhaps another agency was warranted in order to foster efficiencies and fulfill an oversight role. However, this idea was not accepted locally as it was viewed as adding yet another layer to an already over-layered regulatory landscape. In any event, one year later, Ottawa announced the creation of a new oversight bureau, as follows:

> *The new Northern Project Management Office will have direct responsibility for coordinating northern projects and will offer a single point of contact for clients...*
> *Regional offices will coordinate the early engagement of all federal players in resource development, work with territorial governments and boards, <u>and coordinate federal Aboriginal consultation efforts.</u> ... (excerpt: Minister Strahl's press release, Sept. 11, 2009) (author's underlining)*

The fact was that proper crown / native consultation had become lost in the regulatory maze; which was the real reason why the north was getting yet another agency. Year-end 2010 finally saw the National Energy Board issue its approval for the Mackenzie Gas Pipeline project. After six years of review, the project managed to muster 56% native support vs. 44% native opposition (calculated along the right of way). The regulatory review had taken an eternity; except now the NEB was urging the proponents to get a move on in order to make up for lost time, as follows:

> *By the end of 2013 we require the companies to file an updated cost estimate and report on their decision to build the pipeline. In keeping with these needs, we do not agree with the companies that they should be given until 2016 to begin construction of the project.*

*Actual construction must begin by the end of 2015 for
our approvals to remain valid. (excerpt: Part 4: Our
Decision NEB Mackenzie Gas Project dated December
16, 2010) (author's underlining)*

With this decree, the regulators now gave the proponents
less time to start construction (which is a massive
expediting challenge in and of itself) than they themselves had taken to review and approve the project. After
writing down its $127 million loan to finance the APG,
TransCanada described the Mackenzie Gas Pipeline
project's future in its 2010 letter to shareholders thusly:

*The National Energy Board approved the Mackenzie
Gas Pipeline Project late in 2010 subject to certain
conditions. The project's backers continue fiscal
discussions with the Canadian Federal Government to
further advance the project. TransCanada believes
gas from both Alaska and Mackenzie will be needed in
the future. (excerpt: TransCanada 2010 letter to
shareholders, March 2011)*

Once touted as a major plank in Canada's future as an
energy powerhouse, this is 'corporate speak' for how
northern megaprojects languish and die. From the
Berger Inquiry onward, the north has never missed an
opportunity to miss an opportunity (on the Mackenzie
Valley pipeline). But the biggest missed opportunity of all
was the failure to come to terms with the rise of native
empowerment - because that's what killed this pipeline.

Just a half-year after the NEB's conditioned approval,
Shell announced that its Mackenzie Gas Project holdings
were up for sale. Its Niglintgak gas field, at just under
one trillion cubic feet, was one of three gas fields
anchoring the pipeline project. Indeed, Shell's interest in
the pipeline consortium itself was put on the block. Shell

didn't give reasons, tersely stating that it was 'focusing on other opportunities'.

One week later, *Maclean's Magazine* (July 25 2011 issue) ran a pictorial of the Duke and Duchess of Cambridge's visit to Yellowknife. The royal newlyweds were portrayed paddling their canoe with gusto across Blatchford Lake with none other than Dene elder Francois Paulette at the stern; the same *re Paulette* who had launched the ruling that precipitated the rise of native empowerment some forty years earlier. He was still an active native rights strategist having just been profiled in a major David Suzuki feature on the oilsands: seen fishing 100 miles further downstream echoing similar watershed concerns; then over in Norway warning Statoil directors *"How you spend your money here is your business; but how you spend your money in my territory is my business"* (Tipping Point: the Age of the Oil Sands CBC The Nature of Things Jan 27 2011). Whatever he said to his fellow paddlers would not likely have fallen on deaf ears. One thing for sure, the royals were being mentored by the ultimate northern resource ruler as they traversed the very watershed. Indeed that court case back when he was a youth - and now as an elder guiding the royals - make telling bookends for understanding today's north.

It's more than a little ironic that in spring 2012, Inuvik was crying the blues over having to switch to propane; having exhausted the nearby Ikhil gas field. Heating costs are poised to triple, bringing with it all the cost-of-living escalations that inflict northern economies and living standards. But it wasn't supposed to happen this way. That it did is in no small measure due to the NWT's penchant for boarding itself up!

9

CONCLUSION: *R. V. AVATAR*

In the run up to Oscar Night in March 2010, international eco-activists along with several native organizations ran the following full-page advertisement in the Hollywood trade journal Variety that in effect ambushed the oilsands in the reputational-management department:

James Cameron & Avatar... You Have Our Vote!

CANADA'S
AVATAR SANDS

Where Indigenous Peoples in Canada are endangered by toxic pollution and future oil spills.
Where Shell, BP, Exxon and other 'Sky People' are destroying a huge ancient forest.
Where giant 'Hell trucks' are used to mine the most polluting, expensive 'unobtanium' oil to feed America's addiction.
James Cameron, we see you ...

Here was the climax of a strategic campaign to demonize the oilsands on the one night the whole world would be watching. Canada's energy industry responded with an olive branch and proffered the following key statistics:

We invite these activists back to planet Earth to discuss the appropriate balance between environmental protection, economic growth and a safe and reliable supply of energy.

1,500 Aboriginal people have direct full-time jobs in the oil sands industry…

More than half a billion dollars in contracts were awarded to Aboriginal contractors in 2008.

More than $3 billion earned by Aboriginal companies between 1998 and 2008.

More than $3 million in support of Aboriginal community programs in 2008.
(excerpts: CAPP press release, March 4, 2010)

Yet Avatar's opening sequences conveyed a powerful message; showing huge 'Hell trucks' hauling dark 'unobtanium' from gaping open pit mines that were dead ringers for the massive operations in the 'AvaTar Sands' advertisement. And the fact that the trucks' enormous tires had arrows stuck in them as they returned to base with their payload established the overriding social justice theme of the movie - Indian move over! When the Oscars were doled out, Avatar won three, including one for art direction. In fact, the supervising art director hailed from Alberta and even referenced the oilsands for having provided inspiration for specific set designs in a subsequent CBC interview, as follows:

But art director Todd Cherniawsky, from Ardrossen, Alta. ... did, however, turn to oilsands engineers in the Athabasca region for help. "It was very helpful in understanding how a control room would be laid out [and] what type of personnel would be involved to run these factories," Todd Cherniawsky said. "On Pandora, at this base, there's a full refinery in the background, so we had to know what that would look like, what the ore would look like that the trucks were bringing in - so there's all those factors that we had to know." (excerpt: CBC News, March 8, 2010)

Not only did the oilsands serve as the backdrop for this high-tech assault on Mother Nature, but also casting natives in the vital role of land protectors brought indigenous rights to the forefront. It's not science fiction to assert that, more and more, natives are standing defiant before project proponents, regulatory tribunals, and even the courts. Indeed, their recent opposition to two major mines in B.C. has produced scripts that rival Avatar's screenplay.

Kemess North

When Northgate Mineral's former CEO strayed off-script in his address to a Denver gold conference in late September 2007 explaining why his B.C. mine expansion had encountered serious native opposition in its regulatory review, he set off an industry / native firestorm that ultimately swept his project away. No doubt clearly frustrated by the intensity of native opposition, he made the following reference regarding the regulatory process: *"There's things in there that went on the panel like about people talking about speaking to bears. So it's pretty hard to talk science!"* (internet audio of remarks re Denver Gold Forum Sept 25, 2007)

So just what should be emphasized when it comes to addressing the differences between hard science and the native worldview? Indeed, just one week previous Northgate's CEO had won kudos from native strategists (albeit in a backhanded fashion) for his frank assessment of the fate of projects proceeding in the face of native opposition, as follows:

First Nations Summit lauds mining CEO for "telling it like it is" ... "Mr. Stowe hit the nail on the head. He has rightly cautioned major developers and their investors that First Nations need to agree with the merits of their projects," said Grand Chief Edward John, member of the First Nations Summit's political executive. "Otherwise, as Mr. Stowe himself said, 'don't waste your time.'"... (excerpt: First Nations Summit press release, September 27, 2007) (author's underlining)

At this point, the CEO still had reason to be hopeful that his project could win political approval (since Kemess North would be adjacent to the existing Kemess South mine). But the problem was that operating the new mine involved the transformation of a pristine mountain lake (Duncan / Amazay) into a waste rock and tailings dump. And while this disposal plan made sense scientifically (because the slag would be rendered inert in the lake's frigid depths) it was cold comfort to natives who were opposed to the lake's destruction in such a wanton manner. After a full review, the Joint Review Panel (JRP) had sided with the natives and recommended that the proposed project not be approved. Here's the JRP's rationale with respect to the lake's proposed destruction:

Throughout the hearings and in various submissions, the Aboriginal groups involved in this process have clearly and explicitly stated that they do not support *the Project going forward, based primarily on their opposition to the use of Duncan (Amazay) Lake as a tailings and waste rock disposal impoundment. Both the Gitxsan and the Tse Keh Nay have stated that <u>water is sacred to them</u>, and that the destruction of a natural lake goes against their values as Aboriginal people. The loss of the natural lake would be viewed as culturally and socially detrimental by Aboriginal people, and the Panel considers this effect to be significant.*

The Proponent proposed a package of seven proposals for moving forward which, if acted upon, would represent a substantial level of Aboriginal involvement in Project planning and implementation. These proposals are all predicated on the acceptance of lake disposal of mined wastes. Since the Panel has seen no evidence that Aboriginal groups would embrace the Project on that basis, the prospects for negotiation and agreement on a package of such measures <u>do not appear to be promising</u>. ...

Based on an analysis of the pros and cons of Project development, evaluated individually for each of these five sustainability perspectives, and then in combination, the Panel has concluded that overall, from a public interest perspective, the benefits of Project development do not outweigh the costs. The Panel recommends to the federal and provincial Ministers of the Environment that the Project <u>not be approved</u>, as proposed. (excerpts: executive summary, Joint Review Panel Report, Kemess North Copper-Gold Mine Project, September 17, 2007, CEA Registry: 04 - 07 - 3394) (author's underlining)

Now the fate of Kemess North was to be decided by politicians, and it was at this juncture that the "speaking to bears" quip was made. First, the natives demanded a formal apology. Then, when the B.C. mining industry backed the project with a public relations campaign, native strategists responded with an open letter accusing the mining industry generally of attempting to steamroll their concerns and opposition to the specific project:

WE STRONGLY OPPOSE your harmful campaign to undermine the Kemess North Mine Joint Review Panel and its central recommendation to government Ministers that Northgate Minerals Corporation's Kemess North Project not be approved. ... We reject your brochure as bitter rhetoric. ... Your effort to undermine the Panel's recommendation represents [an] ongoing denial of your industry's real impacts on Aboriginal culture, heritage, rights, title, lands, and the environment. ... (excerpt: An open letter to the B.C. mining industry, from Tsay Keh Dene, Kwadacha, Takla, November 30, 2007)

By this time, *The Northern Miner* had entered the fray with an editorial headlined "Northgate in Limbo" that offered a scathing critique of the regulatory process with put-downs that rivaled Avatar's ('You're not in Kansas anymore!') screenplay. Here's that awkwardly worded editorial that gave native strategists another clear shot at the already imperiled project's open net, as follows:

Why exactly a government-funded environmental panel comprised of university educated professionals should blithely accept that <u>stone-age inducing, shamanistic values such as "water is sacred" should automatically trump the values of Western civilization</u> and modern science, is unstated. Pity. (Excerpt: The Northern Miner editorial, October 1-7, 2007 Vol. 93, No. 32) (author's underlining)

For a leading national publication that speaks for the mining industry, this Oscar-worthy editorial was totally out of touch with the impact of the native legal winning streak in the resources sector. Moreover, it conveyed the unmistakable tone of cultural imperialism and entitlement; essentially legitimizing Avatar's social justice theme.

The AFN counterattacked with more denunciations citing the mining industry's "crass attempt to manipulate both governments" (AFN press release, December 15, 2007). Not surprisingly, on March 7, 2008 the B.C. and federal governments issued a joint press release stating that it was thumbs-down for Kemess North; as now both governments would *"accept the recommendations of the independent environmental review panel that the proposed Kemess North copper-gold mine not proceed in its present form."*

But why was "speaking to bears" ever an issue? To answer this question, it is necessary to examine the results of an environmental review that took place a full decade before in Labrador at Voisey's Bay. A quick check of those proceedings would have revealed that bears are sacred to the Innu Nation as they are to many other natives, and that part and parcel of that relationship involves speaking to them and rendering to them traditional offerings. In fact, an entire section is devoted to bears in the Voisey's Bay Environmental Impact Statement *"particularly from the perspective of their spiritual and cultural significance"* (Summary and Conclusions, p. 33). The goal at Voisey's Bay was likewise to minimize bear encounters, not just from a worker safety viewpoint, but to preserve their iconic status within the Innu culture. Any misstep on such an important cultural priority would have damaged the fragile corporate / native relationship that was so long in coming on that project. Tellingly, this project benchmark was there a decade earlier for all to learn from. Indeed, the Mining Association of Canada has since referred to Voisey's Bay as a *"model for delivering economic benefits to aboriginal communities and local businesses in remote areas"* (President and CEO Pierre Gratton's open letter to *National Post*, June 21, 2011). Yet this mining industry setback was soon to be followed by another and on surprisingly similar facts.

Prosperity Mine

The next mine up for environmental review looked like a Kemess North replay; Taseko's Prosperity Mine likewise faced intense native opposition over its proposed destruction of another lake. The Prosperity Mine proposed to turn a high central plateau lake into a waste rock dump thereby reducing the lake to 10% of its present volume. Taseko, in light of what had befallen Kemess North, proposed to transplant the fish to a nearby, man-made replacement lake to be called 'Prosperity'. The project was positioned as a much needed engine of growth in an otherwise depressed regional economy, and it offered the full range of IBA benefits (jobs, training and business opportunities) to local natives. Yet native opposition remained steadfast.

However, on this occasion, the federal review panel included a native (panelist Morin) who was well versed in the mining approval process. The regulatory process was now tailored so as to be more receptive to consideration of native cultural issues and environmental impacts on traditional uses. Once the review process began, it likewise became clear that native opposition was unwavering with respect to the destruction of Fish Lake / Teztan Biny, which hosted a fishery, burial sites, and other landmarks of significance to the Tsilhqot'in (recent victors in that 45% non-binding aboriginal title ruling). It was at this point that Taseko decided to challenge panelist Morin's standing on the review panel. Taseko was concerned that panelist Morin was an advocate for her Tahltan Nation, having previously signed correspondence in that capacity as "coordinator, THREAT". The following excerpt taken from Taseko's lawyer's letter lays out the basis for her proposed disqualification, as follows:

> Our client's concern is that <u>the beliefs of Ms. Morin, and the advocacy role that she plays in her community, disqualify her</u> from being a neutral and unbiased member of the panel. (excerpt: proponent document no. 1445, December 4, 2009 CEAA reference 09 - 05 - 44811) (author's underlining)

The regulatory proceedings went sideways over Taseko's unorthodox procedural application. According to the same letter, the company felt that she "would consciously or unconsciously decide the issues unfairly." Regulatory proceedings were suspended while the remaining board members struggled to come to terms with this request that she "recuse herself" from the panel. Taseko had also filed an application in the Federal Court seeking her disqualification. Now an experienced independent counsel was appointed 'amicus' to assist the panel members in investigating and adjudicating thereon. However, the amicus' report itself completely and systematically rejected Taseko's concerns, as follows:

> ... concluded that the matters identified by Taseko did not raise a reasonable apprehension of bias on the part of Panel member Morin; therefore she was not asked to recuse herself from the Panel. (excerpt: JRP Executive Summary Section 1.9 apprehension of bias CEAA reference no. 09 - 05 - 44811, p. 7)

Now the review panel itself expounded on its handling of the issue and in its decision letter to Taseko, it explicitly referenced panelist Morin's role as manager of the Tahltan Heritage Resources Environmental Assessment Team (THREAT) noting that her credentials had been clearly highlighted in her appointment to the panel, and underscored her qualifications both as a professional metallurgist and as an experienced environmental facilitator in resource developments. So now, not only was the panel explicit in its defense of her appointment, but also it refuted the company's motion to have her recuse herself, as follows:

> *The Panel sees nothing in these terms of reference that would suggest that Ms. Morin's employment as coordinator of THREAT would in any way give rise to a reasonable apprehension that she will not be fair in her assessment of the potential environmental effects of the proposed Project. To the contrary, based on the biographical note referenced above, it seems to the Panel that <u>Ms. Morin's background in environmental assessment for the Tahltan Nation, coupled with her training and experience as a mining metallurgist, is precisely why she was appointed to the Panel</u>. Indeed, this would be consistent with the Panel's Terms of Reference, which state that Panel members shall "have knowledge or experience relevant to the anticipated environmental effects of the project". (excerpt: Panel document #1570) (author's underlining)*

There is an entire section (sec. 1.9) in the JRP's final report that describes both the chronology and the significance of events given that Taseko's challenge to panelist Morin had pre-empted two months of hearings. This counts as a significant native legal win given that Taseko had specifically launched an action in court to

have her "disqualified," which it then abandoned. As a
rule, natives everywhere perceive the regulatory process
to be tilted in industry's favour; no doubt Taseko's
attempt to remove panelist Morin over "apprehension of
bias" only deepened these suspicions. It's difficult to
determine Taseko's lost opportunity cost in this instance;
certainly there was a loss of regulatory momentum, and
likely a loss of regulatory goodwill. In any event, by mid-
2010, the environmental review hadn't produced the
desired results for Taseko. The JRP summation instead
emphasized the importance of fish, cultural heritage,
Aboriginal title and (again) bears, as follows:

> *The Panel concludes that the Project would result in
> significant adverse environmental effects on fish and
> fish habitat, on navigation, on the current use of lands
> and resources for traditional purposes by First
> Nations and on cultural heritage, and on certain
> potential or established Aboriginal rights or title. The
> Panel also concludes that the Project, in combination
> with past, present and reasonably foreseeable future
> projects would result in a significant adverse
> cumulative effect on grizzly bears in the South
> Chilcotin region and on fish and fish habitat. (excerpt:
> Executive Summary Panel Document no. 2369, p. ii)*

Now, as was the case with Kemess North, the final
decision was once again to be made by politicians.
Coincidentally the JRP's report was released July 2,
2010, just in time for the AFN's annual general assembly
in Winnipeg. All the chiefs from across Canada seemed
to be collectively daring the prime minister to approve
the Prosperity Mine - at his peril - and one wonders if the
legal challenge over panelist Morin's nativeness was a
unifying factor. Here's how the AFN framed their
resolutions clearly sending a shot across the PMO's bow:

The Chiefs-in-Assembly:

1. <u>Fully support</u> the efforts of the Tsilhqot'in Nation to protect their lands of profound cultural and spiritual value to its people from the proposed Prosperity Gold-Copper Mine, <u>and will stand behind the Tsilhqot'in Nation in defence of these lands regardless of the decision made by the Federal Government.</u>

2. Call upon the Federal Government to heed the cautions of its independent Panel, demonstrate commitment to environmental protection and the cultural survival of First Nations, and <u>reject</u> the proposed Prosperity Gold-Copper Mine.

3. Advise the Federal Government that First Nations across Canada are watching its decision to see whether there remains any value or integrity in environmental assessments for major projects, or whether First Nations must turn to litigation and other means to assert our rights and protect our cultures.

4. Caution the Federal Government that approval of the proposed Prosperity Gold-Copper Mine, despite the clear warnings of its independent Panel, would demonstrate utter disregard for the survival of First Nations as distinctive cultures within Canada.

5. Direct the National Chief and Assembly of First Nations to advocate on behalf of the Tsilhqot'in Nation and communicate the clear support of Chiefs-in-Assembly. (excerpts: Tsilhqot'in press release, July 22, 2010) (author's underlining)

This was a direct and powerful challenge to the political decision-making process. Clearly, the assembled chiefs viewed the political approval of the Prosperity Mine as their next native empowerment 'line in the sand'. And there was more to come ...

Harvard Law School Report

Right after the demise of Kemess North in spring 2010, the Harvard Law School Human Rights Program released a major report entitled 'Bearing the Burden: The Effects of Mining on First Nations in British Columbia'. The premise of the Harvard report, which undertook an in-depth analysis of the Kemess North project, was that natives suffer disproportionately from the negative impacts brought on by mining. And although it was highly critical of the B.C. government, the report nevertheless gave credit where the authors felt credit was due. For example:

> *British Columbia has taken an important first step by announcing a revenue-sharing plan at the government level, but it should work closely with affected First Nations to implement this plan, and if necessary, to revise it. (excerpt: Bearing the Burden: The Effects of Mining on First Nations in British Columbia, June 7, 2010, p. 134)*

The Harvard report recommended that the B.C. government work hand in hand with natives and argued for the adoption of the United Nations Declaration of the Rights of Indigenous Peoples (UN Declaration). Yet the Harvard report was publicly dismissed as "hogwash" and as "a completely flawed document" by the province's Minister of State for Mines, Randy Hawes, who emphasized that the province, to the contrary, was making *"great strides"* with natives. His quip even made national headlines:

"B.C. mines minister calls Harvard report on First Nations rights 'hogwash'" (Globe & Mail, June 16, 2010).

Three months later, on September 27, with the political decision still pending on the Prosperity Mine, the AFN ran a major article in the same newspaper. It was a powerful denunciation of the proposed project and was accompanied by a large colour photo of the pristine mountain lake. The headline read: *"The cost of 'Prosperity': First Nations aren't anti-development but we are anti-destruction."* The AFN's article was replete with accusations of government "rubber-stamping", "creative" regulations and "shameful" outcomes. To underscore native national unity, it was signed by two regional chiefs from opposite ends of the country, and called upon Ottawa to "strike down the Prosperity Mine" (AFN's open letter to the *National Post,* September 27, 2010). Now the native strategy to block the mine's approval really kicked-in. Throwaway lines can often trigger unintended consequences. Native strategists were able to recycle the minister's "hogwash" quip throughout the entire period during which the federal government was considering its response to the Prosperity Mine. They even highlighted it as a major faux pas in an open letter to the B.C. premier; laying out a litany of media missteps that again seemed right out of the Avatar script:

Dear Premier Campbell,

We are writing to strongly object to the unwarranted and insulting comments by the BC Minister of State for Mining Randy Hawes on multiple occasions, which have only served to reiterate and promote racist stereotypes about First Nations culture. By Resolution 2010-40, the Union of BC Chiefs-in-Assembly call upon you to accept the resignation of Junior Minister Hawes.

The Takla Lake First Nation, the Union of BC Indian Chiefs and others support the independent report released by Harvard Law School's International Human Rights Clinic titled "Bearing the Burden: The Effects of Mining on First Nations in British Columbia." Rather than address the serious recommendations made in the report, Junior Minister Hawes called the report "hogwash" and "completely flawed" and suggested Harvard "look in its own backyard or concentrate on places with more egregious offences against indigenous people." Minister Hawes' comments were shockingly offensive, not supported and clearly historically inaccurate, given the substantial hardship that Indigenous peoples have endured due to federal and provincial legislation and policy.

We were absolutely appalled that Junior Minister Hawes has also gone on record saying "some First Nations reject mining for a more traditional lifestyle - those ways are linked to lower birth weights, higher birth rate deaths and lower life spans. Improving these outcomes requires sharing the wealth and jobs that come from mining." We understand he refused to apologize for these unsupported and ignorant comments.

Junior Minister Hawes has boldly stated support for Taseko Mine's proposed Prosperity Mine and extremely controversial efforts to replace the Xeni Gwet'in and the Tsilhqot'in Nation's Teztan Biny (Fish Lake) and surrounding area with a massive open pit mine and tailings pond, and detrimentally impact nearby Esketemc territory as well. He has publicly criticized the Tsilhqot'in, who he said are "putting a lake before their kids." Again, this comment is

*insulting, unwarranted, inaccurate, and fails to
consider listening to what First Nations want.*

*In 2005, you and the Province of BC committed to a
government-to-government New Relationship with
First Nations in BC based on respect, recognition, and
accommodation of Aboriginal Title and Rights. In the
spirit of the New Relationship, we would like to meet
with you in order to discuss the seriousness of
Minister Hawes' comments and review the absolute
need for mining reform in British Columbia
beginning with a real review of the Harvard study
recommendations.*

*Union of B.C. Indian Chiefs
Grand Chief Stewart Phillip
(open letter dated October 28, 2010)*

Just five days later, no doubt influenced by these same
native empowerment dynamics, the federal minister of
the environment announced his government's rejection
of the Prosperity Mine (as proposed). It was to be Jim
Prentice's last official decision as minister. His rejection
most certainly triggered Premier Campbell's resignation
the following day; and Prentice himself resigned the day
after that. So were these departures related in some way?

Premier Campbell had been heavily invested in the
Prosperity Mine going ahead. Just one month earlier he
had expressed his full support for the project in a speech
to the Union of B.C. Municipalities. Indeed just the week
prior to his resignation he had announced a new
provincial ministry to prioritize Natural Resource
Operations in order to streamline the process of granting
resource permits. It's highly unlikely that a premier
planning his exit would fundamentally re-order his
cabinet just days before leaving. The reality was that
Campbell had urged, lobbied, and assumed that Ottawa

would approve the Prosperity Mine. Instead, Prentice's announcement had drawn political blood. The real-politick issue was whether the approval of the Prosperity Mine would have unleashed a torrent of 'on the ground' native unrest not seen since Caledonia, Ipperwash, Gustafsen Lake, or Oka? 'Better safe than sorry' may well have decided the project's outcome.

Ostensibly, it was the proposed destruction of nearby pristine lakes that was the deciding factor determining the fate of these two mines. Yet there were other factors at play which provided fuel for the native victories in each case: the bear gaffe, industry's brochure, the "stone-age" editorial, the legal challenge to panelist Morin, the Harvard report, the "hogwash" rebuke, the AFN's suite of resolutions, and the two (perfectly timed) open letters - all of which collectively read like an Avatar sequel. But these were real life events and voices from the B.C. interior - not Pandora!

The fact is, strategically speaking, that each of these unscripted inputs served-up a 'freebee' opportunity whereby native strategists were able to further challenge these important projects. They were 'freebees' in the sense that each one provided a fresh incentive, a new platform, and a clear target for escalating native opposition right to the highest levels in government - the PMO. Without these 'freebees' - repeatedly served up by industry and government - it's possible that both these projects might have progressed as highly conditioned projects in terms of permit approvals. Instead, native strategists saw these lob-balls coming and hit them out of the park.

The Copenhagen Conference on Climate Change

The prime minister's arrival at Copenhagen in late 2009 precipitated a series of eco-activist spoofs whereby his government was subjected to international ridicule. A Greenpeace poster portrayed him as older but not wiser: "It's 2020, I'm sorry, we could have stopped catastrophic climate change ... we didn't." Eco-activist shenanigans manipulated Environment Canada's press releases by issuing patently false last-minute reversals of Canada's climate change position. They even fabricated the Wall Street Journal's coverage using fake headlines: "Canada Announces Major Shift at COP15 Climate Summit." The U.N. secretary-general directed pointed commentary his way, and the newly elected U.S. president gave him the cold shoulder. Back in Ottawa, the opposition Liberals reworked the infamous photo of Jack Ruby gunning-down Lee Harvey Oswald by superimposing a grimacing Harper - supposedly portraying his true feelings about having to attend the climate change summit. All of which transpired in the aftermath of a string of daring eco-activist disruptions at various oilsands sites. For the premier of Alberta, seeing Canada named 'Fossil of the Year' was too much to bear. Thus, he penned a full page open letter to Canadians, outlining Alberta's defense of the oilsands, as follows:

If you have followed the news from the international climate change negotiations in Copenhagen, you have seen comments by Canadians questioning Alberta's management of its natural resources. ...

Albertans want to reduce emissions. We offer pragmatic, practical ways to do it. No one should ignore the economic stakes of this debate. Slowing our economy is a guaranteed way to reduce emissions. But if Alberta's economy stops growing, all Canadians will feel this pain. ...

Pressures on the planet have taken decades to build up, but we don't have decades to get serious about

*reducing these pressures. We shouldn't waste time
pointing fingers at one another. The world needs us to
act, and that's exactly what we're doing. (excerpts:
Premier Ed Stelmach's open letter, the National Post,
December 17, 2009)*

Vancouver Olympics

Just two months later, in February of 2010, the outstanding success of Canada's Vancouver Olympics seemed
to right all the diplomatic wrongs. Now the prime
minister basked in the glow of a mature Canada that was
the world's envy. More than any other event in recent
history, the Vancouver Olympics showcased natives as:
heads-of-state, Olympic landlords, and keepers of
cultural icons. Indeed, the real politick subtext was that
Vancouver had won the games largely as a result of
native support. The games wouldn't have taken place
otherwise. By the closing ceremonies, Harper had discovered the vision of Canada that he wanted to represent
internationally. He might even have found common
ground with natives. Soon he would play two important
diplomatic cards: one for the oilsands and one for the
natives. The first card was played when Environment
Minister, Jim Prentice, delivered a clear and pointed
response to Premier Stelmach's open letter at the
University of Calgary, as follows:

*"The development of the oilsands and the
environmental footprint of these industrial activities
have become an international issue ... and as such
they now transcend the interests of any single
corporation. What is at issue on the international
stage is our reputation as a country. ...*

*Given that perception has a way of becoming reality,
unless we take some bold, proactive action, the many
positive steps we take toward addressing climate
change will be eclipsed by that negativity. We will
continue to be cast as a global poster child for
environmentally unsound resource development.
Canadians expect and deserve more than that.*

*And for those of you who doubt the Government of
Canada's willingness, that we lack either the willingness or the authority to protect our national interests
as a 'clean energy superpower,' think again. ...
(excerpt: Minister Prentice's speaking notes
University of Calgary, February 1, 2010) (author's
underlining)*

Here was Ottawa serving notice on Alberta that it wasn't
going to be the international whipping boy for the
oilsands increasingly negative environmental image. For
their part, the oilsands proponents were not in a position
to take issue with this federal dressing down, mired at
the time in the lead-up to the (never-ending) duck trial.
Moreover, the twists and turns of that legal process,
playing out monthly as a major media event, accorded
eco-activists complete public relations immunity from
anything industry might assert in its defense. Indeed in
the court of public opinion, it was as if both the energy
industry itself - and the oilsands - that were on trial.

The second card was played one month later in the
March 2010 federal throne speech. Throughout the
previous two years, Canada had likewise been heavily
criticized internationally over its refusal to sign-on to the
*United Nations Declaration on the Rights of Indigenous
Peoples.* Now as a result of the prime minister's back-to-
back experiences at Copenhagen and the Olympics, his
government was poised to reverse that position. Stephen

Harper's reasoning is reflected in the throne speech itself, as follows:

> *We are a country with an Aboriginal heritage. A growing number of states have given qualified recognition to the United Nations Declaration on the Rights of Indigenous Peoples. Our Government will take steps to endorse this aspirational document in a manner fully consistent with Canada's Constitution and laws. (excerpt: Throne Speech March 3, 2010)*

And while the rise of native empowerment was not cited as a motivating factor in the throne speech, clearly it had brought immense pressure to bear upon his government's reversal. Of course, in the hands of native strategists the UN Declaration portends a remarkable toolbox having the potential to further level the resources playing field. Especially in light of the native rights concept of "free and informed consent prior to the approval of any project." Here's the U.N. Declaration's text for that increasingly contentious clause:

> *United Nations Declaration on the Rights of Indigenous Peoples*
> *Adopted by General Assembly Resolution 61/295 on 13 September 2007*
>
>
> *Recognizing the urgent need to respect and promote the inherent rights of indigenous peoples which derive from their political, economic and social structures and from their cultures, spiritual traditions, histories and philosophies, especially their rights to their lands, territories and resources,*
>
> *Article 32*

1. Indigenous peoples have the right to determine and develop priorities and strategies for the development or use of their lands or territories and other resources.

2. States shall consult and cooperate in good faith with the indigenous peoples concerned through their own representative institutions in order to obtain <u>their free and informed consent prior to the approval of any project affecting their lands or territories and other resources, particularly in connection with the development, utilization or exploitation of mineral, water or other resources</u>. (author's underlining)

3. States shall provide effective mechanisms for just and fair redress for any such activities, and appropriate measures shall be taken to mitigate adverse environmental, economic, social, cultural or spiritual impact. (excerpts: UN Declaration, Article 32)

Initially (back in September 2007) the UN Assembly vote had passed by an overwhelming 143 to 4 (with 11 abstentions). The very next day, the federal minister of Indian affairs and northern development penned an open letter reinforcing Canada's ongoing opposition to UNDRIP citing as his principal reason - the native 'veto':

Given that Canada has more than 600 First Nations and numerous Metis and Inuit groups, this would be an almost impossible undertaking, and goes far beyond Canada's domestic obligations to consult. This provision could be interpreted as giving aboriginal peoples a <u>veto</u> over virtually any legislative or administrative matter.

Critics of Canada's position have said that a declaration is an aspirational document, not legally

binding, and that Canada's concerns are overstated.
Aspirational or not, there could be attempts to use the
declaration in negotiations, <u>in Canadian courtrooms</u>,
and to demand that the federal government bring
policies in line with the declaration. Therefore, the
wording is very important. ... (excerpts: Minister
Strahl's open letter to the National Post, September
14, 2007) (author's underlining)

But that was then. Now in response to Ottawa's reversal, in yet another open letter, the AFN applauded the positive tone of the Throne Speech and indicated that it wanted to be involved every step of the way on UNDRIP's implementation, as follows:

We encourage the government of Canada to work
with Indigenous Peoples on a respectful process for
the endorsement and implementation of the
Declaration. We believe the statement announcing
this change in position must be developed in genuine
partnership, and in a way that honours the spirit and
intent of the Declaration. Many Indigenous leaders in
Canada were involved in the Declaration's 20 plus
years of development in the UN system and have
much knowledge, insight and experience to share. We
look forward to this happening in a timely manner
and are prepared to assist in any way. (excerpt: AFN
open letter, March 22, 2010)

Avatar Comes to the Oilsands

James Cameron's visit to the oilsands came just six months after Oscar Night's Ava**Tar Sands** siren call. And his visit put the oilsands and Alberta on high alert. Cameron had already made headlines by supporting natives fighting a hydropower dam deep in the Amazon.

Now he promised the downstream natives that he would help them too. You-Tube videos depicted him as being open-minded and genuinely committed to what he saw as a critical ecological and human rights issue. His oilsands fly-over even made the national news as it preceded Syncrude's convictions in the duck trial by just three weeks! Two weeks later, Cameron took his message to the inaugural World Indigenous Leadership Summit in New York City featuring such notables as native Nobel Laureate Rigoberta Menchu (1992 peace prize winner) and a host of corporate social responsibility heavy-hitters. Cameron was garnering credibility on the world stage precisely because Avatar had struck such a profound social justice note with the public. The coincidental timing of the duck trial added poignancy to Cameron's savvy media messaging; but it's worth underscoring that the oilsands had served-up that Oscar-worthy performance all by itself.

Canada Embraces the UN Declaration

On November 12, 2010, after three years of nay saying, the Harper government officially reversed its position on the UN Declaration. Canada was now aligned with the rest of the international community. It was hardly a coincidence that this reversal occurred just one week after the Prosperity Mine's rejection. Because without a doubt it was the rise of native empowerment in the resources sector, combined with the opportunity to burnish Canada's international reputation, that were the unstated dynamics driving this major policy reversal. Here's the official text reflecting Ottawa's post-Olympic reconsideration of the UN Declaration, as follows:

In 2007, at the time of the vote during the United Nations General Assembly, and since, Canada placed

*on record its concerns with various provisions of the
Declaration, including provisions dealing with lands,
territories and resources; free, prior and informed
consent when used as a veto; self-government
without recognition of the importance of
negotiations; intellectual property; military issues;
and the need to achieve an appropriate balance
between the rights and obligations of Indigenous
peoples, States and third parties. These concerns are
well known and remain. However, we have since
listened to Aboriginal leaders who have urged
Canada to endorse the Declaration and we have also
learned from the experience of other countries. We
are <u>now confident that Canada can interpret the
principles expressed in the Declaration in a manner
that is consistent with our Constitution and legal
framework</u>. ... (excerpt: Canada's Statement of
Support INAC press release, November 12, 2010)
(author's underlining)*

*The 2010 Olympic and Paralympic Winter Games
were a defining moment for Canada. The Games
instilled a tremendous sense of pride in being
Canadian and highlighted to the world the extent to
which Aboriginal peoples and their cultures
contribute to Canada's uniqueness as a nation. The
unprecedented involvement of the Four Host First
Nations and Aboriginal peoples from across the
nation set a benchmark for how we can work together
to achieve great success. (Ibid.)*

Then at the end of 2010, the United States became the
last signatory to endorse the UN Declaration - in yet
another (Bush) policy reversal instigated by President
Obama. By this time, the president has established a new
office in his administration dealing with - Indian Energy
Policy and Programs - a sure signal to Canada that his

administration meant to do business differently on issues and projects that impacted native rights. His first big test was just around the corner and the outcome would send shock-waves through the oilsands and the PMO. But it was Native Americans who strategically set the wheels in motion to protect the Ogallala Aquifer which ultimately derailed the Keystone XL pipeline. Once again in the gaffe department, this concerted opposition to Canada's leading export got some backhanded assistance from political opinion-setters who should have known better. Alberta's Energy Minister, Ron Liepert, made headlines just when matters were coming to a head with Obama's public defense of his energy record. (Here first are the U.S. president's stated concerns, followed by the Alberta energy minister's remarks in direct response):

"These tarsands. There are some environmental questions about how destructive they are, potentially, what are the dangers there and we've got to examine all those questions. So we've got to do some science there to make sure that the natural gas that we have in this country, we're extracting in a safe way. The same thing is true when it comes to oil that's being piped in from Canada, or Alaska, for that matter. We've got to do these evaluations. If it looks like I'm putting my fingers on the scale before the science is done, then people may question the merits of the decision later on. So I'm not going to get into the details of it."
(President Obama speaking at a town hall session in Fairless Hills Pennsylvania April 06 2011)

"Frankly, I wish he'd get on with action. I saw where he said they need to study the science. I don't know what they're studying. We could give him all the briefing he needs and it would take him 15 minutes to read about it, so I just wish he'd sign the bloody order

*and get on with it."(Alberta Energy Minister Liepert
responding to media the next day in Calgary)*

There's an passage in Avatar's screenplay that juxtaposes
the Na'vi's "deep connection to the forest" versus the
miner's "they're just goddamned trees". If one were to
substitute (taking artistic license) 'unobtanium' for
'tarsands' and using the Na'vi salutation 'Mr President,
we see you' - versus - 'we could give him all the briefing
he needs' so 'sign the bloody order'... then conceivably
this real-life exchange could have taken place on
Pandora! More importantly, on the critical issue of
oilsands reputational-management: here was the U.S.
president being publicly berated by a foreign official on a
matter exclusively within his domestic purview; just as
the Keystone XL decision point was coming to a climax.

What a gift for Sioux strategists: who in September
2011 authored the Mother Earth Accord; who in October
interrupted a presidential fundraising speech that
elicited *"I know your deep concern about it. We will
address it"*; who in November led the massive human-
chain encircling the White House; and who in December
presented the Mother Earth Accord to the president
(with help from native strategists north of the border).
Their relentless pursuit in protecting the Ogallala aquifer
from oilsands output was the major factor in setting the
stage for the demise of the Keystone XL pipeline, and
they didn't need to invoke the UN Declaration to do it.
(They didn't need to given the way the issue played out!)

Back in Canada, today, the AFN considers the full
adoption and complete implementation of UNDRIP: "as
the foundational aspect of our work at the AFN ... that
natives have the right to consent to projects and the
freedom to withhold consent - is the starting point - and
projects will only proceed with the full participation of
First Nations." (Shawn Atleo speaking notes, Law Society
of Upper Canada , Sept 9 2011) (author in attendance)

In this keynote speech in the halls of legal power, Atleo provided counterpoint saying that in his culture "it's the Elders who carry moral authority' - that the Law Society was viewed as an intimidating place - where his people were once prohibited from admission" He then called for a massive transformation in thinking saying that it was a "false choice and a major misrepresentation to see events as a rights agenda versus an economic agenda ... instead it's all connected via sustainable development practices that merge with our world view and perspectives. Each First Nation has a right to advance or impede proposals that are in accord or don't accord with their values. Attempts to impose foreign externalities on our values will not work ... and that nothing without our agreement will happen". (author's underlining)

He zeroed-in on the Keystone Pipeline saying that it represented "another example of inadequate consultation and the failure to listen." He highlighted the AFNs growing alignment with Native Americans (National Congress of Native Americans) and noted that President Obama had sent delegates to attend a recent International Indigenous Summit on Energy and Mining (Niagara Falls June 2011) (author in attendance).

Yet all the business commentary in the wake of Keystone XL's demise chalked it up to U.S. pre-election politics (which indeed may well be the case); although it's just another project train-wreck when looked at through the lens of the rise of native empowerment.

Home and Native Land

Just prior to Canada's signing the UN Declaration - on the same weekend in August of 2010 - two foreign vessels approached Canadian shores. On the west coast, the MV Sun Sea was escorted-in with 490 Tamils on board none of whom had permits or permission to enter. While on the east coast, the German research vessel, the RV Polarstern under contract to the federal government, was impeded from entering by a last-minute court order even though it had all the requisite permits and permissions. It was here to conduct high arctic subsea seismic surveys, which federal scientists asserted would not disrupt marine wildlife. Once again, the ruling's opening paragraph sets the stage for the outcome, as follows:

> [3]   The areas where the seismic testing is to be carried out are plentiful with marine mammals, including seals, walrus, narwhal, beluga whales and polar bears. They are traditional hunting areas for Inuit in the five affected communities. Inuit state that the seismic testing will impact on migration routes and will drive marine mammals away from these areas for a significant time. Canada takes the position that the seismic testing will have little or no impact on marine mammals. ... (excerpt: Qikiqtani Inuit Assoc. v. Minister of Natural Resources 2010 NUCJ p. 12)

> [25]...The opportunity to participate in _the hunt, an activity which is fundamental to being Inuk, would be lost_. The Inuit right which is at stake is of high significance. This suggests a significant level of consultation and accommodation is required. (Ibid.)

> [48] If the testing proceeds as planned and marine mammals are impacted as Inuit say they will be, the harm to Inuit in the affected communities will be significant and irreversible. _The loss extends not just to the loss of a food source, but to a loss of culture. No amount of money can compensate for such a loss._ (Ibid.) (author's underlining)

It's wording right out of Avatar. It's the social justice nexus at which the blockbuster and the rise of native empowerment converge. Compromising the sustainability of the subsistence food chain is a serious attack on native culture. This legal premise is now a fundamental component of Canadian common law from coast to coast to coast.

And while it may appear to be a case of comparing apples and oranges, natives had thwarted a visit by a government-authorized vessel, while Ottawa was powerless to stop a visit by an unauthorized vessel. The unmistakable fact is that the rise of native empowerment today outmuscles the PMO. Not surprisingly, just two month's later, the offshore region in question was designated by the federal government as a future national marine conservation area - of course with ongoing native consultation now being paramount.

No wonder today, The Economist magazine outright calls it what it clearly is: *"the natives' de facto veto power"* (September 10, 2011 issue 'The piper pays'). The article treats native opposition to the oilsands, and by association its proposed pipelines to foreign markets and tanker traffic off of the west-coast, as an international social justice story precisely because of the de facto native veto in the resources sector.

Canada may well have evolved as a country built on resource exports, but our resources future sees natives in the driver's seat as *Resource Rulers*. That's because native strategists have both hands on the secret levers of power; one in the law courts and one (thanks to Avatar) in the court of public opinion. Thus for industry, the old order is over and major challenges lie ahead in earning the 'social license' to operate.

Canada's hit-or-miss experience with the rise of native empowerment indicates that we've been slow learners on the road to resources. Today, there are so many project train-wrecks littering the resources landscape that a comprehensive assessment of the lost opportunity costs to the country is almost certainly the biggest and most under-reported business story of the past decade. There's not one instance of a project post-mortem ever having been conducted that links investor misfortune to the native legal winning streak and the rise of native empowerment. Thus, until we have true resource power-sharing with natives, the fate of Canada's resource sector will be in the hands of native strategists in their new capacity as Resource Rulers.

Power-sharing is what has to happen in order for Canada to play a leadership role in setting the world standard with respect to the universal recognition of native rights. Indeed, the international community would look to Canada as one of the few countries having the moral and legal authority to show the rest of the world the benefits of resource power-sharing. So far only Quebec has risen to address this complex social justice and environmental challenge. Now it's time for the rest of Canada to do likewise; indeed the economic and ecological future of our home and native land depends upon it.

EPILOGUE

There's only one ruling in the native legal winning streak where a CEO's personal intervention turned the tide - culminating in a corporate win. The Quebec Court of Appeal thought the CEO's letter to the chief and council was of such import that it inserted it, in its entirety, right into the judgment. The natives' concerns are directly referenced; thus here's the letter that won the day:

> [26] *It is worth reproducing here the complete letter of August 31, 2004 sent by Kruger in response to Chief Picard's letter of July 27, 2004:*
>
> *[TRANSLATION] Dear Chief Picard:*
>
> *I am writing in response to your letter of July 27, addressed to me personally. First of all, allow me to extend my best wishes to you on your re-election.*
>
> *I have to say I was surprised by your letter concerning the logging operations undertaken by Kruger on Île René-Levasseur almost a year ago, in September 2003, under a timber supply and forest*

management agreement regarding Common Area 093-20 granted to Kruger in June 1997.

Our company's policy is to foster the best relations possible with the aboriginal communities on the land where our operations are carried out. Thus, Kruger did everything it could to establish such relations with the Innu First Nation of Betsiamites and encourage the Betsiamites Innu to take part in the economic development generated by its operations in the Côte-Nord region, while respecting the Innu culture and way of life.

The construction of a sawmill was announced in the Baie-Comeau region in September 1995. Since then, Kruger representatives have met with representatives of the Betsiamites Band Council to discuss the economic benefits of a sawmill in Ragueneau, as well as the socioeconomic benefits of Kruger's forest management activities in the region. In fact, Kruger has worked assiduously to recruit members of your community, and we have employed and still employ Betsiamites Innu workers at our mill in Ragueneau.

Kruger has always apprised the Betsiamites Innu of developments in its forest management activities in the region and has maintained ongoing discussions with your community. Further to requests from your community, Kruger introduced measures to harmonize its forest management activities with the traditional activities of the members of your community, in coordination with representatives of the Betsiamites Band Council. Our relations have been forged through many meetings over the years between Kruger, your band council and your community at various levels, and through regular meetings of the issue table, on which sits a representative of the Betsiamites Band Council and a representative of the management council of the Louis-Babel ecological reserve. To date, our relations have been marked by mutual respect, understanding and a spirit of cooperation and goodwill.

Kruger carries out its operations on Île René-Levasseur in compliance with the applicable laws, particularly in regard to the environment, and is concerned about sustained yield and sustainable development. Kruger opted for a mosaic-type spatial cutting pattern with strict measures for protecting regeneration and soils. Kruger also undertook to conserve exceptional forest ecosystems. In addition, nearly one quarter of Île René-Levasseur has been excluded from the forest management activities, either through the creation of the Louis-Babel ecological reserve in 1991 or, more recently, through the establishment, with Kruger's collaboration, of the Baie-Memory protected area.

Your letter is the first sign since 1995 of any unease in your community over Kruger's activities in the region. Accordingly, I have given special attention to it. I want Kruger to continue to maintain excellent relations with you, your band council and your community. It matters to me that Kruger understand the concerns of the Betsiamites Innu regarding the company's activities on Île-René- Levasseur. I have asked Daniel Tardif, Senior Vice-President, Forest and Wood Products Division, in whom I have complete confidence, to be my representative with you in this regard.

I understand that your community is negotiating comprehensive land claims with the Québec and Canadian governments, and your letter raises matters that are under their respective jurisdictions.

*As I am sure you understand, it is not up to us to
handle these matters. However, I assure you that
Kruger will continue to be available to collaborate
with the government authorities and the Betsiamites
Innu, as we have done in the past, in order to
maintain harmonious relations between all
stakeholders. Mr. Tardif will also represent me in this
regard as needed.*

*Yours truly, (Kruger Inc. c. Première Nation des
Betsiamites 2006 QCCA 569)*

The Quebec forest industry was in steep decline at the
time that this ruling issued. But within the year, the
Quebec government would extend $20 million in funding
and low interest loans to Kruger in order to revamp its
Trois-Rivieres mill. Moreover, because a provincial election
campaign was underway, seats were in play and job
losses were imminent. Yet it's obvious that Kruger's legal
win made it a safe political bet in the corporate social
responsibility department; that's because Kruger, on the
strength of its corporate commitment, had likewise won
in the court of public opinion.

Today, if there's a CEO in the Canadian resources sector
who isn't able to write such a letter, then shareholders,
directors and analysts should be asking why not. If
instead, they're relying on corporate lawyers to carry the
day, then the chances of prevailing are slim. Because
that's where the evidence leads in examining the native
legal winning streak. But more to the point, there are no
second chances once a *Resource Ruler* weighs-in.

ABOUT THE AUTHOR

Bill Gallagher is a lawyer, strategist and facilitator (and a former energy regulator and treaty negotiator). With over thirty years of experience in the turbulent area of native, government, and corporate relations, he is an authority on the rise of native empowerment in Canada's resources sector.

The perspectives presented herein are as a result of having worked in various capacities and experiencing the issues and interface from all angles: general practice, oil patch lawyer, federal regulator for frontier energy permits, treaty negotiator on the prairies, northern devolution negotiator (NWT & Yukon), strategist on oilfield vandalism, IBA facilitator at Voisey's Bay, corporate social responsibility designer; as well as navigating trouble spots in NB's war-of-the-woods, Voisey's Bay Labrador, and Platinex in northern Ontario. Along with a host of conventional resource project roll-outs across Canada; where managing the native dialogue was of paramount importance.

The research is drawn from personal attendances at key court proceedings, commission inquiries, resource conferences (and as counterpoint) personal attendances at on-the-ground protests (Caledonia and Burnt Church) and other manifestations of native empowerment. The author has collated 20 years of event-driven research in an extensive road-to-resources library. This book summarizes that research to explain the profound impact that the rise of native empowerment is having on Canada's resources sector.

INDEX

CPSIA information can be obtained at www.ICGtesting.com
Printed in the USA
LVOW07s2251120115

422492LV00001BA/95/P